Little Man
in a Big Hurry

LITTLE MAN IN A BIG HURRY

The Life of Joseph H. Hirshhorn,
Uranium King and Art Collector

Gene Hirshhorn LePere

VANTAGE PRESS
New York

The article, "The View from the Castle," by S. Dillon Ripley, *SMITHSONIAN* magazine, November 1981, is reprinted with permission.

The obituary, "Joseph Hirshhorn: Canada Recalls 'Uranium King,'" which originally appeared in the *Toronto Globe & Mail* (owned by *The Canadian Press*), on September 2, 1981, is reprinted with permission.

Copyright © 2009 by Gene Hirshhorn LePere

Published by Vantage Press, Inc.
419 Park Avenue South, New York, NY 10016

Manufactured in the United States of America
ISBN: 978-0-533-16079-2

Library of Congress Catalog Card No.: 2008905075

0 9 8 7 6 5 4 3 2 1

Contents

ACKNOWLEDGMENTS

There are many people who encouraged me to keep on working at this book and some without whom this book could not have been properly researched and written. All of them have earned my sincere gratitude and acknowledgment for their time and efforts.

Two people have helped me by editing the manuscript. Tom Johnson spent hours excising any extraneous material that did not move the story forward. At the same time he corrected my poor spelling and made constructive suggestions. My niece, Debora Cohen-Strod, went over the manuscript again, then in its fifth revision, with a sharp, objective eye, further refining the work. To both of them I give my heartfelt thanks.

Anna Brooke, Librarian of the Hirshhorn Museum, earned my lasting gratitude. I asked her for all kinds of assistance: for documents, contacts, photos, suggestions and never did she turn me down. She provided a secure backbone for research connected to the days when the Smithsonian first took over the responsibility for my father's collection and the plans for the museum and its building were begun, a time when she was among the first hires for the museum. She may be the longest-time employee still working there. She has been cheerful, optimistic and willing beyond any expectations, always acknowledging my right, as Joe's daughter, to have access to the materials I required.

Additional thanks go to my friend Jerry Cobb who, after volunteering to read the manuscript in one of its earlier incarnations, suggested the idea of taking what was then a dry recital of a man's journey and turning it into a book that breathed with life. He also gave me the courage to dig in and do it. Thank you, Jerry, and thanks to all the friends and family who encouraged me to push on and get the job done.

I have reserved my most generous thanks for Abram "Al" Lerner for his contribution to the very existence of this book and much of the content it contains. It was Al who insisted, against my honest reluctance, that it was I who should write the definitive biography of Joe Hirshhorn and who gave me, late in his life, the gifts of his time, his energy and his memories that have enlivened the stories of my father, a man whom he knew intimately and loved over many years. Al died October 31, 2007 at the age of ninety-four and a half without having seen the final manuscript or knowing the book for which he had contributed so much was to be published.

Lastly, a nod to Aline Saarinen for the title of my book. It was the title Saarinen used for the chapter about Joe Hirshhorn in her book called *The Incurable Collectors*. I stole it because it is the best brief description of Joe Hirshhorn anyone could ever devise.

A TRIBUTE TO UNCLE JOE FROM HIS NEPHEW, LEO GOLD

Although he was only fifteen years older then me, my Uncle Joe was like a father to me. He was an incredible man, always there for me, motivating me and encouraging me to become the person I am. He was my guiding light and my mentor through all the years.

When I was badly burned at the age of two, I was told that seventeen-year-old Uncle Joe was always around, helping change dressings and just being there, already exhibiting the sensitivity that was ingrained but rarely obvious.

When I returned home after my two-year tour of duty overseas during World War II, he gave me the keys to his estate in the Pocono Mountains so that my wife, my two-year-old daughter, and I could reestablish our lives together as a family. Again his great sensitivity came through.

There are so many memories I shared with Uncle Joe. I loved the times we spent riding the subway, having dinner at the automat, hearing his voice calling out, "Hey, kid." Then there were the special events: the opening of the Algom uranium mine in Canada and the groundbreaking and dedication of the Hirshhorn Museum in Washington, D.C. Because he helped me to establish myself in my stock brokerage business, we knew each other very well, better than most uncles and nephews.

Uncle Joe was a risk-taker, a brilliant investor with a keen mind, an ardent art lover and collector, and a man I dearly loved who is sorely missed.

I am pleased that my cousin has written this insightful book and I'm certain Uncle Joe would be very proud of her and her achievements.

Little Man
in a Big Hurry

Introduction

On October 1, 1974, The Joseph H. Hirshhorn Museum & Sculpture Garden Museum held the first of three successive formal occasions to mark its opening in Washington, D.C. The museum, designed by Gordon Bunschaft in the shape of what architectural critics of the time described as an enormous concrete donut, was the fulfillment of the collector's fondest dream. One hundred and fifty friends, relatives and members of official Washington were invited to a pre-ceremony dinner that night at the Smithsonian's old brownstone "castle" on the Mall. Afterward, nearly 2,000 guests gathered in the open plaza to hear remarks by S. Dillon Ripley, Secretary of the Smithsonian, the Honorable Daniel Patrick Moynihan, Chairman of the Board of Trustees of the Museum, by Abram Lerner, Director of the Museum and by Joseph H. Hirshhorn, the museum's namesake who gifted the institution with his collection of 6,000 works of art. Present, in addition to Hirshhorn's immediate family and friends, were the former First Lady Lady Bird Johnson, ambassadors and justices, senators and congressmen and officials of the Smithsonian as well as representatives of the international press, mainly art editors who had been sent to cover the event.

Invitations to the second opening held the evening of October 2nd, were sent to representatives of the art world; museum directors, gallery owners and artists, who attended in full force. The evening of October 3rd was reserved for Smithsonian Institution Associates. On each of the three evenings, attendees viewed a select portion of the 6,000 pieces of donated art (from modern masterpieces by such artists as Picasso, Klee, Pollock and others) on display for the first time.

The emotions of guests attending all three openings ran the gamut from those who had known Hirshhorn's generosity to those who had been on the receiving end of his withholding ways

1

or downright ruthlessness; from those who had experienced the sharp sting of his rejection to those who had felt his love.

Certainly his children were pleased to be recognized by their father as worthy of inclusion. They were, after all, his immediate family, an inclusion they often felt denied. *Among these I dealt with this inner conflict with equal parts of pride and pain. I looked at my small father, now shrunk below his maximum five foot four height, still jaunty and energetic at seventy-five and impeccably attired. He wore a black tuxedo, an unruffled, beautifully starched white shirt and black bow tie which suited him. His aging face was still mobile and expressive; although he no longer resembled a combination of Jimmy Durante and Spencer Tracy, as I had long ago described him. With his wife, Olga, at his side, graceful in her ankle-length chiffon print, he looked so happy and so cute I was close to tears with pride at his supreme moment of recognition. He had done it all himself.*

Joe's second wife, Lily Harmon, an accomplished artist in her own right, did feel genuine pleasure at seeing the extraordinary collection of art permanently situated in a modern museum open to the public—a beautiful and worthy home, at that. Some of her own paintings were part of the collection and that made her happy also. In truth, however, the fury she felt for her former husband was palpable, contaminating her feelings.

Among other invited artists who were summoned for the second night's opening, all of whom had works included in the display, were a few who likewise harbored varied emotions. Several harbored feelings of having been cheated, of having been taken advantage of, side-by-side with a sense of genuine gratitude and pride to know their work would be honored, hanging for all time in this glorious new museum. Most of them were simply and plainly delighted for Joe and for the museum. There were many art dealers there, most were delighted at the invitation but a few who accepted the coveted invitation wrestled with ambivalence. Somehow Joe had taken advantage of them, undercut their profits. Many museum directors came, some feeling Joe had failed to recognize the superiority of their art expertise as measured against the man—Abram Lerner—he had chosen over them to be director of The Hirshhorn Museum. Even some of the politicians had come merely because it was expected. Others came to see what the government's money had paid for, and more than a few were resentful that the cocky Jew had gotten his way.

Of Hirshhorn's siblings attending the first night's opening, only Dora, Joe's younger sister, was there. Annie was not well enough to be able to attend. Dora's feelings that night were of pure admiration and joy for the achievements of her brother. She had been the recipient of so much kindness and financial help from her "rich" brother, she was bursting with happiness—for him and their family and perhaps most of all for their mother who would have been so proud. Joe's nephews and nieces, who knew him least, stood in awe of his achievement and sensed that his fame shed light on them by association. Leo Gold, whose brokerage firm was one of Hirshhorn's main venues for trades, knew him best. Their connection had helped him achieve a more than comfortable lifestyle, but even he harbored mixed feelings. For all the business Joe threw his way, Joe extracted a fee: he demanded a commission rate lower than any Gold's firm permitted another customer. Joe also told Leo to which charities and in what amounts he was to give donations. The wife of one of Joe's nephews, in spite of the excitement she felt at being in the company of a raft of notables, held a burning resentment against her husband's uncle, remembering (although she didn't know the boy when the event occurred) that "Uncle Joe" had failed to give her husband a bicycle during the poorest years of his childhood.

Other guests had also been invited: men who had worked for Hirshhorn for half a century, men who had given him all their loyalty, who knew his secrets and protected him by their silence. By virtue of the invitations alone they were assured of their good standing with Hirshhorn. Their conflict was mainly seeing him publicly honored, all the while knowing his nefarious and sometimes cruel ways. One day they would discover what they had believed was a mutually close and cherished friendship was not valued by the man who had accepted their trust and loyalty.

As they strolled toward the opening of the doughnut-shaped structure for their first look at both the architecture and the art inside, all the guests were forced to pass, among other large sculptures, the magnificent Henry Moore "Draped Reclining Figure" (1952–1953), one of fifty works of art by Moore that Hirshhorn compulsively and lovingly bought in his lifetime and donated to the "people of the United States." A colorful mobile-stabile by Calder, standing twelve feet wide and sixteen feet high, greeted guests at the entrance. It had been purchased through the private dealer, Harold Diamond, with whom Hirshhorn did a great deal of business; and Henry Moore's "King and Queen" occupied the center of the ground-level lobby. Once inside, visitors rose on the escalator to the second level where the displays of the collection were set out on walls and in cases and where each person could linger to study each piece that caught their interest. Daumiers, Degas, de Koonings, it was a treasure trove of masterpieces.

On October 4, the Hirshhorn Museum was opened to the public at large. In the first year of its existence, the number of people visiting the museum reached two million. In the following thirty years many more millions of people have flocked to Independence Avenue and 7th Street to view the extraordinary treasures sheltered within the Hirshhorn Museum or stroll through the exterior sculpture garden and marvel at the elegant, oversized works that dominate the space. It has become one of the favorite museums among the many under the Smithsonian banner.

Joseph H. Hirshhorn, a five-foot-four-inch supercharged dynamo, streaked across the twin worlds of Canadian mining and art collecting like a comet with a vapor that illuminated people (not always to their best advantage) that trailed in his wake. What kind of a man was Hirshhorn? Where did he come from? What propelled him to attain the luminosity of a star, not just in one field of endeavor, but in two?

"Joe" Hirshhorn, as he was familiarly known (though he was called J.H. by his business associates and "Daddy Joe" or D.J. by his first four children), was a maddeningly complex man. Like Joseph of biblical legend, he rarely showed more than one color of his "dream coat" persona to business associates or family members. Indeed, no single person experienced all of the many facets of his personality. Most who knew Joe typically saw either what they wanted to see or what *he* wanted them to see.

Everyone who did business with him recognized Hirshhorn as smart, tough and above all, suspicious. He was ambitious, shrewd and driven. He could be incredibly, albeit selectively, generous. If he was greedy, his avarice was for beauty. He pursued beauty in art, something he responded to in a profoundly personal way and what he responded to he wanted to own. He accumulated paintings, sculptures, drawings, objects of all kinds and quested for everything he found beautiful. He also loved beautiful women and those women were invariably attracted to him. In the proper setting he became playful. But he was always confident—dynamic and unforgiving, secretive, wary, sentimental and manipulative. In part, what made him successful was his determination and patience. Although he seemed to make instantaneous decisions, no one ever accused him of being rash. Joe's genius was that he was able to understand, process, assess and decide with amazing speed. Hirshhorn's attorney, Sam Harris, a brilliant and accomplished man, called Joe "a genius at what he does." His near-photographic memory contained a repository of information that he could summon almost instantaneously until the day he died.

Hirshhorn exemplified a man who achieved everything he could have hoped for in his business life, and was an abject failure in his personal life. More than one person, looking at his life objectively, commented that had Hirshhorn been a better husband and father, he would never have attained the wealth and stature he did. Almost everyone who knew him, men and women alike, wanted more from him than he was able to give.

But the battery of attributes that made Joe such a success in business took a destructive turn when applied to his spouses or his parenting. One of Joe's daughters called him a "monster." One of his wives (Joe had four) likened him to Hitler. Another observed him to be greedy and so much in need of love that "he even tried to charm the man at the toll booth on the parkway." It was Joe's children, his lovers and his first two wives who felt the most deprived. In those early years, when he was striving to make his place in the world, Joe's absenteeism and disinterest left lasting emotional scars on those closest to him. Throughout his life, Joe was emotionally inaccessible to his children who wanted and expected more from a father than money and *things.* They craved closeness and companionship and a feeling that they were loved, as did his wives. His second wife came to believe her husband was incapable of loving. So did his first.

Nearly everyone who entered Joe's orbit was caught in his spell, yet it is difficult to identify all the factors that made his personality so engaging. It may have been his self-confidence. Hirshhorn's most compelling aspect, one which was most often mentioned when describing the man, was his dynamic energy. That quality, aided by charm, seductiveness and a mind as quick and startling as an electric spark, was a magnet that drew all kinds of people to him, the shrewd as well as the naïve. They wanted the "magic" of his natural life force to rub off on them, believing that somehow, in his wake or by his grace, they would arrive in the "promised land." *I must have inherited some of his skepticism. I knew him as he was, never believed he was Santa Claus, and loved and admired him despite his obvious shortcomings.*

Joseph Herman Hirshhorn was the twelfth of thirteen children and the youngest of four sons born to his parents, Amelia Friedlander and Lazer Hirschhorn, in Latvia. A year after Joe's birth on August 11, 1899, Lazer died and, although she tried, Amelia was unable to carry on the formerly successful provisions enterprise. The twin circumstances of poverty and the political upheaval of the pre-revolutionary Russia drove the family to immigrate to the poor streets of Williamsburg, Brooklyn before Hirshhorn had turned eight.

In 1907, knowing just a few words of English, living with nine members of his family in a three-room apartment, Joe was left to sink or swim on the strength of his own wits and adaptability. He triumphed over his hardscrabble beginnings, and like so many before him, Joe became an immigrant success story in the land of opportunity. It was a success story the likes of which neither Joe nor any of his family could have predicted, and which culminated with the seminal moment of his life—the opening on the Washington, D.C. Mall of his namesake museum. This was a man who gained everything the material world could offer, including fulsome praise and acclaim, but in scaling those heights he lost out on the emotional, human benefits that might have enriched his life.

This seventy-four-year journey taken by a Jewish immigrant child from a small *shtetl* in Latvia is a story worth telling.

I
Shtetl Boy

Joseph Hirschhorn was, genetically and culturally, the product of generations of Latvian Jews. His mother, Amelia, born Haye Friedlander in 1864 in Mitau (now Jelgava) Latvia, was the youngest of seven children born to forty-one-year-old Simon Friedlander and thirty-five-year-old Freda Elison. Jelgava is located in northwestern Latvia, in an area called Kurland, considered among Latvian Jews to have nurtured the elite of their countrymen. Amelia's family can be traced back to a Hessel Friedlander, born about 100 years earlier in 1797, who is considered to be the ancestor of the Kurland Friedlanders. Throughout her life, Amelia was proud of her Kurland identity, often reminding her children they were not mere Latvians, they were Kurlanders.

Simon, her father, and his twin brother, Hersh, also spelled Hirsh, were two of six children born in 1814 to Hessel's son Behr in Mitau. There were also two sisters, Feige and Taube, and a brother, Hessel.[*] Judging from the size of Amelia's home and the relative comfort in which they lived, the family was comparatively well off. Until she was married in 1882, Amelia lived in a large house staffed by servants. She attended school where she learned to read and write Yiddish, was offered some instruction in European history and learned how to calculate numbers. In a family that practiced Orthodox Judaism, Amelia was schooled in

---

[*]A genealogy of the Friedlanders of Kurland can be found in the book *Eliahu's Branches: The Descendants of the Vilna Gaon and His Family* by Chaim Freedman, AVOTAYNU, INC., Teaneck, NJ, 1997. Further research shows it is doubtful that Max, living in New Zealand, was directly related to Amelia.

all the ritualistic, religious and homemaking arts in preparation for her expected future role as a Jewish housewife. Although small in stature, Amelia was a handsome woman, as her photograph at the age of eighteen reveals. Her strength of character and resolute determination are evident in her posture and the set of her mouth. These traits made her seem larger than her diminutive size would suggest.

The family of Joe Hirshhorn's father, Lazer, can traced back to about 1773, at the time of the birth of Joe's great grandfather, Hirsh, in Hasenpoth, Latvia. Lazer's grandparents were Levin, also called Leib, and Fruma-Leya Hirschhorn. They had six sons and one daughter. Elias Hirschhorn (Lazer's father) was born about 1825 and married Rifke Shore. Lazer was the third of the six sons born to the couple. Elias Hirschhorn's family wasn't as comfortable as was Amelia's, but as a "milk seller," Elias' profession followed in the tradition of the family. Many of the Hirschhorns were engaged in some aspect of the cattle business as butchers, dairy farmers or provenders of dairy products.

How Lazer and Amelia met is a mystery but, on October 18, 1882, in the Jewish community of Tuckums, Latvia, Amelia Friedlander, 18, and Lazer Hirschhorn, 24, were married.[*]

The couple settled in the Klein-Leivenhof district of Tuckums surrounded by Lazer's large family where they resided for the first eleven years of their marriage. It was there that Amelia gave birth to the first nine of their thirteen children: Herman, born December 24, 1883. The other children (Rahele, followed by a stillborn child; then Annie, Yudel, Ella, Frieda, Abram and Marianne) were born at regular intervals, two to three years apart. Marianne, the couple's ninth child who arrived in December 1895, was the last Hirschhorn to be born in Tuckums. Marianne died five months later on April 21, 1896 in a small *shtetl* called Djukst (also spelled Djuste or Dzukste) to which the family had recently moved. Yudel also died in childhood. Soon after Marianne's death, Amelia gave birth to Fannie.

---

*The marriage record of Lazer Hirschhorn and Haye Friedlander was obtained from the Latvian Archives in Riga, Latvia.

Amelia Friedlander Hirschhorn, Joe's mother, about 18 years old, taken in Latvia around the time of her marriage.

Djukst is located 100 miles southwest of Riga and approximately the same distance from Libau, the Baltic port to the north. The family settled into a house located on the property of a local baron, and Lazer opened a general store. This is where their last three children were born: Isidore, called Irving, on October 6, 1897; followed by Jossel, called Joseph, on August 11, 1899. Dora, the last of their children, was born on August 9, 1900, at a time which coincides with her father's death at age forty. Amelia was widowed with ten surviving children from newborn to age sixteen.

The world into which Joseph and his siblings were born was harsh and foreboding for Jews. In the early 18th century, when Peter the Great was Czar, long before Amelia and Lazer's marriage, Latvia had been made a part of what was known as the Russian Empire. For hundreds of years, Russian governments under the Czars had taken an official position against Jews that made life difficult for them. Cossacks frequently raided Jewish settlements and *shtetlach* setting fires to their homes and barns, destroying crops and often killing entire families.[*]

As part of its determination to contain and control a people that were regarded as dangerous and difficult, with few exceptions Russia restricted Jews to living in an area known as the Pale of Settlement which lay in the northwestern part of Russia. In the late 19th century, the Pale included countries which decades later came to be known as Latvia, Lithuania, Poland and Prussia. The Czars restricted not only where Jews lived and how they earned a living, but also prohibited them from owning property. Adding insult to injury, Jews were overtaxed and their sons were drafted for obligatory military service in the Russian army. Although alternatives were limited and it took courage to leave one's homeland and family for the uncertainties of a foreign land, many Jews scrimped and saved the amount necessary for steerage tickets to England, South Africa, Palestine and the "New World." Notably, among these "huddled masses," were three of Lazer's first cousins, Chayim, Hessel, and Isaac, the latter two of

Shtetlach is the plural of *shtetl* which means a Jewish village.

whom emigrated to London while Chayim came to the United States. One of Lazer's brothers, Jossel, also called Joseph emigrated to the United States where he raised his family in Michigan. On Amelia's side, an Uncle Schlomo (Solomon) left for London, married there and went on to found a large family in Australia. A sister, Taube, married and emigrated to Cape Town, South Africa along with two of her Friedlander first cousins who made significant contributions to the Cape Colony there.

Lazer worked hard to provide for his family. In fact he was eager to provide Amelia with the kind of lifestyle she had enjoyed growing up. His general store carried such dairy products as butter, eggs, sour cream and milk as well as breads that were prepared in the family's kitchen. The store also sold all manner of farming implements, including tools and wagon parts, in addition to quantities of animal foods and plant seed, all of which he supplied to the rural area around Djukst. Amelia, occupied as she was with her growing brood, could not be a full-time partner in her husband's business, although she supervised the products made in her own kitchen. The baron to whom they paid rent was reputed to be Lazer's single most important customer.

The family's property consisted of the main house together with outbuildings for horses, cattle, chickens, a few sheep, a single wagon and farm implements. The house itself was framed of wood and overlaid with stucco.[*]

Winters were long and cold in northwestern Latvia and, typical of the houses of Russia and its extended Empire, the Hirschhorn's was heated by a brick stove located in the kitchen upon which the family's food was also cooked. There were just two small bedrooms, both childrens' rooms which, when the family was completed, consisted of six girls and four boys. With the two dormitory-like bedrooms fully occupied, the parents slept in a small section of the large living room that was curtained off for privacy. In addition to these interior comforts, the house was dis-

---

*In 1998, Joe's nephew Donald Hirschhorn, visited Tuckums and Djukst where he took photographs of houses in poor repair, one of which certainly might have been the family's domicile.

tinguished by an indoor toilet (quite rare at the time) with seating for three. A door from the kitchen afforded convenient access to the store. In truth, while Lazer was alive, the family lived well. Lazer provided his wife with household servants, a cook and housemaid as well as a wet nurse to relieve her after the birth of each of her children. He also paid a man to take care of the vegetable garden which, in summer, provided fresh, healthy food for their substantial brood.

The Hirschhorns lived a religious, Orthodox Jewish life. In their large living room an area was set aside for worship complete with an Ark containing a Torah. On Sabbaths and religious holidays this reserved area served as the town's synagogue—the center of the community's religious life. It was here that the male congregation of Djukst met for daily morning prayers, regularly each Sabbath and for special religious observances. It was also a place of refuge for itinerant Jewish peddlers who might be caught on the road at the start of the Sabbath on Fridays at sundown, a time when travel was restricted to walking. The peddlers were welcomed to stay at the Hirschhorns from Friday sundown until sundown on Saturday when the Sabbath was over and when they could climb back in their wagons and drive home. Naturally, they paid a fee for the board and lodging. The religious observances and routines continued while Lazer was alive and after his death. The ten Hirschhorn children were exposed to all of this Jewish culture and, among most of them, especially the girls, the lessons were absorbed.

Lazer traveled the area on his horse and wagon both buying the goods to be sold in his store as well as selling his products to farmers and housewives who were unable to make the journey to Djukst. This was his daily practice while, during the week, his children attended school for nine months of the year. The children received their education in Yiddish, their mother tongue, and in German which, instead of Russian, was their second language. The family also spoke Lettish, the language of Latvia. Education was valued, but for the Hirschhorn males, earning a good living for one's family was even more important—it was the mark of a successful husband. Thus, when Herman, their eldest, reached the age of thirteen in December 1896, two-and-a-half years before Joseph was born, he joined his father in the store and on the wagon making rounds. At the same time their daughter, Rahele, was encouraged to continue her education. At twelve, she was sent to the gymnasium (equivalent to an American high school) in Mitau as Amelia felt able to manage at home without Rahele's assistance.

During the good weather in summer the family went on outings, traveling by wagon to a nearby lake where they swam, relaxed and picnicked on the shore. A wedding or *bris* (circumcision), would find them together in the family wagon traveling to the event. In this way the family lived a comfortable and, for middle-class Russian Jews, conventional life. It was only after Lazer died that things changed.

No death certificate has been located which would verify the cause of Lazer's sudden death. It was his grandchildren who reported what Amelia had told them: that his appendix ruptured, became infected and, untreated, led to his death at age forty. Joe believed his father died of diverticulitis, a condition Joe himself acquired in his fifties. Underscoring the fact that in Latvia in 1900, "they didn't know what it was all about," Joe believed he had inherited the condition from his father. "I have twelve feet of it in my lower bowel and so every now and then I get an infection," he told Paul Cummings in his seventy-seventh year. Given the limitations of medical treatment and the remoteness of their village, there is no reason to doubt that either ruptured appendix or diverticulitis, as Joe believed, was the cause of Lazer's untimely death. In any event, Lazer's loss had a severe impact on the family and long-lasting emotional and financial implications for everyone.

With the head of the family gone, it fell to Herman, not yet sixteen, to take Lazer's place as head of the family and chief breadwinner. Amelia also relied upon him to set an example for the younger children. Immature for his age, harboring dreams of self-realization, even heroism, Herman recoiled at his new roll. Amelia's expectations and the tiresome obligations to a large family not of his making felt overwhelmingly burdensome. Herman was not a young man well-suited to the paternalistic role into which he had grudgingly been cast.

Two years after Lazer died, when Herman was barely eighteen, Amelia asked him to undertake an important assignment that put most of Amelia's assets into his hands, a task that would have taken him to the town of Mitau, a week's journey from their home. Family legend posits that Herman was sent on a mission either to sell the family cattle or to take 1,000 rubles of family funds to Mitau to replenish the store of flax. Regardless, Herman was expected back in about two weeks. He never returned to Latvia. In time Herman wrote to his mother from South Africa where he had gone to the Friedlander relatives he knew were there: two brothers, cousins of Amelia's, who were successfully making their fortunes in what became an important town about 400 miles northeast of Cape Town called De Aar. The money Herman confiscated paid for his transportation to Cape Town and from there to his relatives where he hoped they would give him a financial start in this new country.

It was several years before Herman reappeared, and by that time the family was living in Brooklyn. Without the expertise of Lazer or the strength of her eldest son to help carry the responsibilities of running the dairy and store, the family suffered. Although Amelia and her children never experienced hunger, life was full of hard work and empty of luxuries. While the oldest children, Herman, Rahele and Annie, had known the comforts of financial security, the younger children had no such memories, especially Joseph, who was three when Herman deserted them.

Needless to say, with this betrayal by Amelia's eldest child, the family's finances suffered a severe blow and continued to sink into a steady decline that threatened the family's future. Equally threatening was the violent uprising and riots that came to a head in Russia in 1905, riots that foretold the Russian Revolution twelve years later when the Czarist Empire was dissolved and replaced by a Marxist dictatorship. Both of these events propelled Amelia to a difficult but necessary decision: she would have to remove her children from Latvia. It had become clear that she and her daughters, even with the assistance of a hired man, were not able to successfully operate the general store and that Russia had become too dangerous for Jews. Amelia began planning the necessary strategy to take her family to America.

Amelia was faced with a number of tactical problems. Paramount among them were how she would pay passage for the entire family and where she and her family would go. One of her nephews by marriage, Nathan Hirschhorn, was also planning to leave for America, but he was bound for Michigan to join his mother's family who had already settled in Bay City. Amelia had no desire to live in Michigan. She wanted to place her children in a city where they would have cultural advantages and where she and the elder children could readily find work. It appears Amelia had relatives named Jakobson living in the borough of Brooklyn, and it was to the Jakobsons she was determined to go. On the passenger manifest of her arrival in New York, she claimed to be traveling to her "brother-in-law, Louis Jakobson" and gave an address in Brooklyn.

More problems, more decisions. Amelia could not afford steamship passage for the entire family, not even in steerage. Therefore, she had to decide who would accompany her and which of her children would remain in Latvia to be sent for when money was available. She needed the skills of at least two of her elder daughters to work with her in America to earn the funds for passage, not just for the remaining children but also to complete the payment of her own and the girls' passage. She didn't want to be separated from her children a day longer than necessary. The little ones were too young to be without constant care whether they were in America or Latvia. Yet if she took them with her to New York, who would watch them while she and the older girls were working? Even so, she couldn't afford to bring the entire family at once.

Rahele, her eldest daughter, had recently married her cousin, Yehuda Leib Hirschhorn, and it was decided that some of the small children would remain with the newlyweds in the house in Tuckums. As the little ones would need an adult (those considered children today were accustomed to accepting adult responsibilities even at the age of thirteen!) Amelia decided to leave her next-oldest daughter, Annie, behind to bring the little ones over at a future date. Ella and Freida could accompany Amelia to New York. Both girls were able seamstresses and, at ages fourteen and thirteen, old enough to work. Annie, the daughter whom she had selected as the one to be in charge of the youngest children during the crossing to America, was a was sweet-tempered and patient young woman but strong in character and someone whom the little children all loved. So with one deviation—one which had an immense impact on the future of Joe Hirshhorn—it was settled.

Rahele and her husband would keep four of the youngest five (Abe, Irving, Fannie and Dora) in the home they had always known. The couple would live in the house and continue to run the store. Annie, until she would be pressed into service to chaperone the little ones to America, was sent to work in a small grocery store in the nearby town of Dovlin. Joe was sent to live with Amelia's brother Peretz, who with his wife Zetta, had begged to have the boy live with them until he could rejoin Amelia in America. They were crazy about the child: he was cute, bright and energetic. And they were childless.

The couple lived in Riga, a large, historic city where they had their own home. Peretz had a successful lumber business. The fact that he and Zetta had no children certainly added to their eagerness to play the part of foster parents for Joe. Amelia felt pity for the childless couple, since she herself had been blessed with many children. When she agreed to allow Joey to stay in Riga with Peretz and Zetta, it was clearly understood the arrangement would last only until she could send for him.

Amelia, now forty-two, together with Ella, almost fourteen, and Frieda, nearly thirteen, boarded the S.S. *Patricia* on May 26, 1906, sailing out of Hamburg, Germany bound for Ellis Island. Their steerage tickets, partially paid for, obliged them to continue sending money from New York to the shipping company until the balance was paid off. After that they would start saving to pay for the passage of the next wave of Hirschhorns. The three women arrived in New York Harbor June 10, 1906, when Theodore Roosevelt was President of the United States and San Francisco had not yet recovered from the earthquake and fire that had devastated the city, killing 452 people one month earlier.

II
Amerika, Amerika!

Amelia Hirshhorn's introduction to America did not go as planned. The ship's manifest records that Amelia and her daughters were housed on Ellis Island while the authorities tried to locate Louis Jakobson, the brother-in-law who was supposed to meet them at the pier.[*] They never did find him.

She gave the immigration inspectors two different addresses for her in-law, neither of which actually existed. Nevertheless, the three women were released into Manhattan with the help of the Hebrew Immigrant Aid Society (HIAS), a Jewish ombudsman agency established for the purpose of aiding Jewish immigrants. Within a remarkably short time the women found jobs, rented a three-room tenement apartment in Brooklyn, and welcomed two boarders to whom Amelia rented a small bit of space in order to save more money. This was a common practice for poor but determined immigrants. A mother longing for her children was willing to suffer most any deprivation to shorten the time when her family could be reunited.

Amelia was employed in a factory that made pocketbooks. Ella and Frieda both found work at the Triangle Shirtwaist Company. All three women worked twelve-hour days, six days a week, for which they received no more than $3.00 per week, a typical pay scale for workers in "sweatshops." By March of 1911, the Triangle Shirtwaist Company, where Ella and Frieda were still employed, became a household word and tragic events that occurred there ultimately changed working conditions in America.

*Jakobson is the Russian spelling.

Meanwhile, in Riga, Joe was living a life of luxury he had never before experienced. Uncle Peretz was a lumber merchant with a successful business, one that enabled the childless couple to live a comparatively luxurious lifestyle. This, coupled with the Peretz's joy in having a child they deemed "adorable" in their care, gave them reason to shower Joe with treats of every kind including toys and beautiful clothes. For the first time little Joe had new clothes to wear instead of hand-me-downs from Abe and Irving. Uncle Peretz took Joe fishing, something he had never done before. Sophisticated, big-city Riga was a far cry from the rural backwater of Tuckums. In Riga, Joe attended concerts and saw a library and museum for the first time. He was taken on picnics and was entertained in the homes of other affluent Jews. Every day he traveled by cart to a school that was forty minutes from home where he learned Latvian, German, Russian and Hebrew surrounded by various Jakobson cousins.[*] For additional studies Peretz hired a private tutor to instruct Joe. His time—a year and a half—with the couple exposed Joe to a lifestyle that strongly influenced his future aspirations and forever separated him from his siblings who seemed content to live average, middle-class lives. This window into a privileged, upper-class world that Joe experienced, played an important (if unconscious) part in Joseph Hirshhorn's consuming ambition. He found out that with money one could live well.

Years later, when the adult Joe was asked about the time he spent with Uncle Peretz and Aunt Zetta, he described Peretz as a jolly man with a red mustache and his wife as a woman who seemed "a little crazy." He remembered that she would wake him at 3:00 A.M. to give him a bath. "The best thing about living with them," he said, "was that I had a bed all to myself!"

The couple grew so attached to little Joe they not only treated him like a prince but, when the time came to return him to his mother, they begged Amelia to be allowed to adopt the boy.

---

*It was Hirshhorn's own testimony that he had Jacobson cousins. Without that indication from him, because the Jakobsons Amelia was seeking upon her arrival in New York were never found, one would have doubts as to their existence.

Amelia loved this son as she loved all her children, perhaps more. Even Amelia was not immune to her five-year-old boy's precocious charms. And Joe, for all his new experiences and the kindnesses of Uncle Peretz and Aunt Zette, missed his mother terribly and looked forward to being with her again. Amelia was adamant in turning down her brother's request to keep Joe. One of her last letters advising Annie of the arrangements for the voyage ahead, included a mother's cry of near panic. She wrote, "Under no circumstances should you leave Joe behind. You *must* bring him with you to America."

Following the detailed instructions Annie received from her mother, she collected the children who had remained with Rahele then, traveling together by horse and wagon to Riga, she picked up Joe from a tearful Peretz and Zetta, taking them on to the Baltic port of Libau, a few hours journey away. From Libau they boarded a steamship which took them to Liverpool where they were to go aboard the S.S. *Cedric* bound for New York. Their journey was delayed a week in Liverpool during which time Annie kept the children busy taking walks on the dock. Dora, years later, told her granddaughter, Diane, that on one of these walks she had seen bananas for the first time and had no idea what they were.

The S.S. *Cedric* finally sailed out of Liverpool on September 26, 1907, arriving in New York Harbor October 4th. Clearly Joe, just turned eight, must have been a very appealing child, for during the nine-day voyage, while the six Hirschhorns were booked in steerage, a couple traveling first class became quite taken with the boy. As Annie later told the story to Barry Hyams, who related it in his 1979 biography of Joe, *Hirshhorn: Medici from Brooklyn,* every morning she washed and dressed the children, Joe in the new clothing Uncle Peretz had provided. The instant he was released, the boy rushed to climb out of the hold and onto the steerage deck. The first day, a man with his wife at his side, leaning against the railing in first class spotted the small boy, smiled at him and tossed an orange down which Joe deftly caught. It was the first orange he had ever seen and, after examining it, Joe looked up at the man as if to ask, "What is this?" Again the man smiled and gestured an invitation for the boy to join him. Joe, not one to hesitate even for an instant, quickly ran up the stairs to the upper deck and befriended the man whose name he never knew. For the remainder of the crossing, the inquisitive, energetic, charming child delighted the passengers of the upper decks on a daily basis. Annie concluded her story with the telling comment, "Joey always wanted to be in first class."

Upon her children's arrival in New York, Amelia anxiously waited in the Great Hall of Ellis Island during the seemingly interminable delay until the newcomers finally cleared immigration. When at last the children were seated on one of the long benches behind a barrier awaiting release, Amelia was questioned by an official intent on knowing how she would be able to support so large a brood. It was a tense moment. The historic experience Latvian Jews had of government officials was, to put it mildly, threatening, and Amelia hadn't been in America long enough to overcome that foreboding. But the fear was unfounded since the inspector was satisfied with Amelia's answers to his questions and her children were released to her.

The entry process had been lengthy, the hour was late and everyone was tired. No matter, Amelia herded her newly arrived children on foot across the Williamsburg Bridge to join their sisters, Ella and Frieda, at an apartment at 32 Morell Street in Williamsburg, Brooklyn, which she had rented in anticipation of their arrival.

But it wasn't long before Amelia found the tenement apartment on Morell Street too crowded for nine people and moved the household to a larger five-room railroad flat in a three-story brick building at 17 Humbolt Street, also in Williamsburg, a building that dwarfed the adjoining row of houses. Joe vividly remembered when his older brother Herman, (who had absconded with the family funds and run off to South Africa) suddenly reappeared. "On Humbolt Street, number seventeen," Joe told Barry Hyams, "my older brother, Herman, slept on a couch in the living room. There was only one brass bed, I think the girls used it. I always slept on a folding cot." On May 3, 1908, a fire destroyed the Humbolt Street building as the family slept in their second-floor apartment. It is no wonder Joe remembered the apartment. Dora, who was eight at the time, told her granddaughter, Diane, in 1975, "There was some kind of Italian holiday and the streets were decorated. Somebody got a crazy notion to set a fire with gasoline on the steps of the building so [the residents] couldn't get out. The only way out was though a window or get burnt." It was Herman who, upon hearing the noise outside, discovered the blaze. He gathered the family in the front room which overlooked the street and, leaning out the window, waved to the firemen below who spread a net into which Herman, literally, tossed the younger children. "He threw us out like a bag of potatoes, each one," Dora remarked. Herman then persuaded his three older sisters to jump into the net. Helping his mother to the sill, he urged her to jump, which she did. But, somehow Amelia missed the net and landed on the pavement where she lay hurt and unconscious until an ambulance took her to St. Catherine's Hospital where she was treated for internal injuries. "Uncle Joe was hurt, too," Dora said, "but he didn't stay long in the hospital. The apartment had a fence with metal spikes. I was caught on one of those," Dora added.

It was good that Herman had been restored to the family. The heroic part he played in the trauma on Humbolt Street needs to be underscored. It is interesting to note that not a single member of the family ever learned exactly where Herman was living or what his life had been like while he was living in South Africa. Interviewing his sisters, nieces and nephews, even his daughter-in-law of thirty years, no one had any information about where Herman had gone or what Herman had done in South Africa. He never spoke about those years and it was easy to conclude Herman had something to hide. In researching the family's history, it became evident Herman had entered the United States illegally. Exactly when he entered is not certain but he lived in the U.S. from about 1907 until his death in February 1957, a total of fifty years during which time he never voted because, unable to prove his arrival date, he was unable to become a citizen. In fact, Herman was a fugitive from the Cape Colony, having been at the wrong end of three criminal episodes, each involving a shady financial deal. But, luckily, he was in Brooklyn to save his family on the third of May 1908.

The fire was a serious one, the first of two New York fires

that threatened the family, but the second didn't occur until 1911. In the Humbolt Street blaze, while the Hirschhorns, due to Herman's quick thinking, escaped alive, the fire gutted the building killing an entire family trapped on the third floor. Joe later told a biographer, Barry Hyams, that he had known "the bitter taste of poverty," that there was never very much to eat and that in the aftermath of the fire the family was separated and the children had to fend for themselves. "I stayed alive on garbage," he reported. Annie, upon reading this account after the book's publication, took serious umbrage at Joe's statement. Though she rarely demonstrated anger, especially at her younger brother, Annie was deeply offended and snapped, "None of us ever went hungry or ate garbage! He shouldn't have said that."

In future years, when Joe's business exploits in Canada and voluminous art acquisitions brought him great notoriety, he gave numerous interviews to various media. He nearly always spoke about how he'd been driven to earn sufficient money to be able to rid himself "of the bitter taste of poverty." None of his siblings ever referred to the early years in Brooklyn as an impoverished time. Annie resented all such references when her brother made them and denied the family ever went hungry. Poor, yes; a time of suffering, no.

Annie was ten years Joe's senior. Her memories of Latvia were lucid. But even the youngest of Joe's siblings never reflected a displeasure equal or even similar to his. Yes, there was a decided difference between the family's lifestyle in Tuckums, which was fundamentally a country life full of fresh air and plenty of farm-fresh food, and the tenement life of crowded Brooklyn streets and hard work in dusty, airless factories. It seems that Joe's experience in Uncle Peretz's home had given him a higher standard to aim for and one which caused Brooklyn to suffer by comparison.

When Amelia was released from the hospital, the family regrouped at another tenement apartment on Montieth Street in the same Williamsburg neighborhood. Like most immigrants, Amelia moved the family many times, always upgrading their living quarters. But whether she did it to stay one month ahead of the rent collector, as many immigrants admitted, is doubtful.

Amelia was a good money manager and scrupulously honest. During the year that followed the fire, seeing the long hours for little pay that his mother worked, energetic Joe, eager to ease her burden, began selling newspapers in his free time and running errands for a nickel, dime or, if he was lucky, a quarter when the offer was made.

By September 1908, when Joe was nine, the Hirschhorns were living at 482 Bushwick Avenue in Brooklyn and the youngest children—Fannie, Irving, Joseph and Dora—were enrolled in P.S. (Public School) 145. It was there they made several significant, lifelong acquaintances. Joe met Jennie Berman, also nine years old, who would eventually become his first wife and the mother of his four natural children. It is fascinating to note that on the occasion of the first meeting of the two mothers-in-law-to-be, Amelia told Rose Berman, Jennie's mother, her memory of Joe's first sight of Jennie at school. When he arrived home from school that day he proclaimed, "Mama, I've just met the girl I'm going to marry." Hearing the story, Rose burst out laughing; Amelia joined in, commenting, "Well, Joey always knew what he wanted, even at nine." At the same P.S. 145, at the same time, Irving met Bessie Passoff whom he would one day marry.

By 1910, the relocations from one tenement to another ended and, with Herman still living at home, (being the eldest male in the family, he was identified in the 1910 U.S. Census as "Head of Household"), the family routine was well established. Amelia "got up at 6:00 A.M. to make our breakfast and put things up to cook so we could eat at night," Joe remembered. "Then she went to work and came home late. She earned twelve dollars a week making pocketbooks. On Saturday nights she was a cook for weddings and parties. She'd bring back big bags of food—chicken and leftovers. She worked like hell. It killed me the way my mother worked. I swore one day I would make a million dollars and make her life easier. And I did," Joe said many years later, the pain he felt so many years before plain on his face. He finished describing their life in the early years.

"My little sister, Dora, and I set the large table in the

kitchen for the evening meal. It was the only one the family took together."

Annie had been working since her arrival in New York in a small factory sewing silk bow ties and *jabots* that women wore at the throat of their shirtwaists. Abe tended to be sickly and worked only intermittently. The four youngest children continued their education at P.S. 145, although Fannie, at fourteen, looked forward to graduation when she would join her two elder sisters, Ella and Frieda, still employed at the Triangle Shirtwaist Company. Irving, at thirteen, became a Bar Mitzvah and would, in another year, go to work for a grocer, learning a business which, in time, became his permanent occupation. Joe, in addition to his schooling, was interested in athletics. In spite of his small stature—he was invariably the smallest boy in his class—Joe was well-coordinated, graceful and quick. He liked to play handball and stickball and ran in school track meets. "I went to Public School 145 in Williamsburgh, Brooklyn. It wasn't far from the Overmyer & Evans Brewery. The neighbors were Irish kids, Jewish kids, Italians, all kinds of children. I was on the relay team at school. Anyway, we had a track meet at a school on Staten Island. We had to take a Myrtle Avenue train that was in Williamsburgh in those days, to get on the Brooklyn Bridge. From Brooklyn Bridge on the Manhattan side you had to walk from Nassau Street to Broad Street to take the Staten Island ferry at Bowling Green. Well, we walked down Broad Street. I saw a lot of people with red hats and green hats. I stayed there."* That was Joe's first glimpse of Wall Street, an encounter made an indelible impression on him. Indeed, it was a fork in the road that gave unexpected direction and impetus to his life.

In those early days, stock trades were conducted out of the windows of the buildings by brokers who signaled to men on the street the various buy and sell orders. Hand signals akin to those used by the deaf, communicated the name of the stock and number of shares in the trade. As Joe's teammates continued walking

*Quotation from a transcript of an oral interview of Joseph Hirshhorn by Paul Cummings on December 16, 1976 for the Smithsonian Archives.

through the district, Joe stood transfixed at this mesmerizing secret code and the fevered activity that followed in the wake of the cryptic signals. He had the feeling, the sense, that these men were making the world go around. Struck dumb with a sudden and overwhelming desire to be a part of what he saw as a wonderfully exciting world, Joe never noticed the class proceed on to Bowling Green, board the ferry and sail off to the track meet on Staten Island. He remained where he was, literally stopped dead in his tracks until the Curb Market closed for the day hours later.[*] What Joe had witnessed was a tantalizing preview of coming attractions. He had seen his future. He made up his mind that very day that being a stockbroker was what he wanted to do with his life.

*The Curb Market is now the American Exchange.

III

If You're Clean, You're Smart

Joe Hirshhorn's size caused him to suffer a good deal of teasing and embarrassment throughout his school years in Brooklyn. Children were lined up according to height in those days and, as shortest person in class, Joe was always either first in line or last. In the teeming, immigrant-populated Williamsburg neighborhood where he lived, Joe was told by fellow students and street ruffians, "Ask your mother to bury you in the sand in Coney Island, that'll make you grow." When Joe shared his humiliation with Amelia, she comforted him by saying, "You don't have to be tall to be great." He apparently took this lesson to heart. Joe's supreme self-confidence as an adult underscored his mother's prescient comment and that comment may indeed have been a catalyst.

When, in his teens, Joe was invited by his future sister-in-law, Ruth, to attend her graduation from Eastern District High School, the doorman at the entrance refused him admission because a guest had to be sixteen years old and the doorman just didn't believe Joe was that old. He didn't reach his full height of five feet, four inches, until he was *more than twenty years old.* Joe's mother-in-law, Rose Berman, believed the cardinal motivating factor behind Joe's drive to make money was because he thought being rich would compensate for his lack of height by adding figurative inches to his height.

Amelia instilled the values she carried with her from "the old country" into her children, or at least she tried to. The habit of observing the Sabbath in the strictly Orthodox tradition continued as it had in Latvia. Every Friday at sundown in the Hirschhorn home candles were lit, the table was set with Amelia's best white cloth, *challah* was served and the family abstained from work until sundown the following Saturday. Yiddish was the language spoken at home and only kosher food was bought, prepared and served. The family belonged to an Orthodox synagogue on Varick Street where, before he turned thirteen, Joe reluctantly prepared for his Bar Mitzvah, learning how to read Hebrew and how to *daven* the Hebrew prayers. Joe later admitted he went through the rite of passage to adulthood only to please his mother. So Americanized had he become in the five years since stepping off the S.S. *Cedric*'s gangway, the ritual meant little to him. In addition to religion, Amelia stressed the importance of strong family bonds, education, culture and cleanliness. Out of her meager salary of $12.00 a week, she spent fifty cents on piano lessons and fifty cents for payments on a rented piano. As for the matter of cleanliness, Annie's daughter Esta Carlen, who lived her teenage years with Amelia and three of the aunts, said the standard was clear, "If you were clean, you were smart!"

It is impossible to overestimate the importance of Amelia's influence on her children, particularly on Joe. This strong, ethical woman was the nerve center of the family. Amelia was the pillar against which her children leaned and the warmth around which they huddled until the day she died. Her unconditional love infused them with strength and much of what they did was to gain Amelia's approval. The respect and love the Hirschhorn children had for her never diminished. Even after they were grown, married, moved into their own apartments and raised their own families, Amelia's children continued to gather around her and each other. When she moved, they moved to neighborhoods within blocks of her. Although Joe was the single exception to the practice of living in close proximity to Amelia, he never abandoned her or his siblings.

As early as the age of ten, when the only money he was able to earn came from selling newspapers on one of the five corners that converged at Broadway and Flushing Avenue in Brooklyn, Joe gave everything he made to Amelia, keeping only twenty-five cents for himself. Of this amount, twenty cents was spent on admission to B.F. Keith's Gates Theater, the Fox Follies or the neighborhood burlesque house. With the remaining nickel Joe bought a small pie, something he never got at home where Amelia only baked strudel.

The impact of Brooklyn tenement life and the characters Joe met on the streets of Williamsburg played a significant role in the development of his personality. In addition to having to "tough it out" among the delinquents who regularly taunted immigrant children, a teacher once insulted Joe by calling him a "little shrimp," a name that was likely to be remembered and adopted by his classmates. Never one to back down, Joe fought back, calling the teacher a "big shrimp," for which he was severely chastised not only at school but also by Amelia who, shocked by his disrespect for a teacher, struck him across the mouth, a punishment Joe felt was unjust.

It was during Joe's childhood that his sense of wariness (that would later, at times, verge on full-blown paranoia) began to take firm root. Joe's quizzical nature and refusal to take anything at face value certainly contributed to shaping the toughness, shrewdness and suspicion that became ingrained in his character. Just one day after his arrival in America, Joe received a first and lasting lesson in the price of gullibility.

As he ran down the stairs from the third-floor apartment of his new home on Monteith Street to the street, Joe noticed several boys huddled behind the stairs which he had just descended. He had no English at his command nor was he familiar with the game the boys were playing but he was curious. It turned out these little ruffians were shooting craps, a game Joe had never before encountered and knew nothing of. Letting the players know he had three pennies in his pocket and would like to join them in play, they willingly agreed. They were more than happy to take advantage of this little "greenhorn" and have his three pennies for themselves. They made room for him and demonstrated the method of play.

To their chagrin, Joe, their "easy mark" didn't lose his pennies but instead won eighteen of theirs! Determined not to let the newcomer win over them, the boys abruptly broke up the game, roughed Joe up and stole back his winnings together with the three pennies he had contributed. He was left on the floor of the hallway, his body intact, his pride somewhat damaged; surprised, angry, and a far wiser child. This, his first exposure to the venality of some strangers, was a lesson in skepticism and wariness that stayed with him the rest of his life.

Another lesson that had a lasting impact on the young Joe occurred when his sister Annie worked for the company that made silk bow ties and *jabots*. Annie decided she could make extra money by crafting the same bow ties and *jabots* at home, then selling them wholesale to shops in the area. One day, having completed an order for one of her customers in lower Manhattan, Annie offered Joe fifty cents to deliver the order for her. His destination was some distance from home, and Joe set off with Annie's bundles at his usual hurried pace. While running along Allen Street near Delancy, not far from the customer's shop, he was stopped by a stranger who asked him how he would like to make "an easy quarter." All Joe had to do was deliver a message to the fourth floor of a nearby house while the stranger held Joe's bundles for him. Depositing Annie's packages in the man's arms, Joe bounded up the stairs and returned quickly, winded but expectant. The man was gone and with him Annie's bundles and Joe's naivete. The fact that this story was told and retold as a cautionary tale by the adult Joe Hirshhorn underscores the incident's importance in developing in him the highly suspicious side of his nature which encompassed everything and everyone—including his own children.

Although Annie gently forgave a shame-faced Joe, he was unable to forgive himself. Joe had learned another hard and bitter lesson: he didn't like to be fooled.

By 1910, the family unit was changing as Amelia's older children began to form attachments outside the home. In November 1910, Frieda married Nathan Goldzweig. They actually married twice. Amelia didn't accept the first marriage, which took place in the clerk's office at city hall. Three days later the couple was married again by a Rabbi in the apartment on Bushwick Avenue. Their children, Sally, born in 1911 and Leo, born in 1914, ultimately shortened their name to Gold. Then on January 1, 1911, Herman married Goldie (called Gussie) Gilden, a young woman described by his sisters and nieces as a beautiful woman and devoted mother. Unfortunately, Gussie's health was fragile and she died in 1925 leaving an eight-year-old son, Leo.

Amelia chose not to move from the apartment on Bushwick Avenue, making more space available for her and the remaining children. But soon afterward, the family experienced another event, one which was tragically shocking to the city of New York but unbelievably lucky for the Hirschhorns. Three months after Herman and Gussie's wedding, on March 25, 1911, as employees were getting ready to leave for the day, the Triangle Shirtwaist factory, where Ella and Frieda worked, burst into flames. The upper three stories, the seventh, eighth and ninth floors, were engulfed within minutes. Hundreds of workers, mostly young, Jewish and Italian immigrant women were trapped inside, together with examiners, bookkeepers and foremen. The Triangle was a model factory in its day turning out women's blouses, which at that time were called shirtwaists. There were approximately 250 sewing machines on each of the three floors, and because not all were in use at any given time, no one was able to say exactly how many of their hundreds of employees were in the building at the time.

Seamstresses working on the seventh and eighth floors, locked into their workrooms, were unable to escape the blaze. In the eighteen minutes it took to bring the fire under control, 146 workers, 123 of them the Jewish and Italian immigrant girls sewing blouses, were killed either by incineration, by suffocation or by jumping to their deaths from windows high above the street. Although firemen arrived at the scene, their ladders weren't tall enough to reach the people hanging desperately out windows, pleading to be rescued from the flames.

The fact that the workers had been locked inside the workrooms preventing them from reaching stairs up to the roof or down to the street and safety, and that there were no safety measures protecting innocent laborers, was a scandal that rocked the garment industry. The fire outraged the citizens of New York and shocked political leaders across America. It was this conflagration that led to massive changes in the legal protections afforded workers in the United States. And, although the owners were brought before the bar of justice, no one was ever convicted of negligence in the tragic fire.

Ella and Freida escaped this disaster by minutes, having left work without permission to attend a party shortly before the blaze began. Family lore reports the two girls heard the sirens as they made their way from the factory in Greenwich Village to the subway that would take them back to Brooklyn in order to change into their costumes for the party. At the time, they had no idea the fire engines were speeding toward the building from which they had providentially just departed.

For the first time Amelia understood that luck might not always protect the family (although the Hirschhorns' good fortune vis-à-vis deadly fires seemed to be a constant). The 1908 fire on Monteith Street from which she and her children narrowly escaped, together with this horrifying Triangle Waist Company tragedy, highlighted for Amelia the vagaries of chance. Realizing that should fate rob her of one of her children, she might not have the funds for a burial, Amelia took out insurance on each of them. This decision, Joe regularly claimed, led to his first brush with art in his adopted country.

"My mother had insurance on all of us," Joe said. "Every Saturday evening the Prudential man came to the house to collect his money. Once a year, at Christmas, he brought a calendar with beautiful pictures, romantic paintings by French Salon artists—the Barbizon School—like [Adolfe-William] Bouguereau, [Jozof] Israels, [Patrick] Nasmyth and [Edwin] Landseer, pictures of a world, places and people all new to me. Every month I couldn't wait until we tore off another page. I used to cut up those pictures and hang them on the ugly green walls in the bedroom where I slept with my brothers and on the walls of the other rooms where I could look at them every day. We lived in a railroad flat and the walls were painted an ugly green. [The pictures] brightened the whole apartment and I loved them. Those calendars were the first art I had seen, they excited me and I wanted more. I kept dreaming about them, looking at them morning and night. It intrigued me. I think this is how my art world started."

As this was Joe's first exposure to world-recognized art, it left a lasting impression on him, as if it were the only real and significant art in the world. It is no wonder that among the first works Hirshhorn bought and hung on the walls of his house in Great Neck in 1930, were prime examples of the precise, realistic style of the 19th century French school. One was a large Adolfe-William Bouguereau painting called "The Madonna of The Lilies" that depicted Jesus' mother, Mary, seated like a queen on a throne. Her hands were raised and her robes were in vibrant, beautiful colors which contrasted vividly with the almost luminous skin tones for which Bougereau was justly famous. In addition, Joe hung a Landseer interior of a dog stretched out in front of a crackling fireplace, and a painting by Jozef Israels of a wooded winter scene with a late afternoon sun that reflected pink on the surface of the snow and off a stream running diagonally, from top left to bottom right, through the painting. Years later, Joe recognized the limitations of the Barbizon School as he was exposed to the work of living artists and his taste matured. He not only learned to appreciate contemporary art; Joe reconsidered his old standards of beauty. While not disparaging their artistic value, he eventually called Israels' work "sympathetic, sweet," and "schmaltzy," and came to wholeheartedly embrace the new art. But that came much later.

IV

Stepping onto "The Street"

In 1913, at the age of fourteen, Joe graduated from the eighth grade. Since that day of the aborted Staten Island track meet, he was eager to make his way back down Broadway to Wall Street, a place etched into his memory. However, it wasn't his mother's wish. Amelia wanted him continue his education. To oblige her, Joe began attending classes at Bushwick High School but, determined to make some money, he took jobs in the afternoons and on Saturdays. This arrangement still didn't satisfy the ambitious teenager. He wanted more time to make money, so after a few months, he quit Bushwick and transferred to night school at Eastern High School so he could work full time. Joe found a job in an optometry and jewelry store owned by S. Lesnick & Sons of Bay Ridge, cousins of Myron and David Selznick of Hollywood.[*] Joe's salary of $20.00 a week was a great deal of money at the time and his duties included running errands which took him across the East River to Manhattan and Maiden Lane, an area which enabled him to become even more familiar with the financial district that he had first glimpsed when he abandoned his teammates.

Whenever Joe passed by, he was reminded again of what awaited him when he would find himself free to venture permanently into the caverns of Wall Street.

Before the age of fifteen, too impatient to wait any longer, Joe quit his job and—forever—his formal education. Amelia was appalled and angry both at his dismissal of the importance of for-

---

[*]David would eventually marry L.B. Mayer's daughter Irene as well as produce *Gone With The Wind*.

Joe at his graduation from P.S. 145, circa 1913.

mal education and by his disregard for the family's financial needs. Imagine giving up a job that paid $20.00 a week! But Joe couldn't wait any longer to become a part of the purposeful madness of stock trading; to find himself every day in the financial district able to gamble on his own future.

People often like to think success is fundamentally being in the right place at the right time with luck a major element. But clearly, Joe's ultimate success wasn't so much luck as it was the product of determination and hard work. He had tremendous energy and not an ounce of false pride. No job was too small or too petty for him to master because he understood that details were the bricks and mortar of the career he was starting to build. Each business exposure became a school, a place where lessons could be learned, lessons from which he would grow and develop. He was getting a pragmatic education, not a theoretical one. He was open to everything, every new thought. He was a sponge absorbing new ideas, soaking up new knowledge in a mind that, like a computer, was assessing, storing and forever figuring out ways to apply all of it to his advantage.

In 1914, when Joe finally made his assault on the financial district, World War I had shut down most of the markets. The hyperactivity which had attracted him at fourteen when he first encountered the "street" was gone. Grown men were killing time playing cards on the steps of the imposing marble buildings of the area. He looked at them and saw they were not working, but Joe was determined to find employment. Walking into the new Equitable Building at 120 Broadway, he rode an elevator to the very top and, starting on the 35th floor and making his way downward floor by floor, he began knocking on doors asking for work. "The Guggenheim Brothers had three floors and they had one man who was interviewing all the help. I was a little bit of a boy, I think I was maybe four feet eight. I had one suit that my mother bought me. I had to cry for three months to get a four-dollar suit because we didn't have any money. It was a green suit with short pants. I'll never forget it."* With that suit Joe felt able to seek employment because regardless of how today's fourteen-year-olds would reject a suit with short pants, in those days boys and young men wore short pants until they were eighteen or even nineteen years old.

He left an application at American Smelting, Nevada Copper and about fifteen other offices. Finally, at the Emerson Phonograph Company on the 29th floor, Joe hit paydirt. They needed a switchboard operator. When asked if he knew how to use one, Joe brashly replied, "Yes," and was told to report to work the following Saturday. Immediately he took off at a run, up Broadway to the New York Telephone Company, where an easygoing receptionist let him study the switchboard. By Saturday he had learned how to operate the plugs, lights and toggles with ease, a talent he was able to utilize in the future as a trader.

Because his salary with Emerson was only $6.00 a week, quite a comedown from his previous $20.00 at Lesnick & Sons, he

---

*From a transcript of an interview of Joseph H. Hirshhorn by Paul Cummings for Smithsonian Archives of American Art, December 16, 1976.

supplemented his income by working for Western Union at
Fulton and Broadway, just blocks from the Stock Exchange.
There the night shift hummed with cabled reports of the European market. After leaving work at Emerson, Joe dashed around
the financial district for his second employer from 6:00 P.M. until
2:00 A.M., delivering messages to traders in the area. These errands allowed him to study the cables he carried, cables which
gave him insights into the workings of financial markets. He
marked one truth that jumped out from those messages he carried and studied; that buyer or seller, profit or loss, *the gain was
always the broker's* and, therefore, the more transactions a man
could stimulate, the better.

That quality in Joe's personality that had charmed Uncle
Peretz in Latvia and caught the attention of the first-class passenger aboard the S.S. *Cedric,* continued to command the attention of influential men during his early years on "The Street."

For $12.00 a week, from 6:00 P.M. to 2:00 A.M., Joe delivered
his cables, often to the venerable brokerage house of Cyrus J.
Lawrence, in business since 1830. In his frequent comings and
goings, Joe caught the attention of W. J. Hutchinson, the senior
partner of the firm who took an interest in the bright young man.
Hutchinson took Joe under his wing and ultimately taught him
the meaning of the movements of stocks on market graphs. With
the additional training in how to assess stock movements and
charting acquired at the behest of Billy Colen, when Joe was
working for R. D. Wycoff, Joe found it a method so useful that he
continued charting stocks in evaluating the trends in the overall
market and as a basis for his purchases and sales of shares for
the rest of his life.

His current job brought Joe into contact with a man whose
influence upon him was fortunate and far-reaching. That man
was Richard De Mille Wyckoff, a cousin of Cecil B. de Mille, the
"tough crazy genius" who owned the *Magazine of Wall Street* and
who had his office on the floor below Emerson Phonograph where
Joe held his daytime job. In addition to the magazine, the firm
also published a financial trend letter. As a subscriber, Billy
Colen, the manager, brother-in-law of Richard D. Wycoff and
Joe's boss at Emerson, took advantage of the ticker and its tape

of trade figures in the publication office and, when the Stock Exchange was open, he would monitor the market. At every opportunity, Joe would also slip downstairs to listen to the clackity-clack music of the printing of stock trades on the tape.[*]

Joe made his breakthrough into the Wyckoff office when his boss, Colen, asked at Emerson for a volunteer to work the holiday trend letter as a favor to Wyckoff. Sensing opportunity calling, Joe immediately stepped forward, to the other three office boys' relief.

When Joe arrived at the 28th floor, the day before Labor Day, to receive instructions as to what he was to do, he knocked on the door of the publisher's private office and politely but firmly announced: "Mr. Wyckoff, I don't like being just an office boy. I want to learn to be a stockbroker. I don't know anyone, but you do business with Schuyler, Chadwick and Burnham and, please, would you give me a chance . . ."

"Joe," Wyckoff snapped, "you know I was a stockbroker. It's a terrible business. You don't want to be in it."

"Mr. Wyckoff," he replied, "I love it. I love it."

Wyckoff seemed disturbed at the boy's declaration so Joe dropped the matter. But a week later, Colen delivered an offer from Wyckoff on the floor below. Joe could, if he wanted, take a job with Wyckoff watching the market. He jumped at the chance, quit his job at Emerson and went to work for the *Magazine of Wall Street* for a weekly salary of $8.00 which, with his Western Union pay of $12.00, brought his overall weekly earnings back to $20.00, a fact that reassured Amelia. Within a short time afterward, Billy Colen, keeping an eye on the eager, energetic youngster, asked, "How would you like to watch the market and I'll show you how to run the stock charts?" Nothing suited Joe better. He gave a brief outline of what he had been taught.

"They used great big charts and line charts and their tape. Stock charts are a tool in the market and you have to know how

*Ticker tape. An actual paper tape that fed through a machine which printed the stock-trades. Most brokerage offices had these instruments in them so the brokers could follow the action in the market.

to read them. One-point charts can only give you accumulation and distribution. Line charts are another thing. I watched them all day and used to run these things off from the one-point charts or the tape." He added, *"I like stock charts. I get turned on by them like everything else.* I have them on my desk." He added in 1976, "You have to know how to read them. And no matter how you read them, sometimes they fool you. It helped me in my own business, my mining business."

The work was long and difficult. "In those days the market was wild," Joe said, "and I worked like a dog. Stocks like Mexican Petroleum and Pan-American Petroleum hopped like frogs. I had to note each dollar move, up and down, and the averages. It was great!" Joe loved the action.

Now that he had a good job, one that legitimately allowed him to enter the world of finance and that taught him the tools of his preferred trade, Joe decided he needed a more dignified surname—one in keeping with his new status as a broker in training. He did it by adopting a middle initial and dropping the "c" from his last name, spelling it Hirshhorn. In imitation of Jessie L. Livermore, another financial hero, he decided upon "H" for a middle initial, using his brother Herman's first name. He liked the way the H. Hirshhorn looked. For Joe, at sixteen, still only four-feet-eleven, the new name seemed dignified, "I felt it added to my height," he said. And Amelia, who still received all his income, upped his allowance to fifty cents a day. This Joe budgeted carefully. Ten cents went for his daily subway fare, another ten cents for lunch and fifteen cents for dinner. The remaining fifteen cents he socked away as a nest egg. He had big things in mind for his savings.

Joe was in his element. He loved everything about Wall Street and read everything he could get his hands on about the stock market. A series of articles in *Leslie's Weekly* inflamed his imagination. Each article, fifty in all, was a sketch about a successful mogul, one of whom was B.C. Forbes, the founder of *Forbes Magazine.* As it happened, a few floors below where Joe worked in the Equitable Building was the office of the great Forbes himself. Learning that all fifty biographies were to be published in book form, Joe went directly to the Forbes office in order to purchase a copy of the book which was to become almost a bible for him. The receptionist had to look down over the barrier separating her from the entry in order to see the small lad in knee pants who was asking to buy a copy of *Men Who Are Making America.** Thinking he couldn't possibly afford the price, she told Joe the book was $10.00 and was surprised to hear him respond, firmly, "I'll take it." Astonished, the receptionist went to fetch Forbes in person who then listened as Joe quoted, word for word, from the advertisement for the book, "No volume exists to enable the ambitious young man to make the intimate acquaintance of so many of the nation's foremost men of affairs and learn from their own lips the most useful wisdom their eventful experiences have taught them." Impressed with the recital and pleased that this youngster thought so well of his advertisement, Forbes autographed an advance copy of the book and presented it to Joe for half its list price.

Joe studied the book which had a chapter on many men whose names are familiar to this day: Alexander Graham Bell, Andrew Carnegie, T. Coleman DuPont, George Eastman, Thomas Alva Edison, Henry Ford, Henry Clay Frick, Cyrus H. McCormick, John D. Rockefeller, Cornelius Vanderbilt and others. He eagerly memorized the two sets of necessary qualifications calculated to achieve success: the first set available to all, according to Forbes; the second set: "Qualities attainable only by those favorably endowed by Nature." Then he examined them for the qualities they all had in common with him. Among the first set of qualities listed were integrity, self-denial, sincerity, industry, sobriety, self-culture, cheerfulness, self-reliance, good temper, courage, stick-to-itiveness, confidence, concentration, steadfastness, loyalty, ambition, optimism and politeness. Joe focused on the "the rarer and higher qualities, not within reach of every brain," which included foresight, statesmanship, generalship—ability to select, to lead, and to inspire other men; "great mental and physical stamina, superior judgment, abnormal

*Copyright, 1916–1917, by B.C. Forbes. Reprinted by *County Life Press,* Garden City, NY. See Kissinger Publishing's Rare Reprints. ISBN 1428631968.

memory, willingness to incur large-scale risks adjudged capable of being turned to profitable account, personal magnetism, dynamic force, imagination and common sense," essential patience, perseverance and unflagging courage. At the age of seventy-four, in an interview with Barry Hyams, of those qualities, Joe remembered best the qualities of superior judgment, personal magnetism, essential patience, perseverance and unflagging courage, several of which are contained in a brief paragraph within the Introduction to the *Men Who Are Making America* written by B.C. Forbes himself.

> Indeed, one great lesson the lives of these notable men convey is that patience, perseverance, stick-to-itiveness, and unflagging courage are essential qualities.[*]

At the age of sixteen or seventeen, having studied the book with great care, he examined himself for the virtues he felt he didn't yet exhibit, then committed himself to acquiring them in time. He was pleased to note that, like himself, few of these business titans had formal schooling, many were short in stature and had been born poor, many had begun working in menial jobs and others had lost their fathers in boyhood. These commonalities gave Joe the feeling he had a right to strive for inclusion among this exclusive and celebrated group. Intending to become the fifty-first among these fifty admirable men, he noted that they had achieved their success at the average age of sixty-one. Not he. By his own admission, Joe was in a hurry. He intended to get there much faster. He told Paul Cummings in an interview for the *Smithsonian Archives of Art* in 1976, "I was a little man in a big hurry."

Years later, Joe was approached by the Horatio Alger society to be honored. Initially he was pleased as he truly was a great example of a Horatio Alger success story. But when he learned he had to make a sizable contribution to the society for this honor—if memory serves, it was $10,000—Joe's pragmatism set

[*]Ibid. p. viii.

in. He went through with the ceremony (which I attended) but was not "honored" by it. He considered it a sort of joke on him.

Joe's personal charm, that magnetic quality that had attracted a variety of influential men, also garnered the attention of Thomas L. Sexsmith. It was Sexsmith who wrote a trend letter that shocked skeptics by predicting U.S. Steel would go from forty to ninety. He was right, it did just that. It was Sexsmith who, working with Joe, taught the younger man more about charting stocks, how to read the ticker and interpret the track on the graph, thus sharpening and adding to skills that Hirshhorn employed to his advantage the rest of his life.

Now sixteen years old, Joe was impatient to try his wings. He quit his Western Union job without even bothering to receive his final two weeks' pay.[*] Gathering together his small hoard of savings, he started to gamble on the market. Joe didn't earn much but later said, "It was a great learning experience."

When Wyckoff moved his trend letter to the Marbridge Building in midtown Manhattan, he took Joe with him, raising his salary in stages until it reached $50. The youngster was worth every dollar. He raced around in his usual fast-paced manner, taking the time to stop at the Waldorf Hotel, close to the office at Fifth Avenue and 34th Street where he could study the trading board, hang around the tickertape and chat with one of the old timers, Jacob Fields, a respected member of the Stock Exchange. Fields, after watching Joe's interest and ability for a few months, suggested Hirshhorn go down to the Curb.[**] "Go on over," he instructed, "and tell my son Eddie that I'll guarantee your account." It was obvious Fields liked what he saw in the young man. That was all the push Joe needed. Returning to Wyckoff at his office, Hirshhorn announced he wanted to start trading on his own, even though he had insufficient funds of his own to do so. Wyckoff interrupted him mid-sentence, "I'll stake you," he said, "to the tune of $250 on the condition you stay on

[*]Years later, at a businessmen's lunch, Joe met the president of Western Union and accused, "You owe me $24.00." The next day a check arrived in the mail.
[**]The trades once performed on the curbs of Wall Street, eventually moved inside and became The American Exchange.

here at the magazine." Out of loyalty to the man who had shown such confidence in him, Joe agreed to Wyckoff's terms. In time, when Joe finally went out on his own, Wyckoff had to hire a man and two girls at a total cost of $150 to replace him!

From Fields and Company, run by Jake's two sons, Leonard and Edward, Joe left for the Curb market to join the crowd of traders on Broad Street. He was sixteen years old and still in short pants. "When I was working on Wall Street I was a curb broker. I was a kid seventeen years old. I went out of there with $255 that I saved. I'd buy nine-cent lunches at a place where Max used to be. There was a place on Ann Street and there was a place on New Street. At Max's in those days you'd get a frankfurter for three cents, a glass of orange juice for three cents and two rolls for three cents. I saved up $255." Spending so much time in that area, Joe began to notice places with art for sale.

Besides working with a broker in a fourth-floor window making trades, Joe charted stocks for W.J. Hutchinson for a weekly salary and acquired the business of Case-Pomeroy, investment bankers. During this time, engaged in a struggle for business with a pair known as the Gallagher Brothers, experienced men and cut-throat traders, Joe developed a technique which he also employed to advantage for the remainder of his business life. This is how he described the ploy. While holding a substantial block of a specific company's stock, he sent a broker—someone who, in a carnival show would have been called a *shill*—into the crowd to shout as loudly as possible, "buys" for that stock at the lowest bid. Then Joe would offer to buy at a price slightly above the shouted offer but below the price of the block he was holding. After a time, the "shill" broker offering the low-buys disappeared and the stock returned to the original price. By this method, Joe earned not only the broker's commission, but the gratitude of his customer and was turning over a steady gross in weekly trading of $20,000. Ten months after his 17th birthday, with Wyckoff's original $250 paid in full, Joe's net worth was $167,000, a remarkable climb, and an astonishing achievement for a man who was still a boy.

About that time, again demonstrating the esteem in which Joe was held by his financial mentors, Wyckoff took him to lunch at Fraunces Tavern, a venerable New York institution where George Washington bade farewell to his officers after the Revolutionary War. Wyckoff wanted to ask his advice. Joe could hardly believe his former employer's request. "What advice could I possibly give you?" he asked in astonishment. Wyckoff explained. He wanted to do something like what Forbes had done with his series and book, *Men Who Are Making America*. Joe, drawing upon his own desire to learn as much as possible about trading in the stock markets, suggested that he put together a book on the technique of buying and selling stocks, adding that he should make it a limited edition which would be sold for $500 a copy. Wyckoff followed this advice precisely. The book, marketed just as Joe had suggested, was a huge financial success. The entire edition sold out. In gratitude, Wyckoff autographed the first copy as a gift for the "boy-man" who had given him the suggestion.

Now, with his confidence in his future even greater than before, Joe decided it was time for him to discard his wardrobe of short pants, three over-laundered and mended shirts, as well as cheap shoes which had never fit properly. It was time for him to dress like a man of means. Joe took himself to Weber and Heilbroner, the authority on clothing for the well-dressed Brooklyn blades of the day, and bought himself two suits, a suitable supply of shirts and neckties, cuff links, tie clips, gloves and a Dobbs hat. At French, Shriner and Urner, Joe bought his first pair of properly fitted shoes to complete his new wardrobe. Still living at home on Lewis Avenue, the apartment in Brooklyn to which Amelia had moved, his mother and sisters would no longer have to patch his pants or wash and iron his threadbare shirts. "I became a gentleman," he remarked when speaking about these events. It is understandable that his mother and sisters were more than impressed with Joe. Their assessment of their son and brother had slowly, during the three years of his steady climb, began to verge on awe, which increased with each passing year and each new business triumph.

As for Joe's new interest in his appearance, it may have harked back to his days living with Uncle Peretz. For the rest of his life, Hirshhorn paid special attention to his wardrobe, buying the best custom-made suits, ties, silk shirts and underclothes from Sulka and other exclusive men's stores, always initialed in tiny, discreet letters, J.H.H.

With so much cash in his bank account, Joe was able to offer his mother a larger allowance, buy her a house and to indulge in his early interest in art. His first purchase came about serendipitously. While browsing among the secondhand book-shops along Fourth Avenue looking for more biographies of business tycoons, Joe came upon the Phaidon series of art books imported from England. He bought the entire series. Studying the profusely illustrated volumes, with black and white, not color illustrations in those days, in his few hours of spare time, Joe was exposed to Albrecht Durer, the sixteenth-century German engraver, whose work struck a sympathetic chord in him. Months later, near Exchange Place in the financial district, Joe happened upon two Durer etchings in the window of Assenheim and Son, whose sign at 37 New Street claimed they had been "Sellers of Paintings and Art since 1870."[*] Entering the shop, Joe made his interest in the Durers known, bargained the price down to what he thought was the "best he could do" and walked out with both etchings having paid what, for him, was a substantial price. "So that was my first art purchase. I paid $70 apiece, $140. I still own them," Joe said when interviewed by Paul Cummings for the Smithsonian Archives in December, 1976, "That didn't go to the museum. They're probably worth $1,500 apiece now." Joe had made his first purchase as a collector, establishing a pattern that was to characterize nearly all of his future acquisitions—bargaining and buying in quantity.

Although later determined to be either fakes, copies after Durer, or works of apprentices in the master's workshop, Joe kept the two etchings and stipulated in his will that upon his death, they be buried with him. And they were. Apart from a sentimental attachment to the etchings as his first art purchases, the Durers were an object lesson in the fine art of

---

[*]During the same interview with Paul Cummings in 1976, Hirshhorn claimed the Assenheim shop was still open for business.

connoisseurship and the pitfalls that existed in the rough-and-tumble world of art.

On September 12, 1918, Joe, just turned nineteen years old, and registered for the draft of World War I (1917–18). He gave his birth date correctly as August 11, 1899, claimed he was employed as a clerk for R.D. Wycoff at 42 Broadway, New York City and declared he was living at home with his mother, Amelia Hirschhorn, at 19 Lewis Street, Brooklyn. He signed his name Joseph Herman Hirshhorn, having dropped the "c" some three years previously. Given that World War I ended in a truce signed November 11, 1918, lucky Joe never had to interrupt his upward professional climb or wear military khaki by becoming a soldier.

Joe's next lesson in the world of business he loved so passionately was a hard one. As World War I was nearing its end, Joe, not yet nineteen, acted on a "tip" he believed came from an impeccable source. He bought into Lackawanna Steel at $62.00 a share having been told by George Bartman, married to the daughter of the President of Lackawanna Steel that he was getting an "insider's tip." His first purchase was 200 shares and, as the price dropped to $58 a share, he bought another 500 shares. As the price kept dropping, Joe continued to buy, acquiring more as the price continued to drop. It finally occurred to him that as he was buying, someone else was selling. "Two weeks before the war ended, the false armistice busted the market wide open and I was knocked out of the box, sold out of my position." Joe said, ruefully, "What did I know, I was a kid of eighteen. But it taught me a lesson I've never forgotten, *never buy a stock on a scale-down unless you're an insider.* Wyckoff wrote that in his book and I read it. How stupid could I be?" Luckily this happened after Hirshhorn had already bought his mother the house in Laurelton, Long Island for $4,500.

"That Lackawanna steel deal taught me a great lesson," he said, in 1976. "I'm Chairman of Callahan Mines. I'm also Chairman of the Board of Algoma Rainy and Rio Tinto in Canada. So I get a report every week and I can call up a friend and say what the hell's going on and blah, blah, blah. So I can get all the information. *So you can buy stocks on a scale-down only if you are an insider.*"

V
Rags to Riches to Rags

Nearly wiped out by the Lackawanna stock speculation, Joe dove right back into the market. He reread the Forbes book and memorized what became for him, an iron-clad rule: deal in money, not in goods or services. He had $4,000 left after the Lackawanna debacle and, despite unstable conditions and a sluggish market, he slowly increased it to $10,000.

By 1921, when he was twenty-one years old, Joe submitted his Petition to Naturalize, anxious to become a citizen of the country he had come to love. He also began a partnership with Thomas L. Sexsmith, his former associate at the *Magazine of Wall Street,* who at that time, was a counselor to Patrick Cusick. He brought two men into the firm, J. Victor Galley to work as office manager and George Courtney to act as cashier and bookkeeper. Courtney, a lifelong friend of Joe's, was a man who "knew where all the bodies were buried." He was also one of the several people who were shocked and bitter when they discovered, after Joe's death, they had not been acknowledged in his will. It is interesting to note that among all his business acquaintances, friends and associates, none at that time were interested in art.

Joe had met the older Courtney, an ex-vaudevillian, near the end of World War I, when, after charting stocks for W.J. Hitchinson, he would hang out in the back room with the other men, enjoying their camaraderie and horseplay. On those evenings George taught Joe to do a buck-and-wing,* something he

*A "buck and wing" is a classic dance step employed by vaudeville dancers.

48

often brought out of his repertoire in future years for the purpose of charming businessmen, art dealers or anyone else from whom he thought playfulness would gain him an inside track. Some of Joe's other antics were busting out the crown of men's straw summer hats and tearing the collars off their shirts. These kinds of rough-house antics were common among the "back-room boys." Later, Joe, a married man with three children, was still treating his guests to these aggressive "jokes" which he thought were hilarious. Although Joe always replaced a damaged hat with a new one or bought a new shirt to replace the one whose collar he had ripped off, the victim, who typically hid his true feelings from his host, was often not amused.

Courtney, at the time of his meeting with Joe, had recently returned from a hitch in the Merchant Marines. The two men often took their girls out on dates together. It was through this friendship with Courtney that Joe and his girl Jennie met several vaudeville performers, among whom were George and May Usher who became good, if temporary, friends. Joe also became friends with Georgie Price, another vaudevillian who happened to be no taller than Joe, who had yet to reach his full height. Courtney became, over time, so trusted an associate that he handled Joe's funds, wrote his checks and kept his office books. Theirs became a deep friendship. The Jewish Hirshhorn trusted the Irish Courtney implicitly, more than any other man.

Besides Courtney, Hirshhorn was also "in bed with" another colorful character, Patrick Cusick, who contributed $40,000 to underwrite the new business. Joe ponied up $20,000. Courtney described Cusick as "a Scranton brewer during Prohibition" and as "a mortician who had a contract to bury all members of the mob run over by the Lackawanna Railroad." Damon Runyonesque characters were to be found not only on Broadway, they were well distributed among the flotsam and jetsam of the wild traders of the Curb market, and Joe knew more than his share.

Although the intense focus of Hirshhorn's life was the various business enterprises he initiated during the 1920s, he did make time for a personal life. Joe was courting the same girl he had proclaimed at the age of eight as the one he would someday marry, Jennie Berman. Although in 1914, Jennie had move to the Bronx with her mother and sister, he still saw her frequently. Taking the subway to her mother's apartment almost every weekend caused Jennie's mother, Rose, to ask him one winter day why he made the trip so often. When he replied it was because she had heat in her apartment and his mother did not, Rose didn't believe him. She could see all too well that her daughter and the young man were in love. In fact, Joe had not changed his mind about making Jennie his wife. On January 14, 1922, they were married at a ceremony in uptown Manhattan. Joe's niece, Sally Goldzweig, the daughter of his sister Frieda, was flower girl; the luncheon after the wedding, out of deference to Amelia, was kosher, and all the bills were paid by Joe.[*]

Jennie Berman was a pretty, diminutive girl. She had fine brown hair, fair skin, hazel eyes, a quiet manner, soft voice and a ready sense of humor. She and Joe intersected at many points. Both were the children of immigrants from the Russian Empire; each while still very young, had lost a father; both had strong mothers who kept the family fed, housed, clothed and intact by their wits and sheer hard work. Jennie's parents had emigrated from Lithuania, each arriving in the United States in 1884.

Rose Hannah Jaffe, at thirteen, landed alone in Philadelphia on May 15th. Isaac Hirsch Berman came ashore at Castle Garden, New York on May 26th the same year. Although they both came from Lithuanian *shtetlach*[**] only twenty-five miles apart—Rose from Vainutas, Isaac from Silale—they didn't meet

---

[*]On the marriage certificate, Joe's residence is 1921 Lewis Ave., Brooklyn. Jennie Berman's address is 602 East 140th St., Bronx. The wedding took place at The Royal, 58 West 120th St., Manhattan; ceremony conducted by Rabbi (Rev.) J. Rosenblatt. Both the groom and bride give their ages as 22; Joe said his profession was "stockbroker," that he was born in Russia, his father's first name was "Leon" and mother's maiden name was Amelia Friedlander. Jennie gives no employment information but says she was born in New York City, that her father's name was Isaac and her mother's maiden name was Rose Jaffe. It was a first marriage for both. Because Jennie married a man not native born, according to the laws of the time, she lost her citizenship. In 1929, she applied for and was granted citizenship. That law was subsequently changed.
[**]*Shtetlach* is the plural of *shtetl*.

until 1886 when they both were living on the Lower East Side of Manhattan. Rose and Isaac earned their living in the garment trade as did so many immigrants from the Russian Empire: Isaac as a fine tailor to the carriage trade, Rose as a seamstress. Indeed, it was because she had to maintain her family with these skills after her husband died that Rose urged Jennie to learn a profession that would support her no matter what twists and turns life dealt her.

Jennie's parents were married on December 3, 1893 and took up residence at 88 Ludlow Street, Manhattan where their first child, Ruth, was born on January 6, 1895. Jennie, their second child, entered the world January 12, 1899, when the couple was living at 187 Orchard Street. A son named Solomon was born the following year on October 25, 1900, but died a year later of pneumonia. Jennie did not remember her brother. A sensitive child, she still felt the palpable sorrow of her parents' loss.

When Jennie was nine, Isaac, who had suffered for years with heart disease and diabetes, died. The family was then living in Brooklyn where they had moved in 1904 on the recommendation of Isaac's doctor who thought the countrified environment would benefit his patient. But nothing was able to restore Isaac's health, which steadily worsened.

Her father's death was devastating to Jennie, who adored him. Rose, now solely responsible for providing for her family, at first was able to sustain them by managing the small clothing factory which Isaac had established. When that failed, she experimented with a small notions shop and then sewed children's clothing to order. Finally, Rose took jobs in two different factories. The first made hair pieces and wigs, the second manufactured umbrellas. While Rose worked, Jennie, after school, helped out at home.

A quiet, studious child, Jennie enjoyed school and wanted desperately to continue her education after completing the eighth grade. But Rose believed it was more important for Jennie to learn a trade. Reluctantly, Jennie began to attend the Manhattan Trade School for Girls from which she graduated at fifteen when she went to work as a fitter for Bergdorf Goodman, the most prestigious shop for women's clothing in Manhattan.

Jennie Berman, Joe's childhood sweetheart and first wife, at age 18.

She continued working while Joe courted her but, attached as she was to him, she had reservations about marriage, believing their individual visions of the future were incompatible. Jennie craved intellectual stimulation and improvement. She was a voracious reader and her choices in literature enlarged her ideas about life and the world. Moreover, Jennie had a strict moral code and wondered if Joe, given the business he had chosen, the company he kept and his rapid success, wasn't a bit shady in his dealings. She was more interested in ideas than in large sums of money or being rich. Jennie understood Joe's ambition and admired his success but wondered at the single-mindedness of his determination to make money. The letters she wrote Joe during their courtship, which survived her death, are rife with admonitions that "money is too important to you, Joe." Her mother, Rose, believing that Joe's desire for money lay in the notion it would make up for his short stature, didn't fault him. Indeed, Rose thought his ambition and dedication to hard work were admirable. She was also aware that the two young people were deeply attracted to each other. At last, Jennie dismissed her doubts and finally said yes to her persistent beau.

With characteristic generosity, Joe insisted Jennie stop working for the two months prior to their marriage in order to prepare her trousseau and, at the same time, look for and furnish the apartment in which they would live. He compensated her for her lost wages by giving her $25.00 a week in addition to underwriting the cost of all expenditures for the home they would make together.

The couple took a month-long honeymoon traveling in Southern California, during which time they acted like the tourists they were, neither of them having been far from the teeming streets of New York in their lifetimes. A photo of the couple survives showing them seated in a two-wheeled buggy pulled by what appears to be an enormous ostrich. But the most telling memory of the honeymoon was a serendipitous stop the couple made to a fortune teller who reportedly looked at Joe's hands and said, "Your hands are unusual. They tell me you will make a lot of money in your lifetime."

Because that story became family lore, one I heard more than

once during my childhood, I made it my business to examine my
father's hands with care. They were unusual. Only once after-
ward in my life did I again see hands that even faintly resembled
his.

Joe was short and so were his fingers—not unusually short, just proportional to the man's height. His hands looked strong, moved with deliberate assurance, yet were as graceful in motion as was their owner. What distinguished his hands from other hands were the palms which were fleshy, very soft to the touch and covered with tiny, fine, closely hatched lines. It was the palms that gave Joe's future away to the fortune teller.

Something else that characterized Joe's hands was his handwriting: a swiftly written script that was elegant and grace-ful, not pretentious but rather spontaneous, clear and easy to read. Schools were deadly serious about penmanship in those days. He wrote his numbers also in clear, swift strokes that fairly jumped off the pages, bursting with energy. Whether it was words or numbers, Joe's writing was strong and masterful, seem-ingly the work of a man who knew what he was doing. If hand-writing is, in fact, a method of reading character, Joe's script suggested that what you saw was what you got.

Back in New York after their satisfying California trip, the couple moved into a five-room apartment at 2357 Walton Avenue in the Bronx. Left to Jennie who, even at twenty-two, had refined taste, their new home was beautifully furnished. Joe readily ac-knowledged that Jennie's taste was exquisite and gave her the rare compliment of admitting it was better than his.

It was judicious that the apartment had been furnished be-fore Joe and Jennie left for California because while they were away, Joe's office manager, J. Victor Galley, "traded the com-pany into the cellar," as Joe put it, causing him to struggle for the next year to salvage the business. Joe needed as much time as possible to attend to his shaky venture but, to his chagrin, dis-covered that Jennie, though generally healthy, was plagued with severe colds, some of which left her weak and unable to manage by herself. At the time of Jennie's first serious illness, when the doctor said she was suffering from pneumonia, worried as he was, Joe felt he couldn't stay home. The crisis in his company was too critical to warrant his absence. He prevailed upon Rose to take a few days off work to care for Jennie. Afterward, given the frequency with which Jennie felt weak and ill, Joe felt obliged to find a more permanent solution to the personal conflict he felt between Jennie's need for nursing and his need to work. His solution: Joe asked Rose to move in with them.

Joe offered as an inducement to a reluctant Rose, the "carrot" that she could stop working. Rose hesitated, uneasy about giving up her independence, but Joe could be very persuasive when he wanted something and this was something he wanted badly. In Joe's mind it would solve all their problems.

Joe liked Rose. She was practical, a hard worker, a proven risk-taker—hadn't she taken a gamble on herself when she crossed the Atlantic Ocean alone, at thirteen? Because she exemplified the standards he set for himself, Joe felt a kinship with Rose. What was certainly equally important was that Rose ran a clean home, as clean as one managed by a Hirschhorn! Rose talked it over with her elder daughter, Ruth, with whom she was sharing an apartment. Although Ruth was against Joe's proposition, Rose considered Joe's proposal to be eminently practical. Realizing that if she took time off from work too often in order to care for Jennie, she would lose her job anyway, Rose agreed and became a permanent member of Joe's household and in some respects, his ally.

In spite of the stress caused by their financial reversal, Jennie became pregnant with their first child. A girl they named Robin Gertrude, in the Eastern Jewish tradition of naming children for a dead parent, after Rose's mother, was born September 26, 1923. Six months after Robin's birth, Joe's fierce struggle to save his company failed. The partnership was dissolved, Patrick Cusick had to settle the debts and Joe decided they had to give up the apartment whose rent was $30.00 a month. They would have to find someplace cheaper to live.

He had just enough money left to go into a partnership in the jewelry business with a first cousin, Harry Hirshhorn.* Although

---

*Harry was the son of Chayim Hirschhorn, one of Lazer's brothers.

he liked his cousin very much, the jewelry business didn't appeal to Joe. But, knowing he had a family and one in-law to support, Joe felt he had to try it. Jennie, aware of Joe's distaste for the enterprise, volunteered to open a dress shop. In deciding where they would move, space for Jennie's dress shop was a prime consideration. They moved into a small house at 8780 Sutphin Boulevard, Jamaica, Queens. There, in a room facing the street, Jennie aided by her sister and mother, with funds borrowed from David Markel, a longtime friend of her father's, opened a successful business called The Rose Lantern Dress Shop.*

It wasn't long before Joe faced the fact that he disliked the jewelry business to such a degree he couldn't continue working with Harry. Jennie urged him to go back to "the street," back to the work he loved. With the dress shop temporarily providing financial support for the family, late in 1925, Joe formed a partnership called McCann and Company, his partners being John McQuade and Michael J. McCann, who was chosen primarily for the $1,300 he could contribute. Operating out of a tiny office at 30 Broad Street, one barely large enough to accommodate a desk and two chairs, Michael acted as cashier while Joe scrounged for customers and new business on the telephone.

By early 1926, Jennie was pregnant again and Joe's business showed a net profit of $50,000. When the monthly action reached $200,000, Joe dissolved the partnership by buying McCann out for $18,000 and McQuade, who stayed on as cashier, was given $12,000. With the $20,000 that was his share, Joe established Joseph H. Hirshhorn and Company, taking a larger office on the fifth floor of the same building on Broad Street. He increased his staff by three bookkeepers, two men at a trading table, a switchboard operator and he also hired David Tarlow who remained with Joe for the next fifty years, as auditor. Joe was feeling secure in a well-established business when his sec-

---

*Solomon David Markel was a friend of Rose and Isaac Berman from their earliest days in New York when he was a boarder in their apartment on Orchard Street.

ond daughter, named Gene Harriet after Jennie's father, was born on October 16, 1926.

By early 1927 Joe felt sufficiently secure to move his family to a better house and a better address. He found a newly built home in Great Neck, a suburb of Manhattan on Long Island, where he and Jennie settled in with their two daughters and Jennie's mother, Rose. Robin was approaching the age of four, I was not yet a year old.

During these years when his two daughters were small and his business was thriving, Joe enjoyed fatherhood nearly as much as Jennie enjoyed her children. He could be found playing with them and even bathing them although his devotion stopped at changing diapers.

At about the age of two, I liked to climb into bed with my father. I adored him and wanted to be close to him. At some point, he complained to Jennie that he wasn't able to sleep with me clambering under the covers. He'd carried me back to my crib on more than one occasion and I kept crying to be allowed to return. My mother told him she'd put an end to it but he had to allow her to complete the process no matter how much I rebelled. I have a strong memory of being told by my mother that I had to stay in my own bed (crib) and no matter how much I cried and screamed, no one came to get me. Finally I lost my voice entirely from the screaming and that scared me so much I stopped trying.

The family's home was in Great Neck, Long Island, a community where wealthy actors, writers and financial geniuses like Jessie L. Livermore, Joe's idol, had homes. The family had moved early in 1927. With Rose at home to look after things, the next summer Joe took his wife and mother to Djukst, Latvia to visit his sister Rahele who, with her husband, was still running the general store. They had continued living in Djukst ever since their marriage.

Crossing the Atlantic both directions in first class, the trip was a gift to Amelia, who had never seen Rahele's six children. The eldest, Rebecca, was born in December of 1906, after Amelia had already arrived in America. It was during this visit when a variety of Hirschhorn relatives came to Djukst to meet their rich, successful American cousin, that Joe made a stunning offer to the entire Hirschhorn clan still living in Europe. He would pay passage for one representative from each family to come to America and there, give them a start which would ultimately allow them to send for the rest of their households. The Hirschhorns who received the offer were disinclined to move. Regrettably, no one, not even Joe's sister Rahele and her husband Leib, took Joe up on his generous and, as it turned out, timely offer. Like the others, Leib was opposed to leaving because the general store in Djukst was thriving and he could see no reason to start over in a new country. As a consequence, many of the members of the extensive Hirschhorn clan that remained, died later in the Holocaust. Of Hirschhorns alone (not including Friedlanders) more than 100 can be found on the list of Holocaust victims.

Between 1927 and 1929 Joe's life seemed charmed. His home, comfortable and elegantly appointed by Jennie with reproduction English Jacobean- and Chippendale-style furniture, was a center for the entertainment of friends and, occasionally for any members of his family who were willing to eat from a non-kosher larder on non-kosher dishes. Not many were, most of his siblings were maintaining kosher homes and lifestyles, as was Amelia.

Also in 1928, Joe's beloved sister Annie needed her brother's help. Annie had married Nathan Seligman, a man from a family successful in the textile business. During the time her husband worked for the family firm, Annie had given birth to two daughters. But in the eight years that had passed, Nathan had broken with his family and was bringing no money into the household. Annie had gone back to work as a "peddler" of inexpensive goods and the arguments between the couple had become intolerable to Joe's sister.

In order to spare Florence and Esta, Annie's children, the proximity of an acrimonious divorce, Uncle Joe sent the two girls to a summer camp for two months in the Pocono Mountains of Pennsylvania. It was a first for them and, while necessary, not a happy occasion because the girls had never been away from home before and never to the country. At the same time Joe purchased a modest house for Annie and her daughters where they

Joe Hirshhorn in Florida, circa 1929.

could live rent free in St. Albans (Queens, New York), across the street from Jennie's sister and her husband, Ruth and Frank Chaykin. With family just across the street, family who had a telephone, Annie could continue her exhausting door-to-door peddling all over suburban Long Island knowing her children were safe under the watchful eye of Jennie's sister.

In his own Long Island home on Sundays, Joe would walk four blocks from the house on Pont Street into the town center in Great Neck to buy a paper and his cigars at the B & B (Boshneck & Berliner) stationary store. Joe smoked Corona Belvederes by the dozen each day, something his children disliked because of the acrid smell of the smoke.[*] *I often would beg to walk with him and he let me until he learned that by the time we were too far*

[*]He smoked cigars until, during World War II the scarcity of cigarettes challenged him to switch to cigarettes. As long as they were hard to get, he prized cigarettes. After the war he went back to cigars.

Joe's elder sister, Annie, circa 1948.

from the house to turn back, I would plead that he had to pick me up and carry me the rest of the way. I was probably no more than four years old. It got to the point where he said I couldn't come unless I walked all the way. I would eagerly agree but invariably at some midway point on the way home, I'd plead fatigue and had to be transported. I just wanted to be close to him.

The early years in Great Neck are filled with memories of Joe as "father." He was not good with hammers and nails and, to my recollection, was never called upon to be a "Mr. Fix-it," as he paid to have skilled people take care of such things. Yet I have a memory of him making what today would be called a skateboard from a short piece of wooden board and two skates which he attached to it. I am certain he learned to do that on the streets of Williamsburg, Brooklyn before he was ten years old.

Also, when I was growing up in Great Neck, people were allowed to buy and set off fireworks on the Fourth of July. I have a clear memory of Daddy Joe, as we, his four natural children called him, taking charge of rather tame fireworks for us which were set off on the street in front of our house. He allowed us to set fire to pellets that became "snakes" when lit. And, of course, we were permitted to burn sparklers, which he supervised.

Joe hired housemaids, a cook and a chauffer; he bought a Cadillac for both Jennie and the chauffer to drive. Joe had tried driving for a short time but after he'd run the car into a tree, decided he would never drive again. He never did. Jennie was an excellent driver and Joe, for the rest of his life, relied on a chauffer or one of his wives to drive him about. As for his business, Great Neck was a thirty-five-minute train ride from Manhattan and a ten-minute subway ride from Pennsylvania Station to Broad Street. His home at 16 Pont Street was a quick walk to the train station, an equally speedy commute. An early riser, Joe was usually on the train before 6:00 A.M. He liked to get to the office before anyone else. It may have been at that time that he developed another lifelong habit, that of telephoning people, especially competitors, while they were still in bed. He believed if you caught people unawares, they would blurt out the truth to probing, sometimes impertinent, questions before they had sufficient wits to prevaricate. He did it to me more than once when he was on a fishing expedition for some sort of truth.

No matter how busy he was, Joe found time to assist his family and even the members of Jennie's family. Joe had a first cousin on his mother's side named Itzak Friedlander who had spent seven years in a Russian prison as a result of political activities against the imperial Tsars. While in prison he had developed his nascent artistic skills and continued learning graphic arts, wood-cutting and etching afterward. Hirshhorn brought Itzak out of Russia into Toronto, Canada and ultimately settled him and his second wife, Gilda, nee Barondess, in New York City. The importance of this gesture is underscored by the fact that during the Holocaust both Itzak's first wife and young daughter perished at the hands of the Russians.*

In the Jazz-Age boom of the late 1920s, one of Joe's new business contacts was Lewis B. Hughes, a sage businessman whose financial acumen earned him large sums of money that he promptly bet away at the race track. Through Hughes, Joe was introduced to H. Preston "Chic" Coursen, who became Hirshhorn's attorney, a man who saw him through some of his more adventurous exploits. It was Hughes who alerted Joe to the approaching disaster of 1929. Considering the financial, social and emotional climate of the times when corporate earnings and dividends were soaring and everything seemed rosy, the world was on an extravagant binge. Even before Hughes suggested a looming crisis ahead, Joe was worried. He watched the frenzied stock speculation, people buying as the Bulls ran the market up. When the fever reached the point where shoeshine boys were quoting stock prices and "when doctors and dentists quit their jobs to speculate," Joe's uneasiness increased tenfold. He could feel the collapse coming. Influenced by Hughes' warning and acting on his own gut feeling, in August 1929, Joe sold out all his holdings for a total of $4 million. Jennie was expecting again and Joe was looking forward to the birth of their third child. This

*Joe continued to assist this family financially even after the death of his cousin by sending the widow $100 every month just as he did his sisters.

time he was hoping for a boy, someone who would be exactly like him.

On September 1, 1929, the aggregate stock of twenty-nine utilities were up by $5.8 billion and trading during the month of August had topped 95.7 million shares. According to a *New York Times* report on September 5th, on September 4th, with the temperature at a humid ninety-four degrees, "at 2:00 P.M. out of a clear sky, a storm of selling broke." In one hour the sale of two million shares wiped out thousands of small speculators. Appalled at his narrow escape, Joe watched in horror as his idol, Jessie Livermore, and W.C. Durant were ruined. The New York Stock Exchange immediately closed, only to reopen with a shortened day. The federal government promised to cut income taxes in an attempt to reassure the markets. After this, the *New York Times* proclaimed in a front-page headline: "MARKET SUCCESSFULLY MEETS TESTS OF STRENGTH," but on an inside page it reported the suicide of W. Paul Baron, a prominent Philadelphia broker.

What does a man do with his time and energy when he has foresworn participation in a business that has become his addiction? How does he look for an alternative to the action and excitement of risk?

Shaken by cataclysmic market events, but reassured of the correctness of his selling out *before* its collapse, Joe made arrangements to sail to Europe, leaving a pregnant Jennie behind. It may have been only a desire to escape boredom; perhaps it was a business venture. Could Joe possibly have planned an assignation? When Joe boarded the S.S. *Leviathan* for London, his stated purpose for making the trip was that he had undertaken on an assignment for one of the partners of J.P. Morgan with respect to the International Nickel Company. Rumors soon circulated that Lily Damita, a sultry South American movie actress who later married Errol Flynn, was aboard the same ship and that Joe was hotly pursuing her. To add to the swirl of his activities on board, halfway across the Atlantic, a steward handed him several cables telling him he had just purchased several thousand shares of stock. It took a number of frantic wireless exchanges for him to discover it was Jennie who was purchasing the stocks. Judging by the volume of sales that the market had steadied and would climb back, Jennie decided that now was a good time to buy low. Frantically, Joe cabled orders to sell everything, to stop all stock purchases and he suggested to Jennie that she take care of herself and the child she was carrying.

If the gossip about Joe's pursuit of Damita, not only on the ship but allegedly "all over Europe" were true, it was the first sign of Hirshhorn's philandering of which he was later often accused (and frequently guilty). Upon his return home, confronted by an uneasy Jennie, Joe denied ever having met the lady. This was merely the first time Joe's indiscretions reached Jennie's ears. There were more incidents to come. All in all, it was a rather brief trip as Joe made it home to New York in time to greet the arrival of his only son, Gordon Lewis, who was born September 20, 1929.

One month and a few days later, on October 29th, the market finally and totally collapsed. Joe, smarter or luckier than most, was sitting pretty on his $4 million, a sum that had enormous buying power in the aftermath of the collapse and during the long, interminable Depression that followed.

The market was sluggish—the action and excitement dissipated as traders had little money and less courage to plunge back in. These circumstances made Joe restless. He needed the stimulation and excitement of the action. Missing it, Joe looked for other types of investments. Some were successful, others not. He had the money to take advantage of the low prices in the art world and bought the "Madonna of The Lilies" by Bougereau, the Landseer and the Israels, all romantic painters of the French school. The pictures were echoes of remembered calendar art that had attracted him as a youngster. And he began exploring the world of art. For the first time in his life, Joe had the time and the funds at last to begin to study art through books, the few museums open at that time and by making the rounds of the very few art galleries available.

During this long lull in the market, looking for more avenues of interest and new excitement, Joe also began to invest in rare books. It was all part of what he described as his curiosity. "I was interested in everything. I was curious. Because I was curious I bought first editions." Among his book purchases was the Coventry Bible, "a great book, the first Bible printed in English," he said, and other things which, after he and his first wife, Jennie, were divorced, she sold at auction.

Some of Joe's other ventures, begun more out of boredom because the excitement of the market was unavailable, than real interest, did not work out as well.

Joe joined Jake Newmark, formerly an advertising director for W.C. Durant and General Motors, (and incidentally, another man of extremely short stature) in a venture to promote papayas and their enzymes as a health drink. I can still remember all the talk of papaya during the winter months we spent at our home in Miami Beach, Florida. There were to be face creams and other beauty products to come. Joe underwrote the hiring of a chemist and the leasing of a bottling plant but the laboratory was unable to eliminate the unpleasant odor of the fruit. The nascent effort was sold to General Foods which marketed it successfully.

A second failed venture, which Joe financed, concerned a carbon monoxide eliminator devised by a scientist at Johns Hopkins. It wound up with the Mine Safety Appliance Company in Pittsburgh. Having been burned twice, when a stranger walked into his office one day to show him a small cardboard cylinder which he said would revolutionize feminine hygiene, Joe turned him down. He thought the idea was "kooky," the man smelled of whisky, and even the ownership of 2,500 shares for putting up a mere $5,000 dollars didn't appeal to him. A Canadian family put up the money and realized $15 million from the product known as Tampax.

In the early 1930s, during the long Depression when it was almost impossible to find work, Joe had ample opportunity to lend assistance to his family. His sister Frieda's husband was out of work so Joe gave him sufficient money to buy a second-hand taxi which would enable him to earn some money. Frieda was already working as a door-to-door peddler to keep food on the table. Her son, Leo Goldzweig, graduated from high school in 1932 ready to work but unable to find employment. Joe offered him a job as a runner in his brokerage business at 30 Broad Street. Leo, who later dropped the "zweig" from his name and became Leo Gold, stayed with Joe as long as Joe kept the office and remained in the business the rest of his working life. In 1933, Hirshhorn's brother Herman's son, also named Leo, graduated from high school and, having the same difficulty finding employment, also went to work as a runner for his Uncle Joe. Leo Hirschhorn left the business when Joe closed the office on Broad Street.* Ultimately he went into his father's business, selling furniture to poor people and taking back paper on which they made time payments. It was the installment business and, ultimately, Leo Hirschhorn also did well.

Joe longed to stick with the business he knew, the stock market. But the market was behaving erratically and Hirshhorn's charts now made little sense. Uneasy with too much leisure time, Joe, who had always scorned speculators, took a plunge in several stocks on the advice of his old mentor, W.J. Hutchinson. He bet most heavily in International Nickel, buying 20,000 shares. The stock went nowhere and after a year, the bottom once again fell out of the market. Joe persisted but it wasn't until the fall of 1931 that he swallowed his pride and dumped his shares in Nickel. Several financial markets collapsed and Joe, a bull in a bear market, lost $1.1 million. He didn't cry to anyone; even his close associates were misled. "Joe," George Courtney reported, "came out thin like everyone else. He didn't stand up like the Statue of Liberty and escape the holocaust. He ate his lunch in the B/G sandwich joint. Everyone was going around in $28.00 suits." Joe was able to make back some of his losses, but by 1933, when he went to Toronto looking for gold, Courtney said, "He went up to Canada on a shoestring."

*All the Leos, Louis' and Lewis' in the Hirschhorn family were named after Amelia's deceased husband, Lazer.

VI
Over 30: Getting an Education at Last

Hirshhorn, at the age of thirty-one, found himself ideally positioned to satisfy both his curiosity and acquisitive nature by educating himself about art. That curiosity had never been satisfied since the days when he pasted insurance calendar reproductions of the Barbizon School of painters upon the green walls he found so ugly in the tenement where he lived with his mother and siblings. Joe had a lifelong drive to acquire anything that attracted his fancy.

His first purchases were bought on the advice of a dealer named John Levy who sold him the Israels, Landseer, Bougereau and other French Romantic artists. But he was going to the Metropolitan Museum and the few galleries available and was seeing another kind of painting. "I read a great deal," Hirshhorn said, "but I didn't know much and there were very few galleries, maybe twelve or thirteen. But, I went into one gallery, I forget which one—Durand Ruel or somebody—and all of a sudden I saw Picasso and I saw Roualt." These painters were a revelation to Joe. He returned to Levy, his primary advisor at the time, and asked what he thought about Braque, Roualt and Picasso. Levy's reply, "Joe, they're no good. Stay away from them."

"I knew then," Hirshhorn declared, "I was in the wrong church and the wrong pew. That was the end of John Levy."

After Hirshhorn's decision to move away from the past and venture into the future with contemporary expressions in painting, he sped up his visits to the Metropolitan Museum of Art, started going to the Whitney Museum and continued his avaricious reading. By 1933, when the Museum of Modern Art opened in New York, he was more than ready to further enlarge his range of interest in the work of the new artists. In his own words

Joe stated, "I didn't really have any knowledge until I was thirty-one years old, that was in 1930. I learned a great deal more that year and bought with some knowledge." It may have been the Depression, but that only made Joe's dollars go further. He was able to buy "very cheap" because he had kept the $4 million he had made when he had sold out of the market in August 1929, before the stockmarket crash.

Hirshhorn made the rounds of the existing galleries selling the paintings of living artists. He went to the Kleener Gallery and discovered Elshemius, an artist whom Joe got to know well and from whom he bought nearly 400 paintings. "My first big love was Elshemius. He intrigued me. I knew him. He was the most poetic, lyrical, beautiful painter in America." Joe stuck by Elshemius although he was never recognized by the art world as a "great." "The trouble with Elshemius," Joe said, "was that he didn't destroy." In other words, he kept whatever he painted and, in Joe's opinion, no artist could do that. Even great artists occasionally painted bad pictures and they needed to weed the failures from the successes. "Nobody can paint 4,000 or 3,500 paintings that are great. It's impossible!" Joe reiterated.

Louis Michel Elshemius (also spelled and signed Eilshemius) was born in Newark, New Jersey in 1864 on the large estate of his wealthy Dutch family. He and his brothers were left millions, according to Hirshhorn, who believed the two brothers were oddballs. "They had a beautiful house on 57th Street. I used to meet Elshimius there. But the brothers managed to lose all their money." Elshemius received his early education in Geneva and Dresden, returning to the United States in 1881 where he studied bookkeeping and agriculture at Cornell before going to the Art Students League of New York. He then returned to Paris where he studied under Bouguereau, an explanation, perhaps, for the lyricism of his own paintings.

For the next twenty years, Elshemius traveled throughout Europe, the South Seas, Africa and the United States, painting constantly. His work remained out of sight by the art world until Marcel Duchamp discovered him, which finally brought Elshemius some recognition. His work, today, ranks high in the history of American Romantic painters for its warmth, poetry and sleepy charm. Elshemius died December 29, 1941. Although his brief biography fails to identify the cause, Hirshhorn said, "He was hit by an auto" and reiterated, "I love his work. I love art anyway."

Hirshhorn found that when he met one artist and they became friendly, that artist invited him to meet other artists in their studios who introduced him to others and to additional gallery owners. "They'd pass the word around, 'there's a little crazy guy buying art like a madman.' So I went to see them. And I used to buy from them." In this way he became friendly with a great many artists and was also able to buy their work at discounted prices. By his own admission, these artists were often starving throughout the Depression. They couldn't pay their rent or buy food. Joe bought their paintings if he liked them, loaned them or gave them money and, in general, became a friend to the industry, even helping gallery owners who were also living on the thin edge. Among the artists he met, befriended and whose work he bought was Gorky. "I knew a lot of these artists like Gorky, one of the greats," Joe claimed, "Gorky was a darling human being. A big Armenian, six feet four, always looking sad. He had an apartment at 15th Street, a block away from Klein's."

About this time Joe also met Milton Avery and began to buy his work. Avery introduced him to the Soyer brothers. He met Herman Baron, a dealer with whom he became very friendly, dropping into his gallery frequently and buying his artists' work. By 1933, Hirshhorn was beginning to be known among the New York living artists and the struggling New York gallery owners. During these years, Joe bought only paintings. But he was already buying in quantity. It wasn't until the late 1930s that he bought his first piece of sculpture, a stone object by an artist named John Flanagan. "You have to wake up sometime," he told Paul Cummings. "I discovered that sculpture has a third dimension and I was intrigued with it. It was a snake and it was interesting," Hirshhorn explained further, "I can tell you the *way* I buy. I can't tell you *why* I buy. I buy if I get a gut feeling. It starts with the head, then the gut, and the heart. I want to choose everything in life that way." Even after he opened his office in Toronto and began buying art in Canada, Hirshhorn never deserted the New York art world which had come to count on his patronage and with whom he had fallen in love.

More than just prospective business propelled Hirshhorn toward Canada. On the home front, not all was tranquil. When Joe had made his killing in the market in August 1929, Jennie felt he had made all the money they would ever need. Always interested in advancing her own education, she urged Joe to enroll in college with her.

Jennie habitually read to improve her mind. She favored books written by Freud, Havelock Ellis, Jung and Adler. She was also an early advocate of birth control and had managed to arrange the births of their children in the fall months, three years apart. On June 27, 1931, their youngest child, Naomi Caryl was born. It is possible this conception was unplanned since it defied the established pattern by being a summer baby rather than one born in the fall and by coming three months shy of two years since Gordon's birth. Naomi believed all her life she had been an accident and, therefore, an unwanted child. She often spoke of "remembering" that during her conception, Jennie's egg had shrunk from Joe's sperm. It was an issue that affected her entire life.

Jennie had a household and four children to manage, but she had servants and her mother to relieve her of many domestic chores. Jennie was far from lazy, but she had a strong preference for self-education and improvement; household help and her mother's capable assistance meant that Jennie had ample time to read and contemplate a different shape to her marriage. Her dream was that she and Joe be students together and she didn't hesitate to remind Joe there had been a time when she believed he wanted the same thing. Perhaps at one time he had given the notion some credence or at least allowed Jennie to believe it was a possibility, but now a return to school held no appeal for Joe.

Two people couldn't have been much more different than my mother and father or less suited to work together like horses in the same harness. Where D.J. was realistic and pragmatic to a fault, his decisions calculated on hard information and fact, Mother's decisions were based on emotions; on the way she felt. In the practical matters of running her household she seemed to be up to the task. However, in managing her personal life, her children, her relationships with her husband and her mother, Jennie seemed unable to separate her fantasies of what "should be" from what was. She had a fantasy of how marriage should be and couldn't adjust to or accept how her union with Joe was.

These were two people who quite likely shouldn't have married and I am certain it was their youth, mutual sexual attraction and inability to see where the future would take them that caused them to wed and that bonded them in the earliest years. Neither Joe nor Jennie had the capacity for understanding the other. Over time, Joe began to think Jennie was "crazy" and Jennie began to think Joe was "evil."

Joe, practical and realistic, understood their goals in life were different but he couldn't understand why his wife didn't see that fact. In an effort to accommodate her, in 1930, he agreed to accompany her to Ithaca, New York to check out Cornell University. But his very presence on the campus made Joe uncomfortable. The student's life was not for him. In that environment he was a fish out of water and the idea came to nothing.

Joe and Jennie's arguments, the core of which was a defense of their individual, utterly opposing views of "the good life," increased in frequency and volume and fostered a bitterness between them. Joe felt Jennie was disparaging his achievement, wanting him home at regular hours, asking him to give up his incessant telephoning and his obsession with the stock market. He resented her efforts to fence him in, to make him an ordinary husband. He did not see himself as an ordinary man let alone an ordinary husband. She thought him stubborn and unyielding, she questioned his values. Both were dissatisfied.

A second factor pushing Joe away from New York, where he had formerly operated so successfully, was the languor of the stock market itself. He had an inability to find a substitute venture to raise his excitement level and give him the incomparable thrill of winning. He had tried all sorts of ventures without success and felt he had done all he could in his old venue. He had made his wife and children safe and secure, had bought his mother a house in Laurelton where his unmarried brother Abe lived with her. Examining his options again, Joe identified gold as a possible avenue to pursue.

Joe's old friend, Hutchinson, and a newer acquaintance, Robert Stanley, suggested he explore the gold-mining possibilities in Canada. A three-week exploratory trip to Toronto excited Joe and he returned to Great Neck with a head full of new plans only to learn Jennie was once again pregnant. This time she was determined to abort the child, justifying her decision by claiming she questioned the validity of her marriage and, more emphatically, she doubted Joe's fitness as a father or husband. Joe volunteered to have a vasectomy so that if Jennie carried this child to term there would be no further pregnancies (mind you, it was not yet 1932). But Jennie, unhappy and full of doubts, aborted anyway and Joe, for his own reasons, went ahead with the vasectomy.

When Joe returned to Canada in early 1933, ready to commit to the country and its mineral resources, little of the vast land had been settled or explored except for the border area adjoining the United States. Ottawa may have been the capital, but it was still undeveloped and provincial. Montreal was a city of some size, quite beautiful in the European manner, but it was Toronto that was the center of the Dominion's financial life. In 1933 though, it was not a boomtown. The Toronto Stock Exchange was trading mostly penny issues, the industrial market was negligible, the New York Stock Exchange was foreign to the local traders and Canadians were generally hostile to Americans and Jews in particular. Signs could be found on the city's park benches that read, "No Dogs or Jews Allowed."

No matter, Toronto was the financial center and that is where Hirshhorn, the Jewish New Yorker, set up his headquarters. If Eastern Canada was provincial, Western Canada was a virtual wilderness, wide open for exploitation.

It was a day in March 1933, the same day Franklin Roosevelt declared the "bank holiday" in the United States, that Joe opened an account with a $60,000 deposit in the name of Joseph H. Hirshhorn Limited of 302 Bay Street at the Canadian Imperial Bank. Barry Hyams wrote, "In his Bay Street office, Hirshhorn installed his specially designed console of phones with ninety-three direct lines to banks and brokers." This is where Joe's early telephone switchboard training came in handy. He also issued weekly "blue sheets" with 500 listings from New York and Toronto which he brokered like a one-man exchange. Using Wall Street houses accustomed to the volume of his trades, Joe gave business in previously unheard-of amounts to local houses such as Tom & Barnt and Lattimer & Company. He was determined to succeed and poured all his energy into doing so.

"Toronto's society and its conservative fraternity," wrote Emmet Hughes, the "gold" commentator on Canadian radio, "did not celebrate his intrusion." Joe worked like a robot, chattered like a Brooklyn peddler and let his high spirits explode in such phrases as "I feel felonious!" He also met resistance among his fellow brokers. The lesson Joe taught the Gallagher brothers years before in New York when he used a shill to manipulate the price of the stock he was promoting, he delivered in exactly the same fashion to a local broker who cheated him. And still, Joe kept his eye on his real target, mining. To remind himself of the potential, Joe hung a sampler on the wall of his office which read, "Imagination is the first law of creation." Now he felt ready to launch himself as a creative promoter, someone who would be sure to entice the masses to buy the stocks he would be selling.

In the November 16th issue of *The Northern Miner* Joe placed a full-page advertisement he conceived. It read:

MY NAME IS OPPORTUNITY AND I AM PAGING CANADA

Canada, your day has come. The world is at your feet begging you to release your riches cramped in Mother Earth. . . . Carry on until the pick strikes the hard, firm, yellow metal, until the cry of "Gold!" resounds through the virgin forest. . . . As for us, we believe in the future of this great country to the extent that we have made investments in gold mining and other industries in the Dominion and shall continue to do so . . .

Emmet Hughes called the advertisement a "mating call." Joe had a different slant on its meaning; he believed it would make him rich. "Blue chips and dividends are all right for grandma and the kiddies," he said, "I've always wanted the proposition that costs a dime and pays $10.00." He believed the only way you made *big* money was to use your head, make up your mind and have patience. Joe had made up his mind and he had patience to spare.

That same year, Joe brought to Toronto from London, a boy named Meyer Hershon, the only son of Herman, one of Joe's uncles, who had recently died and left his widow and three children penniless. Herman had been Hessel Hirschhorn before arriving in England where the immigration officials had phonetically spelled a name that Herman and his twin brother Isaac could only pronounce but not spell and Hessel had changed his first name to Herman. Joe made the sixteen-year-old change his last name back to Hirshhorn, spelling it like he did, without the "c." He also suggested the boy "anglicize" his first name to Martin, knowing the Semitic-sounding Meyer wouldn't go over well with the Canadians. Within a year, at Joe's suggestion and with his help, Herman's widow and her two daughters followed Martin to Toronto. Their descendants are living there today.

Hirshhorn, in Toronto on his mission for gold, knew nothing of geology, nor did any of the other traders and promoters. But unlike them, in the pattern he was already exhibiting with respect to learning about art, Joe was, in his own words "curious," anxious to learn whatever would be useful. He surrounded himself with geologists and proceeded to pick their brains. His mind was open and porous, he soaked up everything they could tell him. They gave him the kind of education he desired: not theoretical, but practical. Joe read for information he could put to work in support of his ambitions. Joe's only son, Gordon, once described the difference between his parents on this issue: "Both of them read vociferously. She read to support her attitudes, he read to learn."

Out of his newfound education Joe soon understood that "a miner with a grubstake was a baited hook" which the promoter cast into a sea of hopefulness. Most promoters were only interested in making a killing on the sale of their stock. So, after circulating reports of drilling which stimulated interest in the stock, they would walk away with the profit, having never dug a hole. A public that frowned upon gambling of any other sort, willingly tolerated the manipulation of these penny stocks which, time and again, robbed the gullible of their hard-earned money. All it took to keep the public appetite whetted for the game was an occasional promotion which concluded with a legitimate ore strike. As described by Barry Hyams: "In this sea of offerings, stockbrokers swarmed like sharks, nosing about the market to detect a promoter's weakness, whereupon they struck, swiftly, surely, selling his stock short and sending their victim to the bottom." Joe's hard-won experiences on Wall Street well prepared him to out-shark those sharks.

Within days of Hirshhorn's advertisement, two mine propositions were brought to his attention. The first was Longlac, a straight investment which made money for Hirshhorn. The second, Tashota, Joe described as "a creative situation." Joe was so involved with Tashota it became a household word in Great Neck. But, Tashota failed and cost him all he had earned on Longlac. Again, Joe recognized he had violated one of Wyckoff's rules, the one which instructed the reader to be an insider, "to deal the cards, not to draw them." If Joe was to be a "creative promoter," he required more than "guts," he needed more and more knowledge.

Joe's next project was Gunnar Gold Mine in which he partnered with the LeBine brothers, Charles and Gilbert. With Joe acting as underwriter, for $90,000, he acquired 600,000 shares of Gunnar stock. From March through May of 1934, he advertised the stock at fifty-five cents a share and although the Bay Street sharks, smelling blood, attacked to drive the stock down by selling short, Joe supported the price. The sales alone earned him $25,000 in commissions. Within months he had managed to promote the price to $2.50 a share. Fluctuations continued to confuse the marketplace. On the last day of October Gunnar opened in the morning at $1.43 and two hours later, plummeted to ninety-four cents. When the confusion was over, Hirshhorn had netted $1.1 million and Gunnar was fully financed.

The Bay Street traders, sorely wounded, cried "foul" and called for an investigation. The Ontario Securities Commission obliged and four months later, in February 1934, Commissioner

J. M. Godfrey delivered his report which stated Joe was not liable to prosecution. "He has not committed any criminal act. Manipulation, per se, is not a crime. It is the conspiring with one or more persons to manipulate which is punishable," Godfrey said. Gilbert LeBine was also cleared and the Gunnar Mine continued to produce bullion for the next seven years for a total yield of $4 million.

Within days of the Securities Commission's decision, the Canadian government in Ottawa notified Joe that he was to be deported. His "non-immigrant" status barred him from more than "casual business and pleasure." Clearly the scale of his activities was hardly casual. Upon appeal, Joe was reclassified as a "landed immigrant making his home in Canada" which allowed him to continue his activities. Joe thought this was a propitious time to move from the Royal York Hotel, where he had been living since his attack on Canadian mining began, into a rented a house on Old Forrest Hill Road. He hired a housekeeping couple, installed as many books as he could locate on geology and mining, and began to spend Mondays through Thursdays in Toronto, providing a basis of truth to his new status as a "landed immigrant making his home in Canada."

On weekends Joe was in Great Neck with his family. He tried to get home before Friday night services began at Temple Beth-El but, if that failed, he attended Saturday morning services with Jennie and Rose Berman. It was not that Joe was deeply religious, but he had a stake in the continuing success of the temple which he had been instrumental in bringing into existence. Having a dignified edifice where Jews could worship was a project Joe had entered into a few years after he and Jennie had moved to Great Neck in 1927. The few, perhaps a dozen, Jewish families then living in Great Neck had started talking about a temple and by 1932 had started raising funds to build one. By 1935 Temple Beth-El was up and running.

When Joe selected Great Neck for his new residence, he did so because he felt it was a town suitable to his up-and-coming status as a successful broker's broker. He had chosen it for its location and the ease with which he could commute to his office in Manhattan. More important, the town was already noted for the well-known families who lived there; families like the Walter Chryslers and Eddie and Ida Cantor with their six daughters. It was also the place F. Scott Fitzgerald had written about in *The Great Gatsby*. But Great Neck was absent a temple where Jews could worship—a deficiency he and the other Jewish couples with young children living in Great Neck wanted to fill.

While using a community hall as a temporary place of worship, this small group of Jews began to raise money for a temple and it was Joe and Jennie who fueled the fund raising. *I can remember a large outdoor benefit party held on the grounds at 16 Pont Street. There was a dance floor built on the grass in the center of a concrete ring normally used for the Hirshhorn children and their friends to ride bikes and skate; there was a band playing, Japanese lanterns lit the entire area, a bar served drinks and food was available to the paying guests from a buffet. From the windows of our house overlooking the party, through the trees surrounding the house I could hear the band, occasionally glimpse a beautifully gowned woman or perhaps a waiter and listen with envy and curiosity to the laughter of the people enjoying the evening festivities.*

Although Eddie Cantor never belonged to the temple, (at that time, when the movie industry was transplanted to the West Coast, he moved along with it), he generously contributed $75,000 to its building fund before the 1929 crash wiped out his investments. It was Joe who wheedled funds out of the contributors and Jennie who organized the events. Joe and Jennie recommended the architectural firm of Bloch and Hesse, who had designed their home on Pont Street, to design the temple building and Edward Tinterra, who had been their builder, to construct the edifice. When completed, Temple Beth-El was beautiful. Its exterior was of stone, the interior revealed details of exquisitely carved wood. The original building stands today at 5 Polo Road, Great Neck. It is still a Reform Temple, the original Jewish house of worship, since enlarged to accommodate the increased number of Jews now living in a town that boasts eleven other various denominations. Joe, together with the other Jewish families, participated in the selection and hiring of the first Rabbi, a young man named Jacob Philip Rudin. Jack, as he was called, became a close friend of Jennie's, a man who first tried to talk her out of getting a divorce and later helped her work through her grief over the break-up of her marriage.

Joe had already purchased a three-bedroom house for his mother in Laurelton, Queens County, Long Island where she lived with her unmarried son, Abe. His sister Ella, married to her first cousin, Nathan (who originally emigrated to Bay City, Michigan) and Dora who had married their first cousin, Nathan's brother, Eli, made certain they would never be far from their mother by buying houses as close to Amelia's as possible. All three women now lived on the same street, in the same block. Dora and Eli managed to purchase a house right next door! Ella and Nathan were only two houses away. Mother and the two daughters had a powerful need to be geographically close. It was a replication of the customs of nineteenth-century Europe.

The weekends spent with the family in Great Neck were not enough to reduce the tension between Hirshhorn and his wife. Jennie felt abandoned and angry at the increasing imbalance between the hours spent together and those spent apart. She felt her children suffered from the absence of their father as much as she felt the burden of raising them almost entirely without his help. A single, week-long visit of Jennie, Rose and the children to the house in Toronto did little to improve things between the couple.

On weekdays in Canada, Joe was busy in the office considering and promoting deals that seemed ripe for success at the same time he was making his own market plays. In the evenings, Joe entertained the men he identified as the best geologists most likely to find mineral deposits. One man in particular Joe regarded as "the most brilliant geologist in the country," Douglas G. H. Wright. Wright reminded Joe of Uncle Peretz. "He not only looked like him," Joe said, "he drank like him."[*]

Douglas Guy Hobson Wright was born in London, Ontario, Canada circa 1892 to Methodist parents. His father was in retail

---

[*]Joe had never before mentioned that Uncle Peretz was a heavy drinker, but it appears he had been.

Joe Hirshhorn in his Canada office with the switchboard-like device on his desk and his art on the walls, circa early 1940s.

millinery but Doug set his sights on becoming a mining engineer. After attending the preparatory school, Albert College, he enrolled in Queens University in 1914. Great Britain was already at war when Wright joined the military on November 1, 1915 in Kingston, Ontario as a gunner for the 46th battery. He moved up in ranks to bombardier, corporal, sergeant and regimental sergeant major, continuing his studies at Queens until he left for France where he arrived on July 14, 1916. Wright left France on February 28, 1919 and, back in Canada, was awarded the Meritorious Service Medal in June, 1919. Wright returned to his studies at Queens in September of 1919 and graduated with a bachelor of science (with honors) in mining and metallurgy in May of 1921. When he began to rely on alcohol is not recorded but it is likely he drank to dispel the images that haunted him from the years he spent at the front in France.

Habitual drinking didn't deter Wright from regular attendance at church nor did it blur his judgment in geology. Joe
picked Wright's brains about the Pre-Cambrian Shield and, having learned its eight-million-year history and that the world's
richest mother lodes of minerals were locked inside it, he understood that whoever could decipher its clues as to the presence of
minerals could save time and money discovering them.

The shield extended for 1.8 million square miles under Canada, from the Arctic to Ontario, Quebec, northern Manitoba, Al-
berta, Saskatchewan and outlying parts of British Columbia.

Over the years Joe developed successful gold mines in Lab-
rador where Mesabi iron was located and in Quebec where he
found the Anglo-Rouyn mine in Noranda. When its gold was ex-
hausted, Joe converted the mine to copper, which it continued to
produce for many years. He was among the first into the East
Porcupine area below Hudson Bay where he acquired additional
gold mines: Armistice, Aquarius and Calder-Bousquet. These
rich mines, all producing gold, Joe developed over a four-
teen-year period. It is no wonder he began to be noticed. *The
Northern Miner* described him as "the daring mine maker." Joe's
method, combining geology with market "smarts," was to invest
in sighting claims and drilling. He explained, "You have to spend
money in the ground. That's the only way to make mines."

The prospectors, promoters and especially the engineers
and geologists held Joe in high regard and for good reason. Not
only had he proven himself successful in developing many gold
mines, they knew he listened attentively to what they had to say,
he kept his word—you could put it in the bank—and he didn't
keep them dangling. He made swift decisions. These men whose
lives were entirely devoted to the identification and exploration
of minerals in the earth, appreciated doing business with him.
But because his approach was contrary to local practice, Bay
Street was suspicious of him. Not only was his approach different, he was a Jew and, worse yet, a Jew from New York City.

"They said I was a hit-and-run man," Joe remembered, "a
fast-buck guy." Fast he was. His mind worked with the speed of a
racing locomotive and, as if someone was always chasing him, he
hated to waste time. Typically, he listened to the men who ap-

proached him with ideas and claims, weighed the information, made his decision, then quickly acted upon it. Barry Hyams related what he called "a typical transaction" with a client. ,

Hirshhorn outlined a deal to an investor, concluding, "And I'll put up a quarter of the money myself." When the prospect hesitated, Hirshhorn snapped, "Let me give you some advice. Stay away from the mining business; it's not for you. Where would I be if I fortzed around like you?" And dangling his final offer, he asked, "Do you want it, or don't you?"

"I—I think," the man wobbled—"you ought to put up—a third."

"It's a deal!" Hirshhorn grabbed the man's hand. "Send up your fifty thousand right away. I'll have my twenty-five in the bank tomorrow." As he escorted his visitor to the door, he said, "I'll show you how money is made."

Phoning his client, Hirshhorn said, "I've got you $75,000 . . . What? What do you mean fast work? I spent an hour with the guy."

These were events to which his children were never exposed in person. Like someone wanting to know more about an interesting stranger, when I read this brief tale, I loved it. I could see and hear Daddy Joe in action.

It was 1936 when Doug Wright suggested that Joe would do well to finance drilling in the area of the long-abandoned Preston East Dome in the Porcupine, one of Canada's earliest areas of successful mineral exploitation. Joe knew Wright had been offering the same deal to others but, because of his drinking, hadn't been able to sell it. However, Joe, because of his reading and "brain-picking," was also familiar with the mine's history. In 1907, Harry Preston had drilled in the location known as "the crown jewel" of old mines, but the ore had petered out and a fire destroyed the out-buildings. After that the mine had been abandoned and forgotten. Doug Wright, who had once worked for Harry Preston, was convinced more gold lay underground awaiting another assault. The mine's outstanding stock could be had for pennies. All Joe wanted to know was how much money it would take. The two men settled on a figure of $25,000.

In time, Joe acquired Preston East Dome from Gordon Taylor and reorganized the company placing William H. Bouck as legal representative and president. After Joe purchased 500,000 shares of the new treasury stock for $125,000, Wright began drilling and Hirshhorn began his promotion, offering the stock at twenty-five cents. Bay Street brokers, calling this "Hirshhorn's Folly," set about to ruin Joe by driving the stock down with a flood of old shares which Hirshhorn bought up as fast as they hit the market. With most of the company's original shares in his possession, it wasn't long before Joe was Preston's principal shareholder.

Joe was increasingly under strain. His activities in Canada, the inquiry of the Exchange Commission followed by the deportation proceedings that had threatened his new business enterprise, had been stressful. The neverending escalating pressure from Jennie to salvage their marriage, added to his turmoil. All of this conspired to make him feel threatened and pulled in every direction. It couldn't have helped that he was shuttling between Toronto and New York almost every week. Stress and tension may have exacted their due. This was a man who had never known illness, except once, when, already the father of three, he was forced into bed for several days after his tonsils were surgically removed. Now Joe found himself felled by a severe case of shingles. His discomfort was acute. During a protracted recovery, Joe's doctor ordered him to take some time off. He tried.

In 1936, Joe bought a house in Miami Beach on Biscayne Bay, at 4344 North Bay Road, in which Jennie, hopeful of more time with her husband, installed Art Deco furnishings. The house was coolly attractive and comfortable. She looked forward to a family life in the relaxed atmosphere of Florida's warmth and sea breezes. Her hopes were dashed. Joe continued his incessant investing and traveling. Whether it was restlessness, ennui or too much money burning a hole in his pocket, for a "hot" moment, Joe considered purchasing the Brooklyn Dodgers baseball team. For a short time, while the idea was floated, Gordon contemplated himself, age eight, as the new bat boy for the Dodgers. But Joe recovered from his brief mania, decided to stick with the businesses he knew, and the moment passed.

More extended-family difficulties demanded his attention.

In late 1936, Joe's brother Abe died, leaving Amelia alone in the house in Laurelton. Very soon after, upon the death of her husband, Leib, Rahele was ready to be brought to New York. At the same time, Annie, living without help except from her teenage daughters and working at the physically demanding, tiring job in order to keep her little family afloat, was worn thin. With Jennie's help, Joe resolved everyone's problems. He moved Annie and her daughters into Amelia's home and Amelia was no longer alone. With a three-day-a-week maid service provided by Joe, Annie was relieved of many of the household chores that ate up her strength and Florie and Esta henceforth had the strong and loving influence of their grandmother every day.

Joe arranged for the transportation of Rahele's family from Libau to England and then from England to New York Harbor aboard the S.S. *Queen Mary*—eleven people in all, including Rahele's six-week old grandchild and his parents—in second-class accommodations. Jennie stocked Annie's house in St. Albans with furniture, bedding, dishes and food for the immigrants to use immediately upon their arrival. Of course Joe made sure everyone had sufficient funds to maintain themselves until they were on their feet.

For Amelia there was always an allowance and never any rent. Joe sent his mother $500 a month. "She couldn't spend more than a hundred dollars a month. I used to say, 'Momma, what are you doing with all your money?' and she'd say, 'What do you care? It's none of your business.'" Joe was certain she was sending the overage to his siblings who always seemed to be in need.

Within the year Joe was called upon again, this time by his sister Fannie who had married Rudolph Lutren. The couple had been living since their marriage in Bay City, Michigan where Rudolph supported his growing family with a general store. When the store burned down in 1933, Joe had offered Rudolph a job as a runner, the same job as the two nephews, Leo and Leo had been given. But after a short time, Rudolph and Fannie admitted they were very unhappy in New York and wanted to return to Bay City. So Joe paid their way back and bought another house, this time in Bay City, where the family lived rent free for several years until Rudolph got back on his feet.

Meanwhile, the shaky marriage between Hirshhorn and his wife limped along. If he was home, Joe was on the phone. The rest of the time, with rare exceptions, Jennie's husband just wasn't home. *But, when my father was in Florida with us, on rare occasions when he put aside business to be a father, his presence infused our otherwise-routine lives with energy and excitement. He gave me memories I cherish today.*

My father was a wonderful dancer, graceful and rhythmic, he especially enjoyed waltzing. It was part of his grace and athleticism. One of the things that remains clear in my memory was of evening trips to an ice cream store which had tables, a large dance floor and a jukebox. I remember dancing with my father whose bouncing steps were always right on the beat and always graceful. Dancing in his arms was an enormous treat.

Another Miami Beach memory concerned a yearly fishing trip. Joe rented a boat sufficiently large to hold Jennie, Grandma Rose, his four children and the seaman who ran the boat. The rear lawn of our house on North Bay Road extended right to the bay where the boat would pull up to our unpretentious dock. Ice-filled metal boxes crammed full with sandwiches, potato salad and cold drinks were loaded on and the children were helped to climb aboard. After the boat had made its way farther out into Biscayne Bay (the children thought they were really at sea), each of the children who wanted to fish was given a rod on which Joe had baited the hook and announced a dollar prize for the first fish caught. *I always arrived home with a terrible sunburn but maybe I enjoyed those trips so much because I can remember being the one who won the dollar prize. These memories stand out, in part, because of how special those rare times were when Joe was home with us.*

Part of the time when Joe was away he was philandering and each time eventually Jennie learned of it. This set off another round of accusations and promises to reform. There were some ugly scenes to which the children were exposed. They were brought on by Jennie who, out of her pain at his betrayal and a desperate need to curb her husband's behavior, was unable to

The Hirshhorn family in Miami Beach, Florida: (l. to r.) Naomi, Robin, Jennie, Gene, Joe, Rose Berman, Gordon, and Amelia Hirschhorn.

withhold her fury until they were alone. These scenes only served to drive Joe further away from Jennie's side.

On November 1, 1939 Irving, the brother to whom Joe was closest,[*] emotionally and in years, died of colon cancer at the age of forty-two, leaving a twelve-year-old son and a three-year-old daughter. During his long and difficult illness, Joe offered Irving and Bessie all the financial help they needed and also brought their son Donald to the home in Miami Beach so he would neither be a burden to his anxious mother nor witness his father's suffering. Joe also sent for Amelia to make the trip with Donald. Because she kept *kosher,* and the three bedrooms in the house

---

[*]Joe was not close to any of his three brothers. He avoided Herman, Abe was private and none of them attained the refinement for which Joe strived and succeeded in achieving. Of his brothers, Joe liked Irving.

Amelia Hirschhorn in Miami Beach, Florida, circa 1938.

were already filled to the brim, she was not able to live with the family but stayed in a kosher hotel in what is now the fashionable Art Deco section of Miami Beach called South Beach.

After Irving's death, Joe supported the family until his widow Bessie was able to get a job that would support them. Because Bessie needed to work and Donald was not equipped to look after his little sister, Joe paid for her schooling where she was supervised until Bessie returned home. He was thoughtful and generous in taking over his dead brother's responsibilities.

Unfortunately, things were no better in Miami than in Great Neck. Joe could no more mitigate the circumstances that led to his continuing estrangement from Jennie than he could be a more available father to his children. During these years he was often under a strain and could be abrupt, difficult and suspicious at times. *I remember one startling example of an encounter I had with him. It happened in Great Neck.*

When I was about eight years old, my brother Gordon and I were engaged by my father to dig up weeds from the lawn of our home. He paid a penny for ten weeds. In the mid-1930s that wasn't bad pay. But suspicious, even of his children, he questioned whether or not we might have torn one weed into two pieces in order to jack up the count. It was an idea that had never occurred to me. Fatherhood seemed an uncomfortable role for Joe. He was especially uneasy with Gordon, the son he wanted to mold in his image.

Joe's problems with his son started very early in Gordon's life. Within a month of his birth, Gordon fell ill. The diagnosis was a blood clot on the brain. The only treatment prescribed in 1929—and I am told, today—was to keep the baby very quiet and allow the clot to be absorbed. In order to keep a young, active baby very quiet, he had to be given morphine. Gordon was permitted a diet of only strained vegetables for the first five years of his life which made him a cranky, picky eater and a skinny child. His father wanted him to be robust and healthy. Joe couldn't stand Gordon's problems with food. For years my brother lived on peanut butter sandwiches and chocolate pudding Jennie made from scratch for him every day. There were arguments and spankings at nearly every meal the family ate together. Thank God Joe was only home for dinner, not breakfast and lunch on weekdays.

Joe was such an absentee father he never knew Jennie crossed the line when it came to disciplining their children. This was particularly true with Gordon, who was a difficult child for both mother and father. Jennie locked Gordon in a closet at least once, although not for an extended period of time, and she also tied him up with sheets on one occasion. She got her ideas about discipline out of some of the many "how-to" books she read. *Gordon and I got slapped with some regularity. I caught it usually because I would stick up for my brother and that made both Joe and Jennie angry.* But, there were times when Joe made an effort to spend some time with his son.

In the winter of 1938–39, when Gordon was nine years old, Joe took him to Cuba on a business trip. They flew from Miami Beach by Pan Am Clipper. Gordon was a somewhat fearful child and while he soon grew accustomed to the pleasure of flight, upon landing in a strange country where he didn't understand the language, he grew very anxious. Joe seemed oblivious or indifferent to Gordon's fears and did nothing to allay them. What characterized the trip Gordon made with Joe, the father he adored, at a time he anticipated would bring them closer as father and son, was that Joe ignored him while he met with various men to discuss business. Gordon reported that there were no opportunities for closeness except the fact that they slept in the same hotel room. At the end of the trip, on the way back to the Clipper, Joe tried to make it up to Gordon by stopping at a store and buying his son a large wooden replica of the Pan Am Clipper, a meaningful gift to my brother. Years later, when Gordon went off to college, Jennie unceremoniously and without asking or considering Gordon's feelings, threw out the wooden plane which was a symbol of one of the few special connections Gordon had with his father. Neither parent was appropriately sensitive to the child's feelings.

In a paroxysm of buying, as if real estate would cure all the ills brewing within his marriage and his business life, Joe also purchased 470 acres—the top of an entire mountain—in the Poconos of Pennsylvania. There, out of native stone, he had a

French Provincial manor built to house the entire family, their friends, their children's friends, visiting relatives and servants. The house sat above a miniature rural village called Angels, next to a slightly larger village called Newfoundland. The locals in this farming area were as opposed to Jews moving in as were the Canadians in Toronto. I always had an inkling my father, irritable and harsh as he could be if provoked, liked to break new ground for the Jews.

Joe added out-buildings, including a barn where he housed cows and horses. He hired a farmhand to care for the livestock and chickens; built tennis and badminton courts, a baseball diamond and archery mound, each with the finest sports equipment, and put a pool table in the basement. *Joe was a good pool player and he taught me how to play. I was an excellent player and it came in handy during World War II when I volunteered a Saturday every week to the servicemen who came to our canteen in Great Neck. Most of the men were from the Merchant Marine Academy at Kings Point.* I used to play pool with them and improved my skills even more, learning from a few of the "boys" who were really good players.* Joe used to play pool on the farm with his friends when they visited. It delighted his children who, in summer, were allowed to invite their friends for a week's visit. It is worth noting that Gordon did not spend summers with us. He was sent to camp instead. Yet, nothing, not even acquiring property and playing with family and friends, made up for the excitement he found in promotion and trading, especially in Canada, where he felt he was also benefiting an entire country.

"It was awful," Joe later rued with some exaggeration, "I just couldn't retire to a park bench and become a philosopher. I'd have gone nuts!" He found another outlet in real estate where he made a quick profit of $77,000, which restored his energy more than relaxation ever could and sent him back to Canada where Preston was steadily producing gold.

Despite the Bay Street bears' efforts to devalue Preston East

---

*The property and buildings were formerly the estate of Walter P. Chrysler, the automobile magnate.

Dome Mine and its stock, the price rose steadily. Joe sold just enough shares at $2 to recoup his investment and still leave him with 500,000 shares. Preston went to $2.50 and stayed there. Then he made an unheard-of move.

With the mine sitting on $30 million in charted ore, knowing he needed to raise $600,000 to build a processing plant, he floated a bond issue, guaranteeing its redemption in five years at six percent interest with a bonus share of common stock to each bond holder. The offer was unprecedented: a gold-mine operator who was indemnifying investors against loss! Joe turned the underwriting over to another firm, steering clear of a charge of conflict of interest. The bonds, after commissions, netted $612,000. Within three years, Preston was producing at full capacity. On January 1, 1940, Hirshhorn redeemed the bonds and two weeks later the common stock paid its first dividend. The once-abandoned Preston East Dome mine produced gold into 1968 amounting to $57 million. It had become one of Canada's "blue chip" mines. This was Joe's most successful Canadian mining venture to date, but not the most successful he was to have overall. That began in 1953 and came to fruition in 1956. But for now he was forced to give some attention to his marriage, which was nearing its end.

VII
Reaching for the Moon
Can Wreck a Marriage

From the time Hirshhorn went to Canada in 1933, things changed radically in his family household. Before Joe began his new venture, although he left for New York City early every weekday morning, he was home for dinner and sufficiently inter- ested in his children that the two elder daughters had memories of his giving them their evening baths. He would instruct the girls to make a "back table" and a "front table" so he could soap them down with a washcloth. The two younger children have no such memories.

There were three occasions on which he saved my life—be- cause he was home; because we were a family then. The first time occurred in Miami Beach when I was no more than three and trying to follow my sister, older by three years, into the ocean. I was wearing a "turtle tube" to keep me from sinking but I guess I must have gotten a mouthful of water. My father, watching me from the shore only a few feet away, moved quickly to pull me out.

A second event happened at Jones Beach. The family occa- sionally went places together on weekends. This time I was drowning in the shallow end of a swimming pool.

The third "saving" came when I was five, standing too close to the flames of our Chanukah menorah, when my dress caught fire at the shoulder. The first I realized something had happened was when I was startled to have a large hand slap down upon that shoulder as my father put out the fire.

I can remember my sister Robin and I, from time to time, be- ing taken to "Daddy Joe's" office on Saturday mornings—the

91

market was open on Saturday mornings in those days. Joe was in the commission business, he was what was known as a broker's broker, someone who completes transactions for other brokers rather than for individual investors. Of course, all the while Joe traded stocks for his own account.

I loved going to Daddy's office. Seated on high stools at a high counter, we were given discarded envelopes, rubber stamps that had various messages on them, and allowed to feel important as we inked and stamped, doing what we thought was really helpful work. We were allowed to play with rolls of ticker tape, making candles and bracelets by rolling or folding it. We even got to take some of the rolls home with us. We were surrounded by Joe's staff, short men with odd names like "Fuffy" and "Zeke." I remember that only two of the men who worked for Joe were taller than my father: one of them was Sammy Engleburg who Leo Gold, then working for Joe, said was "a bright, outgoing guy much loved by my Uncle Joe." It was as if Joe deliberately surrounded himself with men of his height. Hymie Goldstein was the "cashier," that is the head bookkeeper, who made $35 a week when Leo Gold was making $6. It was the pinnacle of Leo's ambition to reach Hymie's salary. George Courtney, the one other man taller than Joe, was like an office manager. He could do anything and was able to fill in if one of the others was out of the office. David Tarlow was Joe's accountant from the first and continued in that position, holding Joe's secrets close until past the time when Joe died and his estate was being settled.

After the market closed, Joe and Jennie would take us to lunch at Schraffts, a New York "tea room" sort of place with several restaurants at various locations in Manhattan where we invariably ordered the same meal: creamed chicken on toast, mashed potatoes, peas and, for dessert, some of Schraffts' famous ice cream with the even more famous hot chocolate fudge sauce. But all of this was before Canada captured our father's interest and took him away from us. Joe closed the office in 1933 when he set himself up in Toronto.

It appeared there was nothing Joe could do, nothing he could say that would mend the torn fabric that had once held the couple together, not even the trip they took together to Europe in the fall of 1934.* By 1940 Jennie was adamant. She had reached her limit. Joe's neglect, broken promises to spend more time with the family, his indiscretions which somehow always found their way to Jennie's ears (there is always someone who can't wait to upset the spouse, under the guise of being a "good friend"), all strengthened Jennie's determination to file for divorce. Her disillusionment was complete. Even the knowledge she would be taking their father away from his children didn't sway her. She began a process that may have been her greatest mistake, even greater than her marriage to Joe. It caused her grief from which she never recovered and robbed her children of their rightful heritage.

Jennie had always been especially interested in psychology. Before she divorced Joe, and afterward, she was very depressed and started seeing Karen Horney, a famous psychoanalyst who, after a brief time, referred Jennie to another psychoanalyst named Bernard Robbins. Years on the couch seemed to do little for Jennie although she said he had saved her life. Jennie urged all her children to also see him. Jennie fell madly in love with her "shrink" while he in turn fell in love with her daughter. Nothing came of any of it.

One year when all four of Joe's children were in New York at the same time and George Bach, a psychologist from Los Angeles was also there, a session was held at Joe's house in Greenwich, Connecticut. The idea was to have Bach do a group therapy with Joe and his children to help them relate better to each other. It was a wonder that Joe agreed to this. After twenty minutes or so, unprovoked, Gordon suddenly began crying, getting very emotional and screaming at Joe. He was verbally attacking his father, who was visibly shrinking from the attack. No one knew what Gordon was trying to say except to express his hurt and frustration with his father. Bach was totally nonplussed and the

*The couple shows up on a passenger list aboard the S.S. *Magestic,* departing from Southampton, England and arriving in New York harbor September 19, 1934. (Microfilm Serial T715, Roll 5,550, page 14)

scene escalated out of his control. Once Gordon was calmed down, the session was over. A total failure. That concluded any effort to work things out, as a family, with professional assistance. Private sessions with a variety of psychotherapists continued.

By 1942, Joe was no more an emotionally supportive husband than he was an attentive father. In later years even he admitted Jennie had been a far better mother than he'd been a father. As they got older, he seemed disappointed in his children. From his point of view everything they needed had been handed to them with little more effort than a request and a supportable reason. And while not everything they asked for was granted, his children's lives were filled with a rich variety of experiences and opportunities to grow.

Joe was not easily approachable and suspicious of anyone's motives when they were asking for help in the form of money. But he did help his children more than once. He assisted Robin and her husband in buying their home in Watertown, Massachusetts—a home in which they raised three children and spent the next fifty-plus years.[*] He also paid for the education of their three children from private elementary schools and high schools, college and graduate school and further, in the case of their eldest son, through medical school. Oddly, Robin seemed reluctant to let people know that her father had been so generous to her and her children. Perhaps she felt—and rightly so—he was only doing what any parent would and should do for his children and grandchildren, that he shouldn't be given any accolades for what was merely the proper thing to do.

Joe helped me when I bought my first house for $13,000 in Los Angeles. At a time when single women were not usually given mortgages, I had a good job and was able to make the down payment and the mortgage payments but I needed money for accessories, curtains, dishes, etc. Years later I asked for $30,000 to purchase a condominium in Mt. Kisco, NY. I knew my father's

---

*Robin died February 5, 2005, surrounded by her husband and children. She was eighty-one years old.

habit of cutting in half whatever was asked for, but I asked for exactly what I needed. When he said, "I'll give you fifteen," I said, "No, if you can't give me thirty, give me nothing, fifteen won't help me." Later Joe called back and said, "You're the one I've given the least help to, so I'll give you the thirty." And he did.

There were other times I borrowed funds from Joe, times we signed papers and I paid him back with interest! I'm certain I'm the only one of his children who ever paid him back a penny. It was important to me to maintain my independence from him.

He tried to help Gordon succeed in business after Gordon's marriage to Helen Klahr when Gordon was employed by Bache & Company, a brokerage house in New York. Joe was always troubled by his son who seemed to him to be drifting from school to school, from profession to profession, from marriage to marriage. He simply didn't understand Gordon and had no insight into the fact that he, Joe Hirshhorn, had certainly contributed to his son's lack of confidence. Joe had been very hard on Gordon throughout the early years of his life. Joe spoke little about it even to Al Lerner with whom he was close, saying only that he was disappointed in Gordon because he seemed unable to make something of himself. Once Gordon stopped trying to imitate Joe, to equal or out-succeed him, he made a success of his life. But it took a long time.

Joe was funny about money, for sure. If you asked for it, he gave you a hard time and he felt women shouldn't have control over their own money. He was so old-fashioned in this respect, when, upon Olga's urging, he made a gift of a large sum of money to each of his four children, he gave cash to his son and to Robin, his married daughter. Joe unapologetically said that it was because Gordon was a man and Robin had a husband. For Naomi who had never married and me, who was twice divorced, Joe put our funds in trust. He firmly believed women were unable to manage their money and no amount of arguing that I held an MBA and was clearly qualified to handle money cut any ice with Joe. He used to call me Hetty Green, an appellation I thought was a compliment because she was known to be a money-maker and made a lot of it. But when I eventually learned she was a tightwad who allowed her son to die because she was too cheap to take him to a doctor, I understood my father was actually giving me the "back of his hand." It hurt.

*When I visited Joe to proudly announce that I'd just been hired for a managerial job in the furnishings division of The Sperry & Hutchinson Company in New York, my father was truly impressed. First, because I'd gotten the job on my own without his help and, because S&H was a company traded on the New York Stock Exchange. It occupied seven floors of a building bearing its name at the corner of 43*rd Street and Madison Avenue in New York. My announcement excited him. He was all smiles. He asked me when I would be starting. I replied that I was going to quit my current job and take a couple of weeks vacation first. "Where are you going?" he asked. "It depends on how much money I have to spend," I said, "If I have enough, I'll probably go to one of the islands in the Caribbean." "How much would you need for that?" he asked. "Oh, $1,500 would do it." "Olga," he said, "go to the safe and get out $1,500 for Gene." He always kept a substantial supply of $100 bills at home and in his pockets.

My cousin Leo Gold told me the following story, which is more an illustration of Joe's disinterest in self-aggrandizement through money than an unwillingness to spend.

At the close of business one day when Joe was staying overnight in his Park Avenue apartment, he telephoned his nephew Leo, with whom he did considerable market business, and asked him to dinner. Dutifully, Leo called his wife in Great Neck and told her he would be home late; he was eating with "Uncle Joe" and would take the train home after their meeting was over. Leo's wife, Bea, envied her husband his opportunity to have a sumptuous meal in an upscale New York restaurant with his uncle and wished aloud she were there to enjoy it, too.

Leo met Joe at the apartment, anticipating the elegant meal ahead only to be told they were going to Horn & Hardart's Automat because, as Joe said, "It's clean and it's quick"—Joe's favorite attributes. Leo and Bea had a good laugh about it when he got home and they got a lot of mileage out of the story for years afterward.

The Hirschhorns were compulsive about cleanliness and Joe was a true Hirs(c)hhorn in that regard. He went so far as to differentiate between his wives by designating their acquaintanceship with cleanliness: one was very clean or was "dirty" and dirty was not a good appellation. *Once when he came to my home for dinner, having excused himself to go to "the little boys room," he returned to the living room with a smile, noting that he found the bathroom, "Clean, very clean."*

Joe himself was immaculate in his personal grooming. At hotels all over the world or at home with servants to tidy up behind him, he always wiped out the sink after washing his hands or shaving. He held others to the same standard of cleanliness. The only exceptions to this and to all of Joe's rules were artists. They were beyond such conventions. Artists and money for that matter, did not need to be clean.

None of his children were driven by his prime motivation: an urge to make money. He had had to work for everything he got and for everything *they* got as well. Somehow it never occurred to him that it was he, their father, who had been the primary instigator of their lack of concern for money; that none of them had the urgent drive to pursue riches because they already had everything riches could provide.

This problem was especially pronounced with Naomi. Joe had a standing account in New York with Tyson's, the Broadway ticket broker. We could ask our father—and did—for tickets to all of the Broadway musicals of the 1940s and '50s. Daddy Joe was very generous to Naomi regarding the show tickets. Even after I'd left home for college, she used the Tyson account at will. She didn't even have to ask Joe first. When I was home from college on holidays and in summer, my sister and I used to go to every show on Broadway. Joe also gave Naomi a charge account at Barrows, a music store in Great Neck that sold records, sheet music and a variety of other musical items like metronomes, violin and guitar strings. Naomi went into Barrows just about every day after school to listen to records and buy whatever she chose. She had a "rich girl's" relationship with the store. They loved to see her come in.

One day she went into Barrows and tried to charge some items only to be told that the charge account had been closed. Naomi went berserk! Back at home she phoned Joe at the office and threw a tantrum, chewing D.J. out for embarrassing her in public by closing the account . . . for not having told her in advance he was going to close it . . . for not being a good father! Joe, feeling guilty as could be, gave in and reopened the account. Naomi had a sense of her entitlement as the daughter of Joe Hirshhorn that none of his other children seemed to feel. *Neither Gordon nor I felt comfortable enough to demand our father do his paternal duty by us. Robin may have felt some of it. But because Naomi saw it as her birthright, she usually got her way with Joe until one day in the 1960s when she went too far.*

As she never married and never held a regular job (Naomi earned money by bit parts in TV and by sales of her paintings), Joe supported her. She got a check every month from his office, the amount was around $250.00. One day she called and told him that the funds he sent weren't sufficient for her requirements. Joe told Naomi, in his usual businesslike way, to "put it in writing," to tell him how much she needed and for what. She then wrote a letter outlining her needs which included a new car every few years and many other items. She said she required $50,000 a year and, as his daughter, was entitled to it. This at a time when most men supporting a wife and three children weren't making more than $30,000 a year.

Naomi never received a reply from Joe to that letter. He may have come to a moment when he no longer chose to support Naomi in the style to which she wished to become accustomed. He never broached the subject with her but he seemed to feel she had overstepped some unspoken boundary. This serves to demonstrate that Joe, not only as a businessman or patron of the arts, but also as a father, had his limits.

Naomi wasn't lazy nor did she lack accomplishments. She had chosen a different life for herself. Always enamored of "movie stars," singers and entertainers of all kinds, Naomi studied acting, singing and music. She was a good musician and had a wonderful voice for the popular music of the time. For a short time she steeled herself to sing in nightclubs which were distasteful to her, to say the least. The clubs where beginners had to start earning their stripes were places that were often called "toilets." They were small, dirty and usually run by unpleasant roughnecks who treated women entertainers like "pieces of meat." Not only did Naomi detest having to work in these unpleasant venues, having to fend off the crude approaches of sleazy men, she also found it difficult to perform in public. It made her so anxious she decided to give up performing even though she had attained a small success with one record.

She was more comfortable composing music, and wrote several plays, the kind of work that could be done in private rather than in public. Naomi generously gave her time to liberal causes as well. Her greatest public success was her participation in the creation and performance of *Spoon River,* based on the book by Edgar Lee Masters called *The Spoon River Anthology,* for which she wrote the music for four original songs and performed—singing and playing guitar and violin—in the original production which had a five-month run on Broadway in 1963.

Naomi was also an unschooled painter. Although her early paintings were predominantly an expression of her emotional turmoil—there were a lot of egg-rejecting-sperm and hole-in-the-heart paintings—in time her skill improved and she turned out work of complex and interesting forms, painted in glowing colors. For the most part, Naomi, like many performers, seemed addicted to approbation and applause. How Joe, as a father, played a role in Naomi's development cannot not be assessed. To his credit, he did buy some of her paintings which have found their way into the Hirshhorn Museum.

Her great interest, as her life developed, revolved around her theatrical and artistic friends who adored her. Naomi was an amusing companion and a wonderful *raconteur.* Although she spent a lot of time with the family before she moved to Los Angeles at thirty-one, her contacts diminished as the years went by and she became far more involved with her projects and friends. Hirshhorn was extremely proud of Naomi's association with *Spoon River.* That gave him enormous pleasure.

But, concerning his children, Joe most of all had no insight into the fact that what was really the cause of his displeasure was his own jealousy of them. A psychiatrist he saw for a short time, at his second wife's request, tried to help him understand that because his children did not have to work from the time they were eight years old, had every advantage money can buy, was no reason for him to be jealous of them. But it was hard to disabuse Hirshhorn of this notion. He didn't expect his daughters to have his propulsive drive. It was fine that they studied their music, took their dance lessons and followed their mother's studious example, he believed his son should have a primary goal of making money, as he had had. Joe's greatest disappointment was in his son, Gordon, who preferred to study *Mechanics Illustrated* magazines, play trumpet, drums and accordion, build boats and model airplanes and read scientific journals. An intellectual male offspring was not what he'd expected. Joe had hoped to have a son who was fired with the spirit of "the game," one who would eventually stand by his side in the fight to win all the "cards." This was not Joe's idea of how the world was meant to work.

Nevertheless, Joe had no desire to break up his marriage. It was his "safe house," the place where he knew everything was orderly, respectable, his children and goods properly looked after, a place that was physically and morally clean. He begged Jennie to reconsider filing for divorce but she was relentless. To understand the dichotomy of Hirshhorn's sexual cheating versus his desire for a chaste wife, one must remember the era in which he grew up. Men are allowed to play but "good" women may not!

By 1941, Joe was living apart from the family at Number 1 Fifth Avenue and a year later he and Jennie were legally separated. This was a difficult time for him. Not only was Joe's marriage in shambles, his mother, Amelia, at seventy-seven, was suffering from pulmonary edema. Although he provided her with all available medical aid, oxygen tanks, nurses and specialists, Amelia was losing ground. Everyone in the family agreed the dissolution of Jennie and Joe's marriage was information that must be kept from her. They feared learning of the pending divorce could be the disappointment that might end her life. To add to these pressures, in June of that year, Joe again found himself in trouble with Canadian authorities. He was accused of illegal activities by two separate government offices.

The first incident occurred when, in Toronto's Malton Airport, Joe was hustled into a private waiting room by Corporal Ed

McElhone of the Royal Canadian Mounted Police and asked to empty his pockets. Found to be carrying, in addition to his airline ticket, two bundles of Canadian currency totaling $150,000, Joe was charged with attempting to export this large sum without a foreign exchange license. Hirshhorn's excuse was that the money was intended to repay a debt in Canada. Since Joe had been unable to take care of the matter before catching his flight, it was his intention to turn it over after returning to Canada. Although the magistrate was skeptical of Joe's story, he dropped the charges and ordered him to pay a fine of $3,500. Joe called the affair a "stupid mistake."

The second matter was more costly and embarrassing. Three weeks after Joe's airport incident, the *Toronto Star* reported that he was being charged with six violations of Foreign Exchange Control Board regulations. Joe was alleged to have sold securities without a license in three periods occurring between March 1943 and February 1944—securities totaling of $137,228.71. Criminal intent never became a factor in the proceedings. The magistrate found that there appeared to have been errors of accounting, that "a mere inadvertence" could have given rise to the charges of violation. Joe paid fines of $5,000 and later attributed the accusation to another case of "the guys" who were always around "wishing I'd break a leg—or drop dead." Unfortunately, this encounter with the control board came back to haunt Hirshhorn during Congressional committee hearings in Washington twenty-five years later.

During the years 1941 through 1944, Joe was traveling between Toronto and LaGuardia Airport on average three times a month, most of the time alone but, on one occasion, he shows up on an October 21, 1941 passenger manifest with his New York attorney, Preston "Chic" Coursen and one of his closest Canadian mining advisors, Charles Hershman.[*]

Anxious over his mother's health, emotionally distraught

---

*Many, not all, of these incoming passenger manifests are now available on Ancestry.com. I am in possession of thirteen. All the more evidence of a man expending energy at a fast pace.

over the break-up of his marriage and the concomitant legal battle over the division of property and alimony, all conspired to put
even more stress on Joe. Failure of any kind was not only an embarrassment, it was a serious blow to his self-esteem. Joe looked
for ways to relieve the pressure which resulted in accelerating
his art-collecting activities—a turn of events that also introduced him to the woman who would become his second wife.

When Joe met Lily Harmon, she was a serious and moder-
ately successful artist in her own right. He met her because he
was regularly visiting galleries in New York. Joe had long before
become friends with Ella and Herman Baron who owned the
ACA Gallery and, over time, he was starting to accumulate
paintings and sculpture at a more rapid pace.

Instrumental in introducing Joe to the work of living artists
was his cousin, Itzak Friedlander, who himself had trained at
the Rome Academy. Related to Hirshhorn on his mother's side,
this was the cousin Joe helped leave Russia in October 1929 for
Canada, where he took a second wife and lived until the early
1930s. After moving to New York, Itzak steered his cousin away
from dead painters who, he importantly pointed out, had no need
for Joe's money. Instead, he opened Joe's eyes to the work of living artists who often badly needed financial support. Itzak understood the living artist's need. He had the same need himself.

Joe was quickly attracted to contemporary artists and their
work which he found stimulating and pulsating with life. Fur-
thermore, the artists were brimming with new ideas. As he did
with everything that interested him, Joe studied his subject by
reading, wandering the museums and galleries of New York,
probing the minds of dealers and artists and by examining and
assessing what he saw. He began acquiring the work of living
artists whether or not they had been discovered and regardless
of critical consensus. Joe wasn't interested in what anyone else
thought of the paintings he bought, he was gambling on his own
judgment, just as he had done with stocks since he was a boy.

In 1943, at a time when Joe was legally separated from
Jennie, he happened to attend an art show opening at Herman
and Ella Baron's ACA Gallery, then located on eighth street in
New York City. Joe was a longtime patron of the gallery and a

close friend of the Barons. The show was entitled "Friends of Burliuk."* Lily Harmon had been asked to paint a portrait of Amrussia Burliuk, the artist's wife. The portrait was hanging in the exhibit. During the evening, as Lily told it, she bumped into a man she didn't recognize but described as "short, just my height." Buttonholing him, Lily introduced herself and asked him, "Who are you?" Joe replied—as he frequently did—"I'm J.J. O'Brien, a herring salesman. I buy *schmaltz* herring by the barrel from Norway." Confused, after Joe left, Lily asked Herman Baron, "Who was that little man? Is he really a herring salesman?" When Baron told her the "little man" was the new collector, Joseph Hirshhorn, Lily remembered hearing about a new collector from one of the other artists in attendance. "He buys like a maniac," the artist had remarked, "Not one, but dozens. If he shows up at your studio," he advised her, "remember what I tell you. He's a sucker for a sob story. Tell him you're pregnant . . ." Lily would do nothing of the kind.

Because of his unique approach to buying, his antics and speech, Joe's reputation always seemed to precede him. Aline Saarinen's description of Joe, although observed when he was fifty-eight or fifty-nine, may nevertheless be the best-articulated depiction that can be found of Hirshhorn even in the early 1940s when his personal style was already formed.

> He is a tough, wise-cracking dynamo with a mind like an accelerated precision tool, the seasoned gambler's sense of the calculated risk and a big heart as sentimental as the calendar art he first admired. Five feet, four inches short, becoming a touch portly but still walking with a fast, bouncing gait, he has the mobile, tragicomic face of the classical Jewish comedian. His rapid-fire speech is a personal vernacular which hits hard with any direct, colorful word or phrase that is used to mean what he wants it to mean. All his life he has been a little man in a big hurry and everything he has done has been a one-man show.

*David Burliuk, Russian-American (1882–1967) with multiple art styles: early years, cubism with a strong realistic basis, his later painting style he called Futurism.

With few exceptions, artists and dealers reacted to Joe's steamrolling natural brio in the way he wanted them to react. This was especially true when he was a buyer or a potential buyer. Joe's way of making up his mind in swift strokes often unnerved some of the smaller dealers in New York. Even after they had experienced his seeming impetuousness, they never got used to it. Saarinen illustrated his impact.

> A friend describes Hirshhorn swooping into the gallery of a rather fragile dealer who holds only a few timid exhibitions each year. "Joe rushed in and bought five Walt Kuhns," he says. "In half an hour that dealer's life changed: he was developing a tic."

Hirshhorn's presentation of himself was memorable when he initially met Abram Lerner the first week Lerner worked for the ACA Gallery in New York. Neither of them knew it at the time, but it was Lerner's destiny to become a close and trusted friend, an essential part of Joe's art life as the curator of Hirshhorn's massive collection and later, the first director of the Hirshhorn Museum and Sculpture Garden. Joe was already a longtime friend of Herman Baron, the owner, but Lerner was new and alone that day in the exhibition rooms. Baron, who knew Joe well, was home sick.

"It was summer and there were few visitors," Lerner said, "when suddenly, like a wind, in came this little guy, my size. He didn't say anything, he looked at me and asked, 'Where is the boss?' Then, 'How old are you?' and 'What are you doing here?' He said, 'Walk around with me.' He inquired about several paintings, said, 'I'll take that one and that one, and those two. My name is Hirshhorn.' And departed as suddenly as he had entered." When Joe walked out, he left Lerner figuratively scratching his head, "I expected there would be a wagon with keepers waiting for this odd little man outside."

Lerner immediately called Baron at home and told him that a "short, stocky apparition [had] just bought four paintings," that he was at a loss since he'd been unable to get his address or phone number. "I was sure it was a prank." The director laughed.

"No need to worry," he said, "That was Joseph Hirshhorn. He's the most dynamic collector in New York."

Lily, having ascertained that Joe was not really a herring salesman, learned only that he "did something in Canada." Weeks passed before she saw him again. The occasion arose one evening when a photographer friend phoned to ask if she had sold the portrait of Burliuk's wife. When she replied that she had not, he told her Joseph Hirshhorn was with him and wanted to speak with her. On the phone Joe told Lily, "I'd like to see Mrs. Burliuk again . . . right now." It was the dinner hour so she offered him dinner and, quickly agreeing, Joe volunteered to bring dessert.

After climbing the four flights to Lily's fifth-floor apartment, they ate, and then Joe looked at the portrait. Later, Lily showed Joe all her sketches and paintings. He identified a sketch he liked and wished to buy but Lily was adamant. It was something she didn't want to sell. Before they parted, Hirshhorn had turned on the charm, handed her cash from the roll of $100 bills he kept in his pocket and, reluctant as she may have been, Lily accepted his money. Hirshhorn walked away with the portrait of Mrs. Burliuk and the sketch she swore she wouldn't part with, saying, "I told you they would go into friendly hands." That was the beginning.

On January 17, 1944, Amelia died, leaving Joe depressed. He had idolized his mother. To him Amelia represented the best in women: goodness, devotion, loyalty and self-sacrifice. For much of Joe's life Amelia had not been far from his thoughts, always the subject of his own devotion and concern. She had never been told of the break-up of his marriage to Jennie out of concern for her fragile health. Her death had been expected yet was still hard to accept.* Then, within the next year Jennie took herself and their three youngest children to Reno, putting a permanent end to a relationship he had once thought unbreakable. What

---

*The single remaining relic of the family's life in Latvia was a brass *samovar* that Amelia had managed to bring across the ocean from Tuckums. After her death it was given to Robin, Joe's eldest child.

Joe had wanted was to go his own way, fulfill his many needs and carry out his own dreams while Jennie preserved his fantasy of a family. Joe had enlisted the help of Jennie's sister, Ruth, and her mother in trying to prevent her from the ultimate finality he dreaded. And Rose, wanting to preserve the marriage, tried her best to dissuade her daughter, to no avail. Indeed, in taking what Jennie saw as "Joe's side," she opened a wedge between herself and Jennie which led to their semi-estrangement.

With no reprieve forthcoming, at forty-six, Joe lost the remnants of the personal life and many of the symbols of wealth he'd built from scratch. Jennie, in the division of property, received the house in Great Neck (the house in Miami Beach had previously been sold), his rare book collection and the Landseer, Bouguereau and Israels paintings. She auctioned off the most valuable items, including the rare books and much of her jewelry at Parke-Bernet. Jennie had turned down the chance to be given Huckleberry Hill Farm, the Manor House in the Pocono Mountains, knowing she couldn't afford the upkeep. She kept the house in Great Neck in which she continued to live for the remainder of her life.

During their marriage, Joe established a family holding corporation called Beacon Investments for the purpose of creating an asset fund for his wife and children in the event that anything happened to him. During the process of their divorce, Jennie had difficulty obtaining what she felt was a reasonable alimony and support for the children, later asserting it was because her attorney was on my father's payroll. But Jennie could be somewhat paranoid at times. She saw Joe as very rich and, if not rich at any given moment, quite capable of becoming very rich again in a short time. Her inability to be granted what she felt was deserved may have been because Joe's finances were in one of his infrequent down spells. He bore no grudge against his children, even if he opposed the divorce.

Jennie was granted $1,000 a month in alimony and an additional $250 per child until each reached the age of twenty-one. Dissatisfied, Jennie decided her best way of addressing this perceived wrong was to institute a suit against Joe for the 50 percent portion of Beacon Investments which belonged to "the family." Joe held the other 50 percent of the shares. In fact, the way Joe had structured the ownership, 10 percent belonged to each of his children (Robin, Gene, Gordon and Naomi), 5 percent to Jennie and 5 percent to Rose Berman, his mother-in-law. Why he split the last 10 percent between Jennie and her mother is a mystery. It may have been because even in the earlier years of their marriage, he sensed Jennie was angry with her mother and Joe feared she might not take care of Rose.

Before actually bringing the matter to court, Jennie took the precaution of having her mother sign over to her the 5 percent that belonged to Rose. Then Jennie inveigled her children to join with her in being named as litigants in the suit against their father.

I was a sophomore at the University of Southern California at the time all this was in the planning stages and knew nothing about it until I received a phone call from one of my siblings asking me to agree to sue my father. I wanted no part of it. "It's his money," I argued, "He earned it and if he doesn't want us to have it, that's his right." My position was rejected by the others and, while I could have chosen not to participate, my siblings argued that the suit would be stronger if all of us presented a united front. My feelings of loyalty to my sisters and brother outweighed my instincts to stay out of the suit. After all, when my parents separated and divorced, I held my siblings close. I wanted to support them. I've often wondered how things would have turned out if all of us had not sued him. More than anything, I've regretted my participation in what I essentially believed was the wrong thing to do. The excuse that I was only twenty-two years old when the decision was made is lame. My judgment, young as I was, was my own.

As it turned out, after nearly ten years of protracted legal battles, Joe either gave up or lost. The family was granted the money. But, in truth, it was his children who really lost out. Joe never forgave his children for suing him. He spoke of it frequently and bitterly, especially when the subject of why he wasn't more inclusive of his children in his life came up. There were other reasons why he wasn't an "available," participatory father, but this was the crucial one. As Naomi was less than twenty-one

Joe with his first wife and family: (front row, l. to r.) Naomi, age 3; Gordon, age 5; Gene, age 8; (back row, l. to r.) Jennie; Joseph; Jennie's mother, Rose Berman; Robin, age 11; and piano teacher, Frances Druckerman; at a piano recital given at 16 Pont Street, Great Neck, New York.*

*One of the very few photos extant of the entire family together (including Rose Berman and the piano teacher, Frances Druckerman) was taken after a piano recital staged by Jennie and photographed by Mr. Takagi, who owned the only photography studio in Great Neck and who took all the professional photos for everyone in town. His was the only Japanese family in Great Neck.

when the suit took place, he forgave her as being a minor and therefore not responsible. The assumption that legal minority could be used as a reason for forgiveness was merely a sign of Joe's rigid mind in such matters. He was hurt and angry for which it is hard to fault him.

Joe was especially tender in his treatment of Naomi. There were several reasons for his patronage. For one thing, Naomi had been desperately ill when she was nine with a staphylococcus infection of the lungs when there were few options, mainly the sulfa-drugs, with which to fight it. Because Joe, with his influential connections, was able to obtain some penicillin, just discovered and only available for wounded soldiers (World War II was raging), Naomi survived. After a long hospital stay and a longer recuperation from the necessary surgery she had undergone to relieve the putrefying condition, she seemed fragile and both parents were protective of her.

A second, ancillary reason may have been her lack of confidence or assertiveness which, until she was over thirty, seemed to characterize her personality. There was a gentleness and sweetness about her that was undeniably appealing. Joe supported her interests and catered to her financial requirements all of her life. Naomi remained at home with Jennie until she was thirty-two when she finally broke away and moved to Los Angeles where she began to find more internal strength as she built an interesting and productive life.

Some time in the mid-60s, Joe took Naomi to Europe with him where they visited Paris and where she met Picasso. She benefited from having the broadening experience of European travel but no more is known about what transpired on the trip. Naomi never shared her experiences and has refused to be interviewed for this book.

Joe's children's hopes for good marriages were unquestionably damaged by both their father's neglect and by his example. Robin married only once. She and her husband remained together for more than sixty years and raised three wonderful children. I married and divorced twice. Gordon had two brief marriages and two lengthy ones. He and his third wife had three daughters. Naomi never married. But she has had several life-long, loyal friendships.

The dual losses, of his mother and of Jennie, were painful for Joe coming one on the heels of the other. They were the two women who had been the central female figures of his private life during the years when he grew from childhood to maturity. He began to sense his loneliness. Business associates were fine but they didn't fill his need for family, for a more well-rounded life. He would do anything for his siblings and their children but he wasn't close to them. They lived in patterns he had outgrown years before. His children were already leading their own lives. Robin was married in June 1944 to a physicist named Robert Cohen and the couple was living in Connecticut where Bob was completing a Ph.D. at Yale. Naturally Joe had paid for their wedding, which took place at the Waldorf Astoria in New York City.

In 1944, I was about to start my freshman year at DePauw University in Greencastle, Indiana and was not available to Joe. Gordon was at an awkward stage, poised between adolescence and manhood but then, things had never been good between father and son. That had not changed. Joe's children were pursuing their own goals and interests, most of which had been encouraged by their mother.

It was Jennie who wanted her children to have every advantage she and Joe had missed in their childhoods. They were exposed to ballet, theatre, opera, the symphony and all manner of cultural expression, which was ubiquitous in New York City, only thirty-five minutes away from Great Neck by train or automobile. More than that, all four of Joe and Jennie's children were given piano lessons, no matter where the family was living—Great Neck, Miami Beach or the Pocono Mountains. The girls learned violin; Gordon played trumpet, drums and accordion as well as piano; the two eldest girls went to ballet school. It was a grand exposure for Robin, Naomi and Gordon. *I wasn't as thrilled with the steady lessons-and-practice grind. As I approached fifteen, I requested that my birthday present that year would be to give up piano for good. My wish was granted. I continued studying violin and viola, for which I had not an ounce of talent, only because I liked the teacher, Jacques Malkin, a*

Russian-born, French-schooled, American Jew who was a dear, lovely man.

The only one who still seemed accessible to Joe was the youngest, Naomi who, at thirteen, seemed to him naïve, unworldly, soft and gentle—much as Joe may have remembered Jennie at the same age. But, standing between Joe and his children was more than the divergence of interests. Separation from Jennie, temporary or permanent, had done nothing to ease the vituperative relationship existing between the couple and it exacerbated Jennie's fury and contempt for her former husband.

Although Joe remained a gentleman when speaking of Jennie, never demeaning or accusing her in front of his children, Jennie was not equally respectful of him. She raged loud, long and vigorously over Joe's character and conduct in front of her children, thereby damaging his image in their eyes. The constant disparagement was followed, periodically, by the suggestion that they call their father and arrange to see him, causing a serious conflict of feelings. The pair's mutual anger and distrust continued until Jennie's death from cancer in 1966. In La Quinta, California, recuperating from a heart attack that April, Joe did not attend her funeral. What he may have felt about his ex-wife's death at so early an age—Rose would outlive Jennie by another four years—he never said. But, by 1943, Joe Hirshhorn was ripe for a strong alliance with a female who might repatriate his soiled image as a devoted husband and family man. He needed to construct a brand-new existence.

VIII
Starting Over

Lily Pearlmutter Harmon was thirty and Joe forty-six when the two met. Born in the Bronx of Jewish parents, Lily's father hailed from Poland and her mother from a Croatian *shtetl* called Drezna. The pair met in the Ukraine, in a town called Rovno, now known as Rivne. Their destination upon leaving Europe was Winnipeg, Canada, where they married. But it was too cold for their comfort in Canada, and the couple finally settled in New Haven, Connecticut where Lily grew up an only child. A slender, graceful woman with sallow skin, an oval face, high cheekbones that betrayed her Eastern European heritage, a profusion of dark brown hair and penetrating eyes, Lily was pretty, graceful and appealing. She began sketching as a small child and, when still quite young, made the decision to be an artist. Educated at the Yale School of Art, she was smart, literate, worldly, sociable, fun-loving and talented. She had many friends among both the successful and the struggling bohemian artistic community of New York City. In Lily's company, Joe's interest in and access to up-and-coming artists increased. As Joe frankly stated, he liked to find "comers," and bought their work not because he was hoping his purchases would increase in value (he never sold the paintings he bought with one exception) but because he liked to gamble on his own judgment of their enduring worth. Indeed, he was prideful in this and resented it when any of his loaned or donated paintings were labeled "from the collection of Mr. and Mrs. Joseph H. Hirshhorn." When that happened, he furiously demanded they be identified as "from the collection of Joseph H. Hirshhorn."

When they met, Joe was living at 1 Fifth Avenue and his worldly experience was limited to Wall Street, Canadian mining, geology, business deals and art. Lily had lived in Paris and, although only thirty, had already been married and divorced twice, keeping the name of her second husband, Peter Harmon. She had completed psychoanalysis with a Dr. Paul Friedman and was living in a five-floor walk-up at 27 West 10th Street in New York City. Lily's father had supplemented her income with an allowance that had recently stopped. She had found representation at The Associated American Artists (AAA) Galleries at 711 Fifth Avenue, and her paintings were selling. By the time they'd been dating a few months, she had tried to introduce Joe to Marsden Hartley, Phillip Evergood, Max Weber, Raphael and Moses Soyer, Tschbasov, Paul Klee, Joseph Stella, John Sloan, Peter Gwathmey, Abraham Walkowitz, Yasuo Kuniyoshi, Milton Avery, Arshile Gorky, Morris Kantor and others, but was surprised to learn he already knew most of them and had already bought their work. Never wanting to be influenced by Lily's judgment as to which works or painters he should collect, Joe rarely bought when she was present. Indeed, there was never a time when Joe consulted anyone about what art to buy. He didn't care, he said, what his grandfather or anyone else thought. But, if he had some doubt as to the authenticity of a painting, he used Lloyd Goodrich, formerly at the Whitney Museum and an author of renown on the subject of art, to tell him if it was correct or not. In one case Joe had bought a Blakelock which Goodrich then told him was, in Joe's words, "a phony." Hirshhorn refused to put it back into the marketplace so he kept it. Otherwise, he bought what he liked. Not even when his relationship with Al Lerner ripened into a warm, trusting friendship, nor when Lerner became the curator of his collection was Joe concerned with Al's critique of his purchases. Lerner, a painter in his own right as well as an art historian, never recommended a purchase (except, when as a curator, to fill a "gap"). Joe only bought when he felt moved or, as he would say, "when the painting sings to me."

Joe courted Lily. He perceived the knowledge and taste she had acquired by years of concentrated reading, scrutinizing, experimenting, painting and interaction with other artists. Already sophisticated regarding the contemporary art market, Joe picked her brains (as he had picked, and was still picking, the brains of geologists in Canada). It didn't hurt that she was attractive, fun, Jewish and the child of immigrants, as he was. It was all comfortably familiar.

With paintings and sculptures threatening to burst apart the walls of his small apartment, Joe asked Lily to look for a larger place for him while he was away during the week in Canada. She found a duplex in a private house on Waverly Place that belonged to an elderly sculptor and his wife who occupied the bottom two floors and rented out the top two. It wasn't long before Joe and his art had moved. With more room, he soon filled, then overflowed, the new space. Meanwhile, Lily and Joe continued to see each other in a weekly pattern that became habitual. Joe flew to Toronto Monday morning to keep his business churning; Lily painted and saw her friends during his absence. Joe would fly into La Guardia Airport every Friday after the office closed and the two spent their weekends together.

After a while, Joe began questioning Lily about the people she associated with when he was away. Irked by the interrogation, she accused him of being possessive. Contrary to what Joe liked to say about his marriages (i.e., that it was never he but rather the woman who proposed) Joe had done the asking with Jennie. And now he did the asking with Lily. Thinking over her two past mistakes, she hesitated, understandably reluctant to try a third time. But in the end, as always, Joe won out. "I'm sick and tired of climbing those five flights," he declared. "You know we're going to get married."

In 1947, the couple married in a private ceremony with only the bride's family in attendance, at the Temple Mishkan Israel in New Haven. Rabbi Robert Goldberg presided.

Joe's children were slow to accept their father's new wife. In part because they were given no hint of the pending nuptials. They didn't even know Joe knew someone named Lily Harmon. Hirshhorn's attitude was that whatever he did was no one else's business. It never occurred to him it might have an effect on anyone else. Not even his children. Not only were they not invited to the wedding, their father didn't tell them in advance he would marry. Joe didn't even tell them after the fact. It was Jennie who offhandedly informed her children. "Oh, yes, your father got married last week."

Although the entire matter could and should have been handled differently, the pattern of haphazard communication between father and children was already well established. As always, his world revolved around business, women and, increasingly, art. As Lily was part of the art world, her place should have been secure. But some of her new husband's activities among the artists in their studios gave Lily pause.

He had a habit of buying in quantity and, because of it, offered prices far below what the artist usually asked. This made Lily cringe, knowing the artists' financial needs and sensing their hidden resentment. It caused her to stop going with him on these buying sprees. She also found it difficult to be happy when Joe came home with the works of other artists, although he certainly didn't ignore hers. In fact, he wanted so many of Lily's works, she felt robbed of the output which would have given her more exposure in the art world among museums and collectors other than Joe.

Joe found a large townhouse to buy on East 82nd Street. The house was twenty-five-feet wide and nearly 100-feet deep. With a graceful, spiral staircase, an elevator and a separate back stair for the servants, it had the size and comforts he'd been missing. But the location made his wife unhappy. All her former apartments, were in the "Village." This was too "uptown" for her. It embarrassed Lily among her bohemian artist friends, so Joe built her a studio on the top floor to assure her (and them) that she would be able to continue painting.

It was Lily who introduced Joe to "real" antique furniture, something with which he'd had no previous experience. As poor immigrant children (in Jennie's case, the child of poor immigrants) he and Jennie harbored an innate suspicion of "old" things, as if they were used hand-me-downs. The English-style furniture Jennie bought for their home in Great Neck and the French Provencal style with which she furnished the French manor house in the Pocono's, were the finest quality, handmade reproductions. At Lily's urging Joe took to the new game—hunting for the very best genuine American antiques with which to furnish his new home. Lily's formal education in quality antique furniture became Joe's newest enthusiasm. He studied books and consulted experts in his quest to acquire the best. Joe had no intention of being fooled. Once excited, he was again a sponge quickly soaking up his subject.

Within a year of the marriage the couple decided they wanted to adopt a child and, through an agency, were offered a six-day old little girl who was born in Chicago. Lily was eager to adopt although nervous at the same time. She had no previous experience with children. Joe, if not an accomplished parent, was an old hand at fatherhood and, enthusiastic about any new adventure, happy to cooperate. They named the child Amy after Joe's mother, Amelia. Three years later they adopted a second child from the same agency in Chicago and named her Jo Ann. With the second adoption, the family was complete.

While Joe continued to commute to Canada, the regularity of those trips was reduced because he had entered into a new enterprise in the Philippines. Joe organized a syndicate that included the former Secretary of State, Edward R. Stettinius and William Rosenwald and Barney Balaban of Paramount Pictures. The project was to explore the Mindanao region of the Philippines to mine its gold and copper. Joe named it The Philippine-American Exploration Company. Later, he dissolved this company due to pressure placed upon him by local Philippine officials who requested participation in the company in the amount of 20 percent for essentially doing nothing. He then reformed and renamed the company with Rosenwald as his only partner, calling it the Philippine-American Finance and Development Company.

Joe was comfortable to leave his longtime, loyal employees in the Toronto office to "keep the store running smoothly." If necessary, communication could be conducted via telephone or by wire. The new Philippine venture was predominantly in the hands of Rosenwald, who was the primary investor. Rosenwald insisted from the start that Joe match any money he, Rosenwald, put into the project. After a time Joe became alarmed. Rosenwald was pouring money into the company and Joe was uncomfortable with the additional sums he was expected to in-

Joe Hirshhorn with Lily, his second wife, in 1955, with Amy next to her mother and Jo Ann between Daniel and Michael Cohen, Joe's grandsons by Robin.

vest in addition to what he had already invested. The total now amounted to a very large sum.

This continuous demand compelled Joe to make a three-month trip to the Philippines to see for himself what was going on. For both husband and wife such a long time apart was hard. Finally Lily joined Joe for a short visit. Back home again, Joe faced the fact the project was not going as well as had been hoped and, not only was he displeased, he found himself out on a financial limb.* "I spent three years in the Philippines," he said, heatedly, "and it broke my heart. These were the most corrupt people in the world. [The syndicate] lost a million three hundred thousand dollars—$300,000 of my money. Awful people from the president down."

The time came when he announced to his wife that he was broke. He could no longer afford the house on 82nd Street, they would have to move. Had Jennie known she would have been amused to learn that wife number two was going through what she had experienced more than once. Joe's financial status was much like that of any other gambler. When he was flush, money was spent like water. The ups were followed invariably by downs at which time the four servants would be dismissed and Jennie and her mother would take over the cleaning and cooking duties. Suddenly Lily's style of living, one to which she had largely felt indifference, was going into reverse.

Of course, broke by Joe's standards was not as broke as it may have been for most people. Nevertheless, they gave up the house on East 82nd Street and were forced to sell a number of their other possessions to raise money. On the auction block went several pieces of the newly acquired, American antique furniture and several fine French paintings. This was the only time Joe sold his art. The New York house wasn't difficult to sell but the French manor, Huckleberry Hill, took considerable time to unload. It required a special kind of buyer, one preferably with a

---

*On April 27, 1947 Hirshhorn flew from Honolulu, Hawaii into Los Angeles aboard Pan American Airways. It was his final return trip from the Philippines. His flight from L.A. to New York is not recorded.

large family. Eventually it was purchased by Rush Kress who was the brother of Sam Kress, of five-and-ten-cent store fame. Kress and his wife had four children and thought the place ideal for their family, just as Jennie and Joe had thought for their four. It is interesting to note that after his brother Sam died, Rush Kress became one of the principal benefactors of the National Gallery of Art—just down the National Mall from the site of Hirshhorn's own museum.

In place of the townhouse on East 82nd Street, Hirshhorn and his wife found a house in Port Chester which both suited their needs and Joe's current purse. He had wanted to reside in Greenwich, Connecticut, at the time identified as the community housing more millionaires than any other. But the town was so anti-Semitic, he turned his back in disgust. A little more than ten years later, encountering much of the same prejudice against Jews, Joe bought a magnificent house and acreage in Greenwich where he lived with his many pieces of art or, as he called them, "his children." In those days Greenwich was a Gentile stronghold opposed to having Jews move into its privileged enclave. The only Jews living there did so in the peripheral areas and were, largely professional men and their families. When Joe began working with his real estate agent to find the home he eventually bought, a memo was discovered lying in a wastebasket in one of the offices which requested that the agents "do their best to discourage Jews from purchasing homes in this community."

Joe's energy was sufficient to serve the two central preoccupations of his life: art collecting and the wishful exploration of the Canadian substrata. It left little time for his family, a pattern familiar to anyone who had known him in his first marriage. But conditions seemed to be breaking in their favor. While Joe was away Lily supervised the running of the house and minded her children. Without his presence, she was able to paint with little interruption. It was a pattern which actually well served both their needs. What preoccupied and excited him at this time? Joe had begun to focus his interest on what he saw as the mineral of the future: uranium.

Joe, as well as many of his associates, realized the war in Asia had ultimately been won by the use of the atomic bomb.

But, it may well have been Hirshhorn's son-in-law, Robert S. Cohen, married to Robin, who actually got him excited about it. Bob was a youthful physicist who was doing military war work during the war years. He claimed that "every alert physicist knew about the nature of the atomic project," the secret exploration of atomic energy for the manufacture of a bomb which would end World War II. It was a weapon for which a scarce commodity had been largely responsible. At some point he mentioned uranium to Joe. Hirshhorn needed no further explanation. He immediately understood that when the war was over, the scent of space exploration was in the air and, most important, as the Iron Curtain descended, signaling the start of the Cold War, it was clear the "free world" would have to be protected. Joe, who had successfully developed gold, zinc and iron mines, believed uranium would be greatly in demand. It had yet to be found beneath the continent northwest of the Atlantic Ocean but Hirshhorn thought if it could be located anywhere, it would be found in Canada.

IX
Very Rich: Uranium Trumps Gold

Prospectors arrived daily at the offices of Hirshhorn's Technical Mine Consultants, the company he had founded in the 1930s, for the express purpose of sifting through any prospects or deals that came in over the transom. Committed to the idea, Joe funded six or seven proposals which failed to pan out, and in doing so, lost a large portion of his gains from the Toronto Stock Exchange. Patience, something he learned from Wycoff's book, was needed and Joe's adherence to that virtue finally brought a geologist named Franc Joubin to his office door with no more than a theory about an indeterminate "Location X." Joe listened to Joubin with the knowledge he had gleaned from Canada's leading geologists and engineers, whose brains he had picked clean during those long nights in the house on Old Forrest Hill Road. He had not forgotten anything he had learned from those sessions or from his omnivorous reading. Underlying all he heard was the memory, clear in his mind, that within the Pre-Cambrian Shield that stretched across most of Canada lay some of the richest minerals on earth. The story of the discovery of Hirshhorn's uranium unfolds like the plot of a suspenseful mystery.

Uranium in general, and particularly in Canada, had a long and frustrating history. For more than 100 years men had scratched at the surface of the earth looking for the elusive mineral. Each foray had come up empty. Only two men were not discouraged, Joubin, a geologist who, since 1933 relentlessly probed the mystery from the Arctic to the Amazon, and Joe who gambled on Joubin's knowledge and his own instincts.

Franc Joubin was born in San Francisco in 1911 of French immigrant parents. He grew up in British Columbia, eventually

121

attending Victoria College and the University of British Columbia. As a boy he had read Jack London, Bret Harte and Robert W.
Service and became fascinated by the California and Klondike
gold rushes which sparked an interest in geology. World War II
focused his attention on uranium when the world learned of the
bombing of Hiroshima. Beyond its ability to wreak devastation,
Joubin was also interested because of radium's potential as a
cure for cancer. He bought his first Geiger counter for $120 and
from then on it never left his side.

Before 1948, the search for uranium had already been taking place in the rocky bush lands northeast of an area called
Blind River. A small community situated between the cities of
Sault Ste. Marie and Sudbury on Highway 17, Blind River was,
in 1926, a thriving lumber town of 2,500 people. During the Depression, without the continuing demand for lumber, the town
collapsed. When uranium was discovered, Blind River was under
the supervision of the Ontario government. Soon after, the town
came to figure prominently in Joe's dreams as his role in the uranium discoveries of 1953 unfolded. Eventually, Blind River became the source of his greatest success and one of his most
painful rejections.

In 1948, prospecting for uranium was freed from the control
of the Canadian government, the Geiger counter had recently
been invented and any prospector who bought one could prospect
to his heart's content. One of those who purchased a Geiger counter to aid in his search was Aime Breton, the proprietor of the
Central Hotel in Sault Ste. Marie. But he was unsuccessful in all
his efforts to locate uranium. Sometime in 1949, at the mining
recorder's office, while idly dangling his Geiger counter over a
heap of rocks another prospector had left to be assayed, Breton
got a sudden and unexpected reaction on his instrument.
Glancing at a smudged label on the radioactive rock, he thought
he identified a word that looked like "Long." Breton had no idea
where the exact location of "Long" was, but he intended to find it.

There is a township of Long in the District of Algoma, Ontario. It lies east of Blind River and at that time was unorga-
nized. It seemed to Breton a good place to begin looking. Unable
to conduct such a large undertaking alone, he hired an experi-

enced man named Karl Gunterman whom he charged with examining all the previous mining claims that had been staked, registered and subsequently abandoned in Long Township.

Based on the information he'd gleaned, Gunterman set out for Long Township, but after weeks of searching in vain among dense woods and rocks, he decided to widen his search to an area north of Lake Superior among some known pitchblend deposits there.[*] But Gunterman's grueling, time-consuming work brought no reward.

Charles and Gilbert Labine, brothers with whom Joe had already done business, owned a mine at Great Bear Lake which they had first worked for radium. This mine subsequently yielded uranium for developing the atomic bomb. Few people at Blind River or elsewhere seemed to know this nor did they know that the Labine brothers had discovered another radioactive mine called Gunnar, in the northwest corner of Saskatchewan. While searching in this area, Gunterman wandered into the tent of Franc Joubin who, by this time, had been seeking uranium for many years without success. When Gunterman told Joubin about the radioactive rock on the counter in the mine recorder's office, Joubin became very excited and extracted Gunterman's promise to let him know if he ever found the exact spot from which that rock had been taken. Time passed and Joubin did not hear from Gunterman, but Franc Joubin was not to be dissuaded. Whenever he was in Saulte Ste. Marie, he would drop into Breton's hotel and ask had the location of the radioactive rocks been found yet? The answer continued to be, "No, not yet."

Hirshhorn's pattern of work started at 7:00 A.M. when he burst through the doors of his office on the 19th floor of the Bank of Nova Scotia Building. He spent the next three hours alone calling Paris, London, Rome and other cities around the world on business or talking with art dealers. By 10:00 A.M. the office had filled up with geologists, prospectors, brokers or artists, all com-

---

*Pitchblend, an amorphous, black pitchy form of the crystalline oxide mineral uranite, is one of the primary mineral ores of uranium, containing 50–80 percent of that element.

peting for Joe's attention. He was involved with fifty-seven different companies and kept his eye on each of them. His statistician, Bruce Attenborough commented on Joe's memory much as did Sam Harris some years later. "Mention one of the [fifty-seven companies] outfits and he can tell you how much it spent last year on erasers." As the day wore on, Joe removed his jacket and broke into song or went into a jig. Joe seemed tireless.

He required little sleep. Once the "mob" had gone home at the end of the day, Joe continued checking over every detail, planning the next day's moves. He never went to bed himself before he'd put that day to "bed" and made preparations for the next.

Meanwhile, Gunterman and Breton plodded on, coming at last to some pits in Long Township near Lake Lauzon where years ago some blasting had taken place by prospectors looking for gold, silver and copper. Suddenly, their Geiger counter began to click madly. Collecting some samples of rocks, they had them assayed for uranium. But their hopes were dashed when, inexplicably, the assay showed "only a trace." How was this possible? Unable to find an explanation, at Joubin's urgent pleading, they took him to the radioactive pits where, Joubin, as professional and experienced a geologist as he was, was equally surprised and unable to reconcile the excited response from his Geiger counter with the low uranium assay reading. It was a riddle to which Joubin had no answer. But, Joubin hadn't given up the idea of finding one.

It was about this time that Joubin came to Hirshhorn with his ideas about where uranium might be found and Joe, struck by the man's professional experience and intellect, invited him to join the Technical Mine Consultants as managing director of operations.

Joubin knew when Breton and Gunterman's radioactive claims were about to lapse and, when they did, "men hired by Joubin with money provided by Hirshhorn, were waiting to stake the area immediately."[*] Thirty-six claims in the area around and

*Dixon, Catherine. *The Power & The Promise: The Elliot Lake Story*; Gillidix Publishing, Inc., Lake Elliot, Ontario, 1996, 396 pp., p. 8.

including the old pits were staked on May 18, 1952, the very day after Breton's claims had lapsed. Although Joubin had no proof uranium was present, he convinced Joe that diamond drilling would be worthwhile. He was banking on his gut feeling that there had to be some plausible explanation for the high radioactive readings. Joe raised the $30,000 necessary to finance the drilling of the Long Township claims east of town. Shares in the mines, incorporated as Peach Uranium and Metal Mining Company, originally sold for $1.00. By 1953, after the discovery of uranium, their value had risen to $135 a share and was still rising. Joe's profit on these mines alone was worth over $4 million that year, a fact which did not increase his popularity with the townsfolk. It only gave them one more reason to resent him.

In January 1953, it was in an issue of the *Industrial Review,* a journal from South Africa, delivered regularly to the office of Technical Mine Consultants, that Franc Joubin got his answer to the riddle that had been plaguing Breton, Gunterman, Joe and himself. The article reported that *"when exposed to the atmosphere, uranium minerals oxidize"* and, therefore *"on the surface, the uranium has been completely bleached out* with the result that practically no trace of uranium can be detected on the outcrop of even the richest uranium-bearing conglomerates."*

That was the answer. The surface uranium had been leached out!

Now Joubin and Joe were under the pressure of time. The claims could run out for lack of development. At Joubin's urging, Joe put up sufficient funds to drill the site with barely a month left before the claims would expire. In 1953, hopes were high as fifty-six core samples were sent to the laboratory in Vancouver for assay. After a month of increasingly anxious waiting, word came back from Vancouver: uranium was in the samples!

The cloak-and-dagger manipulation began. Like two generals and their lieutenants plotting a coup, Joe and Joubin, having decided they must keep the assay results to themselves, worked out a plan by which they would be able to stake more claims in a

*Loc. Cit., p. 8, my emphasis.

wider area surrounding those they had already assayed without anyone knowing what they were sitting on. In the Agnew Lake region, fifty miles east of the assured lode, they staked what Joe named the "Plum Syndicate." According to an out-of-date map, commissioned in 1922 by the Geological Survey of Canada, the region was called the Collins map or the "Blind River Sheet." A worn-out copy was finally dug up in a secondhand book shop in Toronto by one of Joe's associates, Harry Buckles, and with it they identified in amazing detail the geological features of the district.[*] "Rock structures similar to those where uranium had just been found, stretching across the country in the form of a big 'Z' for over 90 miles."[**]

Now the plotting became even more secret and, of necessity, more extensive. Based upon the details of the old map, Joe wanted to stake the whole field, to cover the entire "Z" with claims—a huge amount of territory. By law, claims had to be registered in a mining recorder's office within thirty days of staking. Each claim registration had to identify the exact location, staker's identity and the time of staking, all of which immediately became public knowledge. To add to the difficulty of the requirements, by law, each man was allowed to stake only nine claims inside any mining district. If Joe's group was to capture the entire ninety miles of the big "Z" for itself, a clandestine, complex, well-executed operation would have to be mounted. Secrecy was imperative.

Joe organized and bankrolled the undertaking. The first order he gave was to stop all drilling on the Peach claims and have all equipment removed. This led all outsiders to believe the Peach enterprise had ended in disappointment. Mindful of the law's requirements, eighty men were hired to do the staking, inexperienced men were teamed up with at least one man who was well seasoned. Culled from mining recorders' offices across the province, the required licenses were obtained—a few from each

*The Collins map, when found, was frayed and torn but it told Franc Joubin where to go and how to look.
**Ibid., p. 11.

of many offices. The men recruited knew only that they would be camping outdoors and staking claims at unknown destinations. They were not even allowed to tell their wives about the assignment.

Tents were brought in and arrangements were made to feed the men. When hired, they were told, "Just grab an extra pair of socks and prepare to live in the bush. You'll be out for a month."[*] Bush planes were hired whose pilots were instructed to leave from Timmons field and fly in a northerly direction to throw off any observers. After flying some distance in the wrong direction, they were to turn and fly south toward Algoma. Landing sites on lakes had been selected where the men were to be let off. They were told to set up camp sites on the shores, hidden from the outside world. During the month of the staking, the men lived in those tents, slept on cedar boughs, ate food from cans, were enveloped by black flies and mosquitoes and trudged hour after hour over rugged terrain.

During this operation, a professional prospector named Manfred Johnson, on the payroll of Joe's Preston East Dome Mine, begged to be flown up to the northern arm of the "Z" to see what he could find. He had a hunch. His request was granted, and on May 28, 1953, Johnson staked the first claim of what was to become Algom's fabulous Quirke deposit. As a result, another crew of men was sent out to stake a large number of additional claims fanning out from Quirke Lake to a spot nearly as far as Ten Mile Lake, extending the "Z" an additional nine miles northeast.

On July 11, 1953, Hirshhorn's men came out of the woods to converge on various mining recorders' offices where they filed title to the more than 1,400 claims covering 56,000 acres. In addition, some 200 claims had been discretely recorded earlier. It seemed Joe had thought of everything. He had taken the additional precaution of flying a team of young lawyers into the northern woods to live and work with the prospectors with the instruction they were to execute documents transferring owner-

[*]Ibid. p. 13.

ship of the individual claims to companies controlled by Hirshhorn. Each claim was bought from the man who had staked it for $1.00. Of course, the stakers also received compensation for the month they had spent on the job.

With the filing of such a large number of claims, the secret was out and prospectors from all over Canada and the United States, Geiger counters in hand, descended like a swarm of black bush flies into the remote northern wilderness. The staking rush in Algoma can only be compared to the gold rush in the Yukon. In sleepy Blind River the streets suddenly filled with strangers; geologists, prospectors, fortune seekers, vagabonds and ladies-of-the-night. The small hotel couldn't hold all of them and the once-quiet town resented the intrusion. The townspeople perceived Joe to be a cocky intruder who had no right to act as if he could exert great influence on the community. He was suspect on many counts: he was not a Canadian, he had dug into their earth to rob them of their natural resources, his actions had brought on this invasion of strangers to disturb their tranquility, he was from New York and, worst of all, he was a Jew.

Many times during the good weather of 1952 and '53, Joe never made it back to his family in Port Chester, not even on the weekends when he was expected. Lily, privy to the thrilling events that were taking place, understood the reason for Joe's preoccupation, even if she disliked his long absences. The time soon came when Joe invited her up to see for herself what was going on, what the area was like and to learn his plans for the town of Blind River and for his family. He had raised $700,000 to develop the properties into functioning mines, in the process building roads and outbuildings, incorporating Pronto Mine to envelop Peach and Metal; and creating Algom Uranium Mines (in error someone had dropped the final "a" on the incorporation papers) out of Quirke and Nordic. He was busy, in his element and in high spirits and, throughout it all, continuing to buy art. It was February of 1955, before Lily arrived in Blind River with Amy, age eight, and Jo Ann, age three.

Joe had promised Lily a new house in the area, one designed by Philip Johnson, the famous architect who was also hired to design a new town to house the mine workers—one that offered them a life of beauty, culture and learning. Joe was so enthusiastic about the town he envisioned, he could hardly wait to show the plans to his wife. Lily needed no salesmanship on Joe's part to excite her about any project designed by Philip Johnson. She was a great admirer of his work and saw the new town as a tremendous boon to Algoma and to her family since they intended to settle permanently in the new house to be built on Bootleggers Bay on the north shore of Lake Huron. Johnson had promised that by spring a guest house would be ready where the family could live until the main house was built. It was all very thrilling.

How marvelous to be able to create an orderly town from scratch, not to have it grow, willy-nilly, like most town do. It was to be called Hirshhorn City and Joe elaborated on his plans for the community at length, to the residents of Blind River. It would be constructed around an Italian piazza-like town square. A multi-story glass, marble and chrome building on stilts would overlook the square, the central feature of which would be a million-dollar art center enhanced by large sculptures by Sir Jacob Epstein and Henry Moore. The center, naturally, would be filled with works of art donated by Joe. He was becoming pressed for places to put the multitude of new works he had continuously been buying. Joe's homes, offices and apartments were full and the center seemed an ideal solution.

Joe wanted Hirshhorn City to also have a modern library, a concert hall and a shopping center. The Hirshhorn City children would attend its schools, from kindergarten through high school. There would be an arena and playing fields and, equally important, because Joe believed no town should be dependent upon a single industry, he would develop other industries so the town could grow. Joe explained that Hirshhorn City would be built with his own money, not that of Pronto Mine, and promised a town which would be planned down to the smallest aesthetic and artistic detail. It would be a model city, the finest in Canada. All of this Joe explained in detail to the town fathers at a Chamber of Commerce luncheon.

Joe's enthusiasm was usually contagious, and Lily was as

excited as he, but the townspeople were immune to Joe's dream and Lily sensed it immediately.

Their attitude toward Joe was full of resentment. "Here he was, as always, this tubby little man trying to lord it over them, Blind River's merchants and chief citizens. Why couldn't he rely on them to determine how the area should be developed? Hadn't they been steering the destiny of the Blind River area for as long as it had been settled?"*

Joe, sensing their resistance, offered, "We are here to help you, not to take things away from you. And this comes from the bottom of my heart," he added. It is certain Joe's statement was sincere, albeit that his desire for the town may have been tinged with a bit more ego than he may have realized. But the people of Blind River were unimpressed. They couldn't overlook their own prejudices that a stranger should come into their midst and plan their future lives for them. Their suspicions of Hirshhorn, his motives, his wealth and his religion couldn't be overcome.

Although Joe's "town" was being discouraged by Blind River citizens, by late summer of 1955, things were going well for him in other respects. The guest house on Bootleggers Bay was finished. Lily and the children were living there. He joined them whenever he was able. On the old Andrews farm, a large bulldozer was clearing ground to construct two large apartment buildings for the workers of Pronto Mine.

The first ore from Pronto was scheduled to be raised from underground in September. For this auspicious occasion, the Earl of Bessborough, Board Chairman of the Rio Tinto Company of England, which had entered into an agreement with Joe to purchase a large share of his uranium holdings, was coming to stay at Bootleggers Bay with the Hirshhorns. Lily was hopeful the relocation to Blind River would provide the magic that would save her faltering marriage, and Joe, whose life couldn't have been better—he had more millions than he'd ever dreamed of—seemed to be charmed. Then the axe fell.

*Ibid., p. 37.

The front-page headline on the *Toronto Star* of June 7, 1955, announced in bold letters, "MILLIONAIRE MINING MOGUL SUED FOR PROMISE BREACH." Joe's philandering had finally, publicly, caught up with him! Also on the front page, in case readers might not be able to recognize him by name alone, was a good-sized photo accompanying the facts in the article. Elund Humphries, a former female employee who had become president of Rhodes Exploration and Finance of Canada, Ltd. with its head office in the Bank of Nova Building on King Street, Toronto (the same building in which Joe had his office) had served him with a writ.

In an effort to keep the papers from reaching Lily's hands, Joe sent a man around Blind River to buy up all the available copies, but his attempt was in vain. Lily learned about it anyway and was livid.

Frankly, the new home in Algoma had not shored up her marriage as she had hoped. Joe wondered at times how he could be so successful in business and make such a hash of being a husband and father. *The answer was easy, although it never occurred to him. If Joe had invested even half as much time and energy on his wives and children as he did on the accumulation of money and art, that part of his life would likely have been different. On the other hand, as Joe's nephew Laurence said more than once, "If Uncle Joe had been a better father, he wouldn't have had time to accomplish what he did." There was truth in that, but my reply to cousin Laurence would have been, "Joe's children would have preferred less accomplishment and more 'Daddy Joe.' "*

Troubles they say, come in threes, so it might have been expected that Joe's hopes for a planned city would also be dashed. On Labor Day weekend, 1955, he found out mining officials at Pronto Mine, under the general management of Franc Joubin, were conspiring with town officials to arrange housing for the miners and their families within the existing boundaries of Blind River, contrary to Joe's plans for Hirshhorn City. Joe was shocked. What was the matter with these people? Not long after, he was visited by a delegation of businessmen from Blind River who begged him to cancel his plans for Hirshhorn City. Joe was flabbergasted and crushed to have what he saw as his generous offer so flatly rejected. It hurt him to know the beautiful planned city would never be realized. They even refused his art gallery, concert hall and library. Joe was nothing if not a realist. Reluctantly, he accepted the inevitable. Hirshhorn City would have to be abandoned.

How this would affect his relationship with Lily coming as it did so soon after the public revelation of his infidelity, Joe couldn't hazard a guess. Although he had tried to patch things up by making an out-of-court settlement with Miss Humphries who had gone to live in California, Joe's marriage to Lily was beginning to deteriorate rapidly. It had to hold together for several more months as the Earl of Bessborough was on his way.

On September 20, 1955, the Earl arrived to visit Joseph and Lily Hirshhorn at their home on Bootleggers Bay. The visit coincided with the successful initial hoisting of ore from the Pronto Mine. While in residence, the Earl, an Englishman of noble blood and former Governor General of Canada from 1921 to 1935, would also be visiting the vast uranium fields of the Algom mines—Quirke and Nordic—in which the Rio Tinto Company now held a large interest. On the day of his arrival, Lily and Joe held a reception in honor of the Earl at which some 200 guests, including miners and geologists, distinguished attendees from Canada, England and the United States and local politicians, mingled with His Lordship. Joe had shipped in a large quantity of various foods from a deli in Toronto as there was no local restaurant in this barely settled area of the Canadian Northwest that could have provisioned such an affair. One month later, as a second gala took place at the official opening of Pronto, while speeches rang with effusive praise for the efficient building of the mine, which was now producing ore on a regular basis, Lily informed Joe she was leaving him.

There was no need to look for excuses. Lily had a host of reasons for terminating her marriage. Joe's preoccupation with business which excluded her more than she felt any marriage could tolerate was just one pattern that had soured her. His affairs occurred with alarming frequency. She knew of several women in addition to Miss Humphries who had embarrassed her publicly in front of others. When she and the children arrived in

Toronto for the first visit, Joe disappointed them all by not permitting them to visit his office. He admitted that if he did, his secretary, with whom he'd been having a three-year affair, threatened to make a scene. There were additional disagreeable revelations.

Lily had learned from her friends the Valentis that Joe was giving her friends in the art world tips on stocks that, because of their subsequent purchases, he made money on while they, who could least afford it, lost money. This embarrassed and humiliated her. Lily couldn't understand what she saw as Joe's greed, but was honest enough to admit that it was also the self interest of the artists and gallery owners that made them covet her husband's advice. Lily's greatest pain came from the realization that her children, especially Amy, were suffering from their father's absence. She had been well aware that Joe had neglected his relationships with his first family. She had seen the evidence of that neglect herself in the unhappy complaints of the first generation of Hirshhorn children. She had apparently thought Joe would be a better father to his second family than he was to his first.

Al Lerner, who saw Joe with his two youngest daughters on a Saturday when they lunched together in New York, bore witness to the poor relationship between Joe and these girls. "I couldn't believe how terribly they treated your father," he said, "They wouldn't behave no matter how much Joe protested. They were terrible and he put up with it." *This was something we, his natural children, had never done. We were never rude to him even if we argued our point. Indeed, when we heard that Jo Ann, still a child and a generation younger than we were, had punched Daddy Joe in the stomach for some unspecified reason, we had a good laugh about it. We seldom saw these girls, but the next time we did, Jo Ann was all grown up. We went out of our way to compliment her on the fact that she'd had the strength to fight back.*

In any case, Joe and Lily's marriage was over. Learning from the mistakes of her predecessor, Jennie, to whom Joe was anything but generous, Lily hired a good lawyer who helped her realize a satisfactory settlement for herself ($5 million) and each of her daughters: $1 million in trust for each child.

In addition, Lily kept the large apartment the couple owned on Central Park West in New York City.*

In 1956, Joe invited Gordon to Canada to be present for the Rio Tinto signing ceremony that turned the company over to the British. After the celebration ended, Joe invited Gordon to remain in Canada with the implied promise that he'd place him somewhere in his operation. According to Gordon, no real job came. He said he was given an office in the law firm where Joe's attorney, Johnny Ayrd, was a principal. He met all the mining men, became friends with Ed Parker, Joe's publicity man, and Harry Richardson, head of the brokerage house of Tom & Barndt. But, according to Gordon, he was given nothing concrete to do. Both Parker and Richardson discouraged Gordon from remaining in Canada. According to Gordon, each man cautioned that his father meant him harm. One of the mining engineers, Charlie Hoffman, told Gordon, "You have to leave Canada. Your father will kill you."

What was actually meant by that surprising statement has never been clarified. Gordon took him literally. He honestly believed his father meant to kill him. *A better interpretation, in my opinion, was that to remain under Joe's aegis would destroy Gordon's spirit and health.* He was present for the signing of the agreements between Hirshhorn and the high-powered British magnates representing the Rothschild family and British royalty. Lord Beaverbrook was their representative. Ed Parker, the Canadian in Joe's employ as publicity agent, accompanied Hirshhorn to the meeting and shared the following story with Gordon:

After the forty agreements had been signed, Hirshhorn signaled Ed Parker to accompany him to the men's room. After making certain they were alone, Joe began to dance around the room, laughing with wonder and relief. "Imagine me," he said, "a little Jewish immigrant from Latvia, making this deal with the Royal House of England!"

---

*Lily Harmon died in October 1998, age eighty-eight, with her two daughters at her side.

In fact, Gordon remained in Toronto for two years, from 1956 through 1958. During that period in addition to his disappointment in not being given concrete and trusted work to do, something treacherous and destructive occurred between father and son. *When I asked Joe why he and Gordon couldn't make peace, he answered, "Gordon did a terrible thing to me. When he was in Canada, he bought one share of stock in most of my companies. Then he came to the shareholder's meetings to challenge me. He embarrassed me no end." When he said these words, Joe had a pained expression on his face and it was plain he had been wounded to the core.*

Gordon, on the other hand, denied he had done any such thing. "It was Ed Parker who bought the shares and went to the meetings," he exclaimed. That's possible, but one might question what motive would move Ed Parker, who was Joe's publicist, to buy those shares and challenge Joe's authority in a forum of his shareholders. Knowing both men, even the fact that Joe was a manipulator and schemer, Hirshhorn was more likely to bluntly tell the truth, even an unpleasant truth. Gordon was angry with and resentful of Joe, blaming him for the failure of two important offshore oil exploration deals Gordon had successfully started. Gordon claimed his father had used his powerful contacts to warn off any potential participants, saying Gordon was irresponsible and crazy. It is possible that Joe might have done this as he considered Gordon emotionally unstable and might have feared Gordon could embarrass him with his important British and Israeli connections. When Gordon eventually left his father's business arena—mining exploration and stock-brokering—he became a psychotherapist, a profession that suited him and at which he experienced considerable success.

After his separation and divorce from Lily, Joe moved into an apartment hotel in Murray Hill. The children continued to see their father sporadically and Joe, flush with more money than he had ever dreamed of having, continued collecting art at a rapid pace. With a sureness unusual in most people and which sometimes scared the gallery owners, Joe was buying art like a man pursuing a mistress. "Why," he was asked, "do you think the dealers become anxious when they know you are coming in?" To which he replied, "It's because I buy very fast and they can't understand that. You know," he continued, "a picture, *a painting is like a man building a : . . . like an architect. It has to have a foundation, everything has to be in the right place. Now that knowledge comes with time and looking a great deal.*" He had more to say about how he bought art.

> . . . Once in a while something may be out of place and it doesn't matter; if it holds together I will buy. I will go into a gallery sometimes and see thirty-five or forty paintings. I'll walk around once or twice and I'll say, "Gee, that looks interesting, that looks interesting, and that" and so on. Maybe I'll select five or six and they'll take them out and put them aside. Then I'll start to talk and I'll say, "Well, what's it going to cost me? How much is this? What do you want for the whole works?" And then I'm not sure whether it's very hard for me to select one or two out of the six or eight that I've looked at that have been set aside. Sometimes I'll buy the whole works set aside. And they get paid the next day.

Hirshhorn's insistent, almost compulsive buying was the activity that brought Al Lerner closer into Joe's orbit.

X
Joe Hires a Curator

Joe first met Abram Lerner while visiting the ACA Gallery in New York in 1945. The closeness and duration of the association gave Lerner an unusual opportunity to know Joe, especially in his role as collector, better than anyone else. As they often found themselves together in social situations, Lerner received strong impressions of the way Joe behaved with his wives, children, friends and others. An intelligent and sensitive man, Lerner was deeply fond of Joe but able to objectively assess his habits and character.

From the time he had his Bar Mitzvah and received a ring with his initials A.L., everyone called him Al but he was born Abram Lerner in May 1914, the only child of parents who immigrated to the United States from the Ukraine. Raised on the Lower East Side of New York where the family lived at Houston and First Avenue, he knew from the age of twelve he wanted to be an artist. Too poor to have access to models, Lerner copied pictures from photos and magazines.

Graduating high school in 1932, at the height of the Depression, Lerner was lucky to find work in a WPA project and the same year met his future wife, Pauline Hannenberg, whom he married on December 6, 1941, one day before the Japanese bombed Pearl Harbor. Because he had ulcers, Lerner was declared 4-F when the United States entered World War II and was able to continue working for the WPA for the next two years in the statistical office of a labor union, a job he didn't like. When a friend told him there was an opening in the Army Quartermaster Corps for an illustrator, he was quick to take it. Meanwhile, Lerner was painting at home during his free time.

After the war, Lerner went to work at the ACA Gallery

**Abram "Al" Lerner in his office at the
Hirshhorn Museum.**

where, within one week, as has been reported, he had his first
surprising encounter with Joseph Hirshhorn.

Joe made his gallery rounds mainly on weekends—rarely on
weekdays unless he could find an hour to spare—and often
dropped into the ACA Gallery. The day they met, Hirshhorn was
squeezing his gallery visit into a spare hour and he began by fir-
ing questions at Lerner about his marriage and ambitions. Soon
Joe found they had a great deal in common. He saw that Lerner
was a man with knowledge and taste, and who possessed a soothing, nonabrasive personality. The clincher may have been the
fact that Lerner was the same height as Joe. According to
Lerner, Joe made many friends in a similar manner, by asking
questions and charming them with his dynamism.

"Joe was very personable and curious," Lerner said. "He asked what would have been seen as impertinent questions as soon as he met someone, 'How old are you? Are you married? Do you have children?' and he listened. He was really interested. If he was curious about something he asked a lot of questions and remembered and he followed up on whatever it was. No one seemed offended. Oh yes, he could also be tough, even scary because he came on very strong. But he had people eating out of his hand in no time.

"When we met, Joe was already familiar with a lot of artists and gallery owners. He already knew Moses and Raphael Soyer and owned their work. Moses showed at the ACA gallery and Raphael at the AAA. He knew Chaim Gross. He knew a lot of them."

It was during the late 1930s that Hirshhorn bought his first work of sculpture by the American artist John Flannagan. "Although he did not begin to buy sculpture avidly until almost a decade later, this initial purchase must have been rooted in a fertile, if still dormant, appreciation of structural form and concrete imagery."[*] By the 1940s, sculpture had become a passion which led him to the Gallery of Curt Valentin where he discovered Henry Moore, Jacques Lipshitz, Auguste Rodin, Honore Daumier and others. At the same time he was acquiring paintings by Milton Avery, Arshile Gorky, Stuart Davis, Lyonel Feininger and Philip Evergood.

During these early years of Joe's collecting, he was particularly interested in the up and coming, as yet little known American artists whom Edith Halpert, with her unerring eye, had identified. She was showing them in her Downtown Gallery and, in some cases was supporting a few, proof of her belief in their talent. Among her many artists were a large number whose work excited Joe and he acquired many examples of their art. Among whom were John Marin, Max Weber, Mark Rothko, Eli Nadelman, Ben Shahn, Yasuo Kuniyoshi, Charles Demuth, the

*The HIRSHHORN Museum and Sculpture Garden, Harry N. Abrams, Inc., Publishers, New York, 1974, 769 pp. From the Introduction by Abram Lerner, director of the museum.

husband and wife artists, Marguerite and William Zorach, and, of course, Stuart Davis, already mentioned, just to name a few. What seems astonishing, given Hirshhorn's avarice for acquiring the works he liked, is that he got only two mentions in the outstanding biography of Edith Halpert, *The Girl with the Gallery,* by Lindsay Pollock, published by BBS Public Affairs, New York in 2006. The book's subtitle, *Edith Gregor Halpert and the Making of the Modern Art Market,* does not overstate the case, yet it is hard to explain why Hirshhorn received one mention in the book's index and another cursory mention on page 376 given the enormity of paintings and sculptures that Joe owned by these artists.

Al Lerner had a ready explanation for this seeming oversight. He quickly and vigorously gave the answer, "Oh, they hated each other."

One can understand how these two controlling human beings could easily clash. Edith, an excellent businesswoman, was not going to be controlled by the legendary charm of Joe Hirshhorn although, in times of financial need, he was an ever-ready source of cash. He admittedly demanded the special treatment he was accustomed to receiving from many other dealers, that is, being allowed to buy in quantity with the additional reward of lower prices. This was especially true during the doldrums of the Depression years—the 1930s to mid-40s. Halpert's merchandising method was always, especially during the Depression, to keep her prices extremely low, being more interested in seeing that the art would be widely distributed both to collectors and to museums, giving her artists as much exposure as possible. The Downtown Gallery's low prices gave her nowhere to go but up and that's not where Joe wanted his costs to go.

There was another negative issue between these strong, dominating personalities. As Lerner said, "I wasn't working with Joe at the time, but he disliked ballsy women. She was just too strong for his taste." I interpret this to mean Joe was unable to manipulate her. The conflict between these two "bulldogs" didn't prevent Hirshhorn from acquiring any and all of the artworks he wanted, be they by Edith Halpert's artists or not. And, to his credit, he readily admitted, "She had a great eye, she was knowledgeable, but she was tough. Even so, I bought a lot of things from her." He found ways to get around her constraints; wherever possible becoming friends with the artists themselves. He even managed to buy paintings by Georgia O'Keeffe, the recluse, who came into Edith's stable sometime after Alfred Steiglitz died.

Joe was already supporting and befriending artists whose work moved him and whom he liked and respected. He bought his first Albers (Joseph Albers 1888–1976) in 1940, seven years after Albers emigrated to the United States. In time, Albers and his wife, Anni, became extremely close friends.

An early letter from Evergood to Hirshhorn, dated January 13, 1955, speaks to Joe's support and what it meant to those who had it. "I was delighted and very honored," Evergood said, "to receive a beautiful letter from the Whitney Museum today in which they say, 'We are delighted that through the generosity of Mr. Joseph H. Hirshhorn we now own your wonderful new painting, *New Lazarus*.' " The letter goes on to thank and praise Joe for his donation which could only advance Evergood's reputation and career.

"You are a really great friend Joe and I am deeply grateful. I cannot find the words to express how wonderful you have been to that crazy man Evergood over the years."

Evergood's praise extended to Joe's love, commitment and sensitivity to artists and his appreciation for "good painting with guts." He lauded Joe for "the founding of one of the greatest collections of art in America." It was letter glowing with warmth and gratitude.

One of Joe's first influences for turning to living artists was his cousin, Itzak Friedlander, to whom he disliked giving credit. For some reason, Hirshhorn didn't advance the work of Friedlander, either, or even treat him with the same regard as he did the other artists. Nevertheless, Joe helped support Itzak during his lifetime and continued to support his widow after Itzak's death.

His association with and support of living, struggling artists continued during his marriage to Lily Harmon and beyond. Once Hirshhorn had awakened to the vibrancy and originality of the work of living artists, he pursued them entirely on his own and found reasons to help them survive. He confided, "Those artists were in bad shape. They were all starving. You know, times were very bad. A number of these artists even back in 1940, 1944, 1945 when the war broke out . . . were in bad shape. As a matter of fact, about fifteen years ago I tore up, I think, $88,000 or $92,000 in notes that they owed me. I knew I wouldn't be able to collect anyway so I wrote the whole works off."

When Lerner met Joe, he was not yet married to Lily. As their friendship deepened, Joe's trust in Lerner and respect for his opinion also grew to the extent that he often visited galleries Lerner had tipped him to, where a certain choice work of art might be found. It was entirely up to Joe what he bought or if he bought. Lerner had no input into those decisions, no one did.

"Once every week or two Joe would call and say, 'Meet me at Parke Bernet auction house at four P.M.' and the two of us would go to galleries together. Joe was so alive and so quick, so positive, strong, he intrigued me no end. He liked me because I was informed." And also, in my opinion, because Lerner, a sweet and kind man for all his strength, didn't threaten him. One of the traits Lerner most admired was Joe's energy. "I still retain the image of him," Lerner said, "striding down Fifty-seventh Street with two giant Canadian engineers on either side trying to keep up with him." Many people were struck by Hirshhorn's energy. Even his daughter Robin commented, "His energy impressed me. It was extraordinary."

Hirshhorn and Lerner used to go to certain galleries during the week around the lunch hour, Lerner said. "He intrigued me the way he bought. He would ask for a price and whatever the dealer said, he would draw back like he was slapped. And at that point the dealer would justify himself. Then Joe would say, 'Give me a piece of paper. I'll tell you what I'm going to do. I'll write down a price that I'm willing to pay you.' The dealer would then look at it and say, 'Mr. Hirshhorn, I can't do it.' Joe would say, 'Look, I come here often, don't I?' The guy would say, 'Yes you do, I'm glad you come.' 'Okay,' Joe would say, 'I buy a lot from you, right? Well, you can afford to give it to me. I'm not a guy who comes here today and you won't see again.' That was a strong point. Joe would say, 'You'll see me for years to come, because I'm collecting.' And he'd get it for the price he wanted.

"They may have resented it, but I felt differently about it. When I went into a gallery alone the dealer might ask, 'Why does Mr. Hirshhorn do that?' And I would say, 'Look, he doesn't pull a gun on you. All you have to do is say no. Say no and see what happens, make a counter-offer.' The dealers acted as if somebody came in with a gun, held them up and walked out."

Lerner analyzed the dealers' true positions regarding the prices they asked and received. "Dealers in those days were working at a one-third mark-up, 33 1/3 percent. Now, if a dealer sold the work of art to Joe, the most he would lose was maybe 10 percent. But the artist would suffer. And if the artist was adamant about the price, the dealer would take a little off his own, so instead of getting 33 1/3 percent, he would get 20 percent. It was no big deal." So, it turned out after all that Joe wasn't making ridiculously low offers. Maybe Lerner should have explained that to Lily.

As for Joe's manipulative techniques with gallery owners, Lerner related a story that illustrates how the strength of Joe's personality could overcome the angry or resentful feelings of at least some of the people who were "taken." And many were. It was Joe's habit, one which couldn't have profited him greatly in terms of monetary gain but may have satisfied another urge to "get over" on people, to go around touting penny stocks that he said would be worth $100 in three months time. As the people in his targeted group were buying and sending the price of the stock up, Joe was selling his shares to them at steadily increasing prices. Eventually, when the "suckers" had stopped buying, with no demand for the shares, the price began dropping precipitously and at the bottom, Joe would again buy the shares at the low price in order to eventually repeat the process, each time with a new target group. Few people fell for the same ruse twice.

He had made the same propositions to me! I only bit once and never again. The statement that lured the "suckers" into the scam was preposterous on the face of it. What stock goes from pennies a share to $100 a share in three to six months? But people wanted to "get rich quick" and be let in on what they believed was "the bottom." "Yes," Lerner said, "I knew he did that. I had it from a very reliable source, a nice man who still loved Joe. He said, 'I cannot dislike Joe. He's so extraordinary. He sold me a bill of goods. I lost a bundle.'"

Time passed and Joe continued making the rounds and buying sculptures, oils and watercolors from various galleries. He bought from everyone, including Sidney Janis, Rene Gimpel, Andre Emmerich, John Levy, Curt Valentin, Leo Castelli, the Pierre Matisse Gallery, and Knoedlers. Harold Diamond, a dealer without a gallery, was a major contact to important artists. The Forum Gallery, owned and operated by Bella Fishko, was a place he enjoyed visiting. Fishko and Hirshhorn became friends. It was from the Gerson Gallery that Joe bought the over-lifesize "Burghers of Calais" by Rodin. As time passed and their friendship grew, Al and his wife Pauline, Joe and Lily began to socialize together.

Lerner saw Joe through the boom days in Canada and through his divorce from Lily. But Joe never stopped buying art, he bought more and more, especially when the money began to pour in from Pronto Mine. He bought in New York, he bought in Canada, he bought wherever his interests took him. Lerner was aware that Joe's collection was growing wildly (it could hardly be called a collection, it was more of an aggregate) and wondered about Hirshhorn's ultimate plan for it. The two men talked only sporadically about the future of Joe's art.

In 1955, the Lerners went to live in Rome. Joe not only didn't resent the move to Europe of his companion and confidant in art, he thought their idea of spending a year or so in Italy was fine and even helped to finance their sabbatical. While Lerner was in Europe, the two men kept up a lively correspondence, touching on personal matters but also discussing what Joe might do with his art. Lerner suggested that Joe might consider finding one of the old, substantial townhouses in New York (perhaps along Fifth Avenue) to house the art, much like J. P. Morgan had done, putting his library in his former home, or Frick did with his own art collection at his own residence on Fifth Avenue.

Whether it was because of these exchanges of letters about the Morgan art or if it was something Hirshhorn had already contemplated, my brother often told a story that suggests Hirshhorn was seriously considering the future of his art collection. The story concerns a walk Gordon took with his father one day in the 1950s.

The two men were strolling down Fifth Avenue past the Frick Collection in New York City, when Joe asked Gordon, "Do you know who Frick was? How he earned his money?"

"I'm not sure," my brother replied vaguely, "He was some sort of entrepreneur. Railroads?"

"You see," Joe said knowingly, "Frick will never be remembered for how he made his money. He will always be remembered because of the Frick Museum." This thought may have lain dormant in the back of Hirshhorn's mind for some years.

Not long after Al and Pauline Lerner's return from Italy with their daughter Aline, on May 3, 1956 aboard the S.S. *Independence,*[*] Hirshhorn set Lerner off looking at possible houses (mansions) where his growing art collection might possibly be accommodated permanently in the future. One attempt offered Lerner an occasion to note his friend's power to attract beautiful women. It was something Lerner continually marveled at: the mutual attraction Joe enjoyed with the opposite sex. Lerner saw Joe's attraction to the women as a parallel to his interest in fine paintings and sculpture.

"Joe never had to be without a woman in his life. He was very sure of himself as a man," Lerner mused. "He had no doubts, none at all, that he was attracted to women and women were attracted to him. He was very flirtatious with pretty women. He wouldn't flirt with a woman who wasn't pretty. He liked pretty women and, to tell the truth, he liked beautiful men, too. Joe was attracted to good-looking people. He also had a high regard for wealth. He loved good-looking, wealthy people. He used to say about somebody, 'He's very refined, you know. He went to the best schools.' Beauty was beauty to him. If they were wealthy, he always attributed a certain polish to them. It's the way F. Scott

*New York Passenger Lists, Microfilm Serial T715, Roll 8715, page 34.

Fitzgerald felt about the wealthy: They were different. They weren't like us.

"I was looking at a brownstone on Fifth Avenue with a museum in mind. I had called an agent and she showed up—they are always women. She took me around and showed me everything but she was very cold and impersonal. Then I thought that Joe should see it because I loved it. It was a house that had belonged to Bache, the financier, and Bache had given his collection of old masters to the Metropolitan. Well, Joe came with me and she, the agent, was already there. I tell you, the minute Joe came in she practically threw herself at him. He had her eating out of his hand."

Another of Joe's characteristics that fascinated and astounded Lerner was his shrewdness, his ability to size people up within an instant of meeting them.

"We were together in Italy one time," Lerner recounted with a smile, "staying at an excellent hotel on a square in Florence and Joe was off somewhere. He was always off. There was never a moment when Joe didn't have an appointment or wanted to see somebody. I was standing outside the hotel when he came back. I'd been talking to a little man who said he was in business and had worked hard all his life, so his children had encouraged him to take a vacation in Europe. The man told me, 'I want to go back home.' I asked, 'Why?' He replied, 'I don't like it here.' I said, 'Look, you're in one of the most beautiful little cities in the world.' He answered, 'You got old bridges, old buildings. I just came from Israel. There I saw farms with cows, with machinery, with modern up-to-date . . . everything.' So, we continued chatting and I could see he was just a regular guy, a businessman all his life. That's when Joe came over to where I was standing with this guy. Immediately, Joe sized him up and his first words to the little guy were, 'What room is the poker game in?' And the guy immediately answered, 'forty-nine.' Just like that!

"I said to Joe, 'How in the hell did you know that about the guy?' And Joe said, 'He's a poker player, a pinochle player. He has nothing to do here. The only thing he can do is start up a game.' Joe certainly blew me down with that. He was so quick, so sure. He sized that man up in one glance. I would never have thought of it."

Joe with Brenda Hawley Heide, his third wife.

Before Lerner and his wife returned from Italy, in 1956 when Joe was divorced from Lily and his uranium deal with Rio Tinto was completed, he'd become involved with a woman named Brenda Heide. All that was known of Brenda's family background came from her own assertions and no one appears to have questioned them. Hyams biography says of her: "Brenda was the grandniece of Collis P. Huntington whose son, Henry, bought "The Blue Boy" by Gainsborough which hung in the Huntington Museum in California." In fact, Henry Huntington was not Collis's son, but rather his nephew. Hyams goes on to state, "Brenda, while still in her twenties, had been wife, mother and widow. More recently she had divorced Julius A. Heide, Jr., heir to the candy millions, and was living with her parents on West Twenty-third Street."[*]

*Hyams, p. 89. On her Social Security application made in November 1937, Mildred (Brenda) gave her address as 435 West 23rd Street where she lived with her parents Robert N. and Margaret J. Hawley.

Hyams may have interviewed her and reported what she and/or Joe told him. My research tells a somewhat different story. Brenda was born Mildred Constance Hawley on October 22, 1913, to Margaret J. Gastiger and Robert N. Hawley, in Brooklyn, New York. Marriage records are not easily available, especially when the place of marriage is unknown, so the claim that she was a widow in her twenties with a daughter cannot be verified or disproved. However, her daughter, Susan Heide, was born in 1940 when Mildred was twenty-six or twenty-seven years old and at a time when Julius Heide, Jr. was already married to a Mary Law.[*] Julius and Mary's marriage endured until 1947 when they divorced in Dade County, Florida. Any marriage between Mildred/Brenda and Julius Heide, Jr. would have to have taken place after 1947. As to Mildred's connection to Collis Potter Huntington, there is nothing extant to connect her by blood or adoption to the family. The Huntington family tree was examined carefully for any connection and Robert Hawley's family was easily traced, by virtue of U.S. census records, back to the 1850s in Connecticut where Robert was born and no connection was found.

As to the parentage of her daughter Susan who is alive, she uses the name of Heide and is unwilling to be interviewed about her lineage. One cannot know if Joe was privy to the truth of Brenda's early life. He may have known something was amiss in Brenda's story as, for a brief time, he contemplated legally adopting Susan. Nothing came of the idea. One can only say with assurance that Brenda/Mildred had a paternal uncle named Collis: Collis S. Hawley.

Brenda ran against type for Hirshhorn: she was tall, blonde, Gentile and had the manners of a society girl. At the time they met, she was a hostess in an exclusive men's shop, comparable to Sulka, on 57th Street between Madison and Fifth Avenues, which Joe frequented. She described herself as a "café society" girl and

---

*The couple appear on a 1930 Federal Census as married, living with the bride's family. They appear to be financially dependent upon Mary's father although Julius Heide, Jr. has a mundane job.

admitted, after their eventual divorce, she had probably met Joe too soon because at the time she was not interested in art or literature. Her main fascinations were clothes, parties and dancing. As a girlfriend, she looked good on Joe's arm (today she might be called a "trophy wife"). But with the closing of the Rio Tinto deal and the subsequent invitation to London where a number of high-toned celebrations were scheduled take place (celebrations where he would be rubbing elbows with the landed gentry, earls, barons and other titled Englishmen), Joe, very much the Victorian, felt embarrassed to bring along his mistress. With the impending trip in mind, in May 1956, he married Brenda. Joe had yet to learn that having a mistress was *de rigueur* for upper-class Europeans, whether or not they had wives. It is also interesting to note that not only did Joe fail to inform his children he was marrying a third time, he also pointedly failed to include them in this exciting, interesting aspect of his life. None of Joe's children, with the possible exception of his son Gordon, were invited by their father to participate in any of the celebrations resulting from his uranium discoveries. This was hurtful to his children.

Following the uranium strike there had been an explosion of publicity. Among the plethora of print publications, both in Canada and the United States, *Life Magazine* did a photographic essay headlined on the cover of the August 1, 1955 issue as FABULOUS BLIND RIVER: RICHEST URANIUM FIELD.[*] Although the article focused attention predominantly on Franc Joubin, the mining engineer whose knowledge lay behind the discovery, it was impossible for the editors to ignore the part played by Hirshhorn. The story contained a photograph of Lily and Joe in Blind River with the caption below reading, "New house blueprints are inspected by Hirshhorn and his wife, who is an artist." A second photo shows Joe standing in front of his recently erected guest housing in Bootleggers Bay, entitled, "Uranium magnate Joe Hirshhorn stands on the terrace of his nearly completed guest house."

I, my two sisters and my brother had similar reactions to

[*]Vol. 39, No. 5, page 78.

these spectacular events and the publicity that accompanied them. First, there was a natural hurt to have been excluded from the excitement of our father's achievement. We were no more than spectators, not insiders as we believed Lily's children had been. And we felt angry not to share in the financial benefits that accrued to Joe and his second family.

In the aftermath of these revelations, my brother and I, sitting in my modest home in Culver City, California, penned a short poem to our father:

You think you are our Daddy Joe,
But there's one thing that you should know,
To us you're Santa, Ho, Ho, Ho,
So open your bag and give us the dough!*

It wasn't very nice but it served to relieve some of the negative feelings and cover up our pain by affording us a scornful laugh at Joe's expense. Of course, Joe never knew about the poem.

Robin's take on Joe's behavior was, for her, typically kinder, "I just don't understand Daddy," she said in 1963. Naomi shared what was originally bewilderment and then expressed her new clarity on the subject of Joe's parenting.

"[Daddy] was capable of great generosity at times," she said, "and then, could be deeply withholding at other times: bringing me to tears with his toughness and his anger and, what I perceived as 'hatred.' A confusing thing for a child and, of course, that confusion continued into adulthood and even after he died, given that he left the bulk of his huge estate to the museum and we, his children, got what little was left over and, at that, it was left 'In Trust.' I never understood why, after our parents separated (when I was about ten) and then were subsequently divorced, our 'lifestyle' changed so drastically. It took me until I was fifty years old to come to the painful conclusion that the reason our lifestyle changed was because the enormous wealth that

---

*My siblings and I called him Daddy Joe because that was the way he used to sign his letters to us.

'Daddy Joe' had amassed was never for us, his family. It was all for him. And so, when he left, he took that lifestyle with him. The family was, once again, an afterthought."

Hirshhorn, in New York, Canada or Europe, was a man without pretensions. Regardless of the company he kept, he was always the same: buoyant, energetic and spontaneous with a habit of blurting out exactly what he thought. It was a style that tended to relax the people around him. "He behaved," publicist Ben Sonnenberg said, "as if he were a member of the Borah Minnevitch Harmonica Rascals." These "Harmonica Rascals" were featured in many black and white films of the 1930s and '40s.

E. P. Richardson, a respected scholar and a co-founder of The Archives of American Art, wrote an entry in his diary about Joe during a large exhibition of Hirshhorn's sculpture collection held at The Detroit Institute of Art where Hirshhorn was the guest of honor.

Joe was in good form—got on well with everyone; clowned and urged people to give money (to the institute). He likes to know everyone's first name, also what they do. Alvan MacCauley introduced him to Jack Lord who, as Rhoda Newberry's husband, represents I suppose the ancient aristocracy of Michigan. "What's your first name?"—"Jack." "What do you do, Jack?" "Jack is president of Lee and Cady," said Alvan. "What's Lee and Cady?"—"Wholesale grocers."—"Never mind that, Jack," said Joe, "I know all kinds of people."

I think Joe would have said that to the Queen of England—"Never mind, Liz, I know all kinds of people."[*]

In London with Brenda for the festivities, he didn't have the opportunity to meet the Queen, but he captivated the English as he did everyone else just by being himself.

Here was more cause for bitterness on the part of Joe's children. *There was so much we felt we were missing out on, always excluded from the events that charmed his life and the lives of*

*The Archives of American Art Journal, Vol. 22, No. 1, 1992.

whomever was his current wife and her children. We, his natural children who carried his genes in our bodies, rarely, if ever, were allowed to enjoy the recognition, pleasures and benefits that arose from that primary connection. Lily and Joe's legally adopted daughters and, later, Olga and her three sons (neither blood nor legally his) all enjoyed the accident of being in Joe's inner circle while we were left out. We had no part in any of it, not even as spectators.

We knew only what the world knew; we had our information from the same sources—newspapers, radio and word of mouth. It caused us more than feelings of personal injury, we were embarrassed in front of our friends and, especially among new acquaintances whose assumptions were that we were a part of Joe's life, privy to "up close and personal" confidences with the wonder-man himself. Nothing was further from the truth.

Having the name, Hirshhorn, became a liability. For Naomi, who was not married, and for Gordon who was both proud of and stuck with the name, it was more difficult than it was for either myself or Robin in that both of us were married and carrying a different last name. Eventually, Naomi gave up using her maiden name and began calling herself Naomi Caryl, Caryl being her middle name. Gordon just stayed stuck with Joe's last name.*

After the festivities in London were over, Joe and Brenda traveled to the French Riviera where he bought a house overlooking the Mediterranean Sea, called *"Villa Lou Miridou"* on the Boulevard du Littoral in Cap d'Antibes. He also purchased seventy-seven acres in Vallbone, also overlooking the Mediterranean. Joe bought a Rolls Royce with the steering wheel on the left, which he temporarily left in France. While on the Riviera, Joe rented a cabana at the Hotel du Cap and indoctrinated the dining room chefs into saving fish heads for his lunches—a favorite food of his childhood. If they could have produced matzo balls

*Helen Hirshhorn, Gordon's former wife and the mother of his three daughters, when asked if she was related to the Hirshhorn of the museum fame, always replied, "No, I'm not."

in chicken soup, gizzards and other childhood delicacies, he would have been even more content. After the couple's three-month holiday in France, Joe had the Rolls shipped to New York.

"He had this very fancy car," Lerner said. "He had it in New York and he'd drive around in it with his liveried chauffeur. I thought he loved the car. He said to me one day, 'You know, I don't like that car.' I said, 'Why?' And he said, 'It's not as comfortable as the Cadillac.' After I was working for him and he had rented space off Madison Avenue in the east sixties, occasionally, at the end of the day, Wilbert, Joe's chauffeur, would drop in on his way downtown to put the car away, to have a look at the day's catch (of art). He was a sort of upright, honorable guy. He never hedged anything, always answered. We'd chat for a while and when it was time to close, I'd go down with him and he's all dressed in his uniform, a wonderful gray, with a hat and everything. He had a chocolate skin and against the gray, I mean, he was beautiful looking. He would open the door for me and I would get into the Rolls Royce. We would drive two blocks or something like that, to the 68th Street station of the IRT. He would open the door for me and I would go from the Rolls Royce into the subway with people standing around looking at the spectacle."

At that time Hirshhorn was living in an apartment on Fifth Avenue. In the summer of 1957 he would commute between Nice, France and New York City, at times without Brenda, by Pan American World Airways. There is a record of one such trip of Joe traveling alone and arriving in New York on June 24, 1957.[*] As he was still needed in Canada, the couple frequently spent their time shuttling between their elegant apartment in New York and Joe's suite at the King Edward Hotel in Toronto and the house in Cap D'Antibes. There were other weeks when Joe left Brenda in France while he flew to Toronto, then stole a few days in New York to make the rounds of the galleries before he shuttled back to the Riviera to rejoin his wife. In July 1958, on one of those flights, Hirshhorn was aboard a DC-7C, 460 miles out of

*Microfilm Serial T715, Roll 8,888, page 409.

Idlewild (now JFK) Airport over the Atlantic when the one pro-
peller drive-shaft of one engine cracked and broke. The plane
shuddered, dropped 15,000 ft. and seemed in severe trouble before the pilot regained enough control to level off in the denser atmosphere at 6,000 feet. Knowing it was too dangerous to
continue on toward Europe, the pilot radioed all air and surface
shipping to stand by for emergency aid as he headed for the U.S.
Naval Station at Argentia, Newfoundland. It took
four-and-a-half hours for the crippled plane with forty-five passengers and nine crew members to reach its new destination.
During this lengthy, anxious time, Joe took to the aisles to sing
and dance in an effort to divert his fellow passengers. He kidded
with the children and cracked jokes. Among the travelers on
board were Lucia Chase, director of the American Ballet Theater, Eleanor Lambert and her husband, Seymour Berkson, who
reported to his newspaper, the New York Journal American, that
Hirshhorn "generally made the whole thing seem a picnic as
nerves relaxed and tension eased." When they reached their destination and the pilot announced over the loudspeaker, "That's it
folks!" the passengers let out a spontaneous cheer. Soon after
they boarded a replacement aircraft and set off again, this time
for Lisbon. Joe admitted with some humility when praised for
his poise under fire, that as a mining entrepreneur he was accustomed to brushing off the stress of risks.

    After spending a year and a half in Italy, Lerner, back in
New York, needed a job. He found one working for Hugh Stiks
who ran a co-op gallery which was unusual for the fact that no
money was taken from the sales of artists' works. The gallery
was supported by Stiks' own funds, together with those he was
able to raise through people he knew. During the eighteen
months Al worked for Stiks, he and Joe spoke often about a future for Joe's collection which was growing too large for one man
to properly house and maintain. Following Al's suggestion about
locating a house in Manhattan suitable to turn into a museum, it
was then that Joe asked Lerner to look around for such a building during the week while Joe was away in Canada. In pursuit of
that assignment Lerner identified the brownstone on Fifth Ave-

nue he liked so well, the place where Joe had charmed the lady real estate agent. But nothing came of the idea.

Hirshhorn was buying art everywhere. But in New York, where there was so much art on display and for sale, and where Joe had so little time to scout all the possibilities, it was often Lerner who suggested a show in some gallery he thought Joe might want to see. In June 1957, at Lerner's suggestion, Joe went to the Virginia Zabriskie Gallery at 32 East 65th Street to see a show she called "The City," featuring various artist's works depicting New York. There he made his first purchase from Ms. Zabriskie, a small paining by George Bellows called "The Bethesda Fountain in Central Park." "After the first purchase," Ms. Zabriskie said, "Joe came in and bought regularly. He used to say to me when I quoted a price to him, 'Are you talking rubles?' "

Lerner said Virginia was terribly fond of Joe, "I saw her after Joe's funeral. She was standing outside the temple and sobbing. 'He saved my life,' she said, 'He started me out.'" Joe had, by his patronage, helped secure her gallery which is still open for business today at 41 East 57th Street. Joe made friends with Virginia as he did with a great many people. She was invited to lunch at his home in Greenwich several times, once when his other guest was Louise Nevelson. "I liked him very much," Virginia said, "He wore bow ties and I gave him some clip-on bow ties once. He was my friend." Virginia Zabriskie was an art dealer invited to the museum's opening who had no conflicted feelings about Joe. He was her friend.

As for Louise Nevelson, Hirshhorn had strong opinions about her, except for his assessment of her ability as a painter, all positive. "I've known Louise Nevelson since 1930," he told Paul Cummings, "She was a lousy painter. She was buying Elshemius when I was buying Elshemius." That was certainly a compliment to her judgment. "But," he added, "she is a great sculptor, she's a great artist. Oh, she's developed. She's a great lady, very bright. But she's a nice woman. That's the important thing." Of course, Joe bought Louise Nevelson's work.

Hirshhorn's enthusiasm for acquiring art and his financial ability to pay for it reached its peak in the years following his enormous success in Canada. On a single day in New York in

1957, Joe bought the following works of art: two sculptures—*Head of a Man* by Pablo Picasso and *Hesperis* by Georges Braque, and five paintings—*Blue Air* by Robert Motherwell, *Girl in Orange Gown* by George Luks, *The Sea* by George Bellows, *Two Becomes One* by I. Rice Pereira and, a work of one of his favorite artists, Thomas Eakins, called *Miss Anna Lewis*. The same year he collected works by Herman Rose, Jackson Polloch and his wife Lee Krasner, by Piet Mondrian, Brancusi, Giacommetti, Mark Rothco, Barnet Newman, Adolphe Gottlieb, Alexander Calder, Man Ray, Giacomo Manzu, Kenneth Noland, George Luks, Joseph Stella, Max Weber, Marc Chagall, David Hockney, Gregorie Gillespie, Joan Mitchell and many, many others.* "I gave [the museum] thirty-five Calders, twenty-eight Matisses (and) thirty-two Giacomettis," he stated matter-of-factly. This was a man both driven and in a hurry.

Hirshhorn bought steadily, through the good times and the bad; he bought things that were figurative and abstract, modern and traditional: a Daumier one day, a de Kooning another day and a Kenneth Snelson, entirely different from the rest, soon after. Joe made a great many friends in the art world, among them were some of his favorites: Georgia O'Keeffe, Joseph Albers and his wife, Anni, and Larry Rivers. His relationship with Willem de Kooning was special and somewhat different.

De Kooning was born in 1904 in Rotterdam, the Netherlands. Although his parents divorced when he was three, he remained close to both of them. At twelve he left regular schooling and was apprenticed to a commercial design and decorating firm, but at the same time he expanded his artistic knowledge and techniques by attending night classes at the Rotterdam Academy. Although schooled in the classical traditions, while still a student he became aware of modern art, particularly the Dutch Vanguard Movement, de Stijl, founded by Piet Mondrian and Theo van Doesburg. Ever more interested in modern painting, in 1924 de Kooning left

*A full list of the works given by Hirshhorn to the Museum in Washington can be obtained from the Smithsonian Archives, The Hirshhorn Museum or on the Internet.

the Netherlands for brief stays in Brussels and Antwerp. After returning to Rotterdam to complete his studies, in August 1926 de Kooning and a friend hired onto a steamer bound for America. After first settling in Hoboken, New Jersey, where he got a job as a house painter, de Kooning finally moved to Manhattan and for the next fifteen years steeped himself in learning modern painting by befriending Greenwich Village intellectuals and by studying the work of modern painters already showing in New York Galleries. Due to his academic background, de Kooning had a great breadth of skills and by 1935, during the middle of the Depression, he found full-time work with the Federal Art Project of the Works Progress Administration (WPA).

Joe Hirshhorn first became acquainted with de Kooning's work in the late 1940s but didn't start collecting it until the late 1950s. Attracted to the man as well as the work, sympathetic to his background and his struggle, by 1964 a deeper friendship had developed between the two men. Hirshhorn provided vital support to de Kooning during his experimental period as he struggled to find his own personal style. This support continued and was particularly generous when de Kooning decided to give up the hectic, over-stimulating energy of Manhattan for a more quiet, tranquil place on Long Island. His need for a contemplative environment, a place where he could think and work out the complex problems of his painting projects drove him out of the city. It was Joe Hirshhorn who subsidized the construction of de Kooning's magnificent new studio in Springs, East Hampton, New York. Several letters exist that detail not only de Kooning's gratitude for Joe's continuing support, but also demonstrate a warmth between the men that resulted from frequent visits and phone calls and from mutually exchanged gifts. A telling depiction of their relationship comes from Judith Zilczer, former curator of paintings at the Hirshhorn Museum and Sculpture Garden who said, "In the annals of American patronage, the relationship between Willem de Kooning and Joseph and Olga Hirshhorn has few parallels."[*]

*Zilczer, Judith. Introduction to the Catalog *Willem de Kooning from the Hirshhorn Museum Collection,* 1993. Olga was Hirshhorn's fourth and last wife.

On a more personal note, de Kooning got a huge kick out of
Hirshhorn's acquisitive nature and, once he'd heard the following story from Al Lerner, he would ask to have it repeated nearly
every time the two men met. This is the story Lerner told to me:

> I want to tell you a story about him as a collector, and *what* a col-
> lector he was. We [Lerner and his wife] went to visit your father
> and Olga in Florida. Olga suggested we go crabbing. I've never
> been crabbing in my life. Your father seemed willing to do that.
> Now, the way you catch crabs, or at least, the way Olga catches
> crabs, she used to keep chicken necks and you put them on a hook
> and the crabs evidently love it. So they grab onto it and you pull
> them in and they're stupid and you throw them into a can or what-
> ever you're using to keep them.
>
> Well, Pauline wasn't interested in this at all, so she was sit-
> ting and reading. But it was very hot. So I got crabs and Olga got
> crabs and your father got crabs and we were there for several
> hours. And it was hot. And the pail, the size of a garbage pail, was
> full of crabs. I said, "You know, Joe, I think we have a lot of crabs.
> I think we ought to go." And he said, "**You're making a big mis-
> take. There are a lot more in there.**"

De Kooning *loved* that story!

Finally, recognizing the collection was getting entirely out of
control, in 1959, Hirshhorn created The Hirshhorn Foundation
with Lerner as curator of the collection. Lerner didn't need to be
asked twice. He quit the Stiks co-op and entered into his first formal employment arrangement with Joe.

"When I started to work for him," Lerner said, "I was living
in Queens and Joe didn't open an office for me right away. In the
beginning, I used to come to his office at 165 Broadway. He had
an entrance room where George Courtney sat and a secretary,
Gloria, at a desk. Gloria was very nice to me which she didn't
have to be because I was an interloper. I came in and, so far as
George and she could see, there was nothing for me to do.

In Hirshhorn's business quarters, there was a small reception room, another small room, about eight by fourteen, and a
large room which was Joe's office where Joe sat at a big table
with a golden telephone that had a lot of buttons. Lerner marveled at Hirshhorn's ability to do two or three things at the same

time on the phone. On two phones at the same time, "he used to say, 'Hold it . . . Yeh, Leo? What's happening? Hold it,' It was quite wonderful. Then the golden phone would ring and that would be something special, I don't know who. Family, maybe, or close friends."

Art of every kind filled the office and the only space Lerner was given was the small, eight-foot by fourteen-foot room. Because Lerner saw Hirshhorn had many and various paintings standing on the floor, leaning against the walls and each other, Al told him, "Joe, we have to build bins in this room because your pictures are going to be destroyed." Hirshhorn agreed to Lerner's suggestion and Al arranged for the metal bins to be erected, after which, Lerner began to catalog the paintings, something that had never been done before. It was the start of some organization.

Working at 165 Broadway brought Lerner into contact with the entourage of loyal characters who surrounded Joe, some of whom had worked for Hirshhorn for many years. One of these was general utility man, George Courtney, who had worked for Joe, as George once said, "since he was a little boy." George was truly a Damon Runyon character who had Hirshhorn's complete trust and who, after so many years in his employ, knew "where all the bodies were buried." Lerner genuinely liked George. "He was a man you just couldn't get angry with because he was always being witty and sharp, sometimes against the grain. One day I walked into the office and said, 'Where's Mr. Hirshhorn?' George answered, 'Oh he's out with a couple of Hebes.' I could *not* take offense. He was that kind of guy. Joe told me George was really anxious to be a sort of Broadway man. He loved song and dance. It didn't turn out that way but he kept all the humor. He was always on stage.

"Courtney was a strange man," Lerner continued, "but I loved him. I loved that wit, that humor. He was outrageous. Nothing was holy to Courtney. He would say, 'You're a Democrat? How the hell can you be a Democrat? You know they were the most destructive party we ever had.' He was a very bright, witty Irishman but, I must tell you, he was very anti-government, so that any forms that had to be filled out, he did not want to do it. I worked for Joe for years and he never had me on Social Security because he didn't want to fill out the papers. Joe either didn't know or he didn't care."

Because Lerner was at work in Joe's office he had the opportunity to see Hirshhorn at work and, as he described it, there was considerable humor in Joe's performances there.

"He was never rough with me, never used rough language with me but, with his brokers he could be rough, and most of it was fun. It was like a routine he had developed with them. When he wanted to know how a stock was doing, he'd make up a name for it, he might say, 'How's Schmuck selling today?' And then the broker would say something. Then Joe would turn to me and say, 'Al, it's down today.' It was very funny. And he used to have little sayings of his own like, 'Have you seen the Mahaska brothers?' He would suddenly break into song and he sang like Georgie Jessel or Jolson, that era. He used to break into song especially when the market was good and he was happy."

Joe had old-fashioned ideas about women, understandably so. He felt they should never sit with their legs apart and he never used what Lerner called "rough language" around women. *However, I was told by my cousin Leo Hirshhorn, who worked for him as a runner in the very early '30s, that Joe had a more-than-sufficient vocabulary of swear words at his disposal which he didn't hesitate to use among his business associates.* (Leo, Herman's son, also reported that during the short time he worked in his uncle's office, Joe was known as "the Mockey Pirate of Wall Street.") *I knew from my own experience that my father enjoyed what I called "toilet humor." One of his favorite jokes concerned a man relieving himself in a bathroom—a story he had heard from one of the Ritz brothers when Joe was staying at his favorite Los Angeles hotel, The Beverly Wilshire.*

Another example of Hirshhorn's playfulness was how frequently he introduced himself as J.J. O'Brien, as he had with Lily. But he also often introduced his companion, especially when the man was older than he, as "my son." Lerner confided that Joe had once introduced him as "that famous ball player from Yonkers."

If Joe told a joke, he might tell the punch line in Yiddish because, if it was a Jewish joke, "the punch line was funnier in Yiddish." Lerner expanded on Joe's ability to speak the language of his childhood. "He spoke Yiddish to me, and he spoke it pretty well. He didn't make a point of it. He used to throw it in casually. And once he read something to me in Yiddish, just to show me he could read it. And he loved Georgie Jessel. He used to imitate the way they (the Jewish entertainers) sang. He would sing 'My Yiddishe Mama.' It was never a prolonged thing. He would throw it in. If he got good news on the telephone he would turn around to me and suddenly break into song."

Finally, Joe realized Lerner couldn't continue to work in that small room, he needed to have an office of his own. Although he still saw him regularly, that was the end of Lerner's daily contact with Courtney's acerbic wit and Joe's spontaneous market-related performances.

XI
The Foundation Gets an Office

In 1959, Joe rented an office off Madison Avenue on 67th Street in a "chateau-type" building that has since been torn down. "My office was on the third floor," Lerner said, "and I can't tell you how delicious it was to go there every morning with the art in the room." On the second floor of the building was a dance studio for children which Lerner enjoyed enormously. "I'd see these little ballerinas every day going up . . . oh, it was lovely." On the same floor as the art office was a photographer who did fashion advertising and an art gallery run by a war refugee.

When the new space for the collection was ready, most of the art that had been at Joe's Broadway office was moved over. Many of the works that were in his home were also moved to Madison Avenue. When Lerner began working for Joe, he "tallied up" 1,200 pieces of art. It represented an "awful lot of buying," Lerner commented. "Joe bought almost every week, you know. I was thinking if Joe had time, he would have bought every day." Prior to Lerner's taking over, Joe hired a capable young woman who had worked as a secretary for his friend, Paul V. McNutt, whom he had met in connection with his speculation deal in the Philippines. McNutt had been governor of Indiana before he became the U.S. High Commander of the Philippines in 1937. When McNutt no longer required the young woman's services as a secretary, he prevailed on Joe to take her on and he did. However, as Joe couldn't use her in his business office, he put her to work cataloging the art, of which there was already a great deal. Modern art, however, was something with which the secretary had no previous experience.

When Lerner entered the scene, the young woman left Joe's employ. Lerner soon discovered as he began to sort though the

A view of the "Art Office" prior to the Smithsonian taking over the collection. The main room was crammed with paintings and sculpture of every kind, from every source.

work she had begun, that she had used a pencil to inscribe an identification number on the back of each painting. By pressing the pencil against the canvas, an indentation was left that was visible on the front surface of the painting. "So that was her legacy to me," Lerner commented, dryly.

To her credit, he added, she had set up a warehouse on 21st Street at Tenth Avenue for the art that was, even then, already overflowing Hirshhorn's office. The desks, tables, and floor were covered with art. It was a big warehouse and by the time Lerner took over, Joe had already rented six rooms, each one about seven feet by eight feet. Bins had been built to hold the paintings in each room.

"I worked in the warehouse for a long time cataloging the art," Lerner reported, "and it was not the most agreeable place. It was cold, wet, dirty and the lighting was bad. I had one warehouse man to help me *schlep*."

The problems in keeping accurate records concerning each individual work of art arose from the hopelessness of staying abreast of Joe's lightning purchasing pace. Lerner did all the identifying and writing, consequently he spent a great deal of time in the warehouse, in his office accepting new work and cataloging, and visiting galleries.

Lerner's office was beautiful but it was small and, like the warehouses, was crammed with art—on the walls, on the floor, in every nook and cranny. "I noticed in the upper wall, very close to the ceiling, there was a strange rectangle that I could never figure out," Lerner said. "One day Joe came in and I pointed it out to him. I said, 'You know, I cannot hang a picture on that wall there because I don't know what that stupid thing is.' And he looked at me and said, 'Al, that's a safe.' And sure enough, we pried it open and it was a small safe. I wondered how Joe could have looked at that rectangle and known it was a safe. It could have been a fuse box."

As it turned out, the safe was put to good use. In Canada, Joe had met a curator of antiquities at a Montreal museum. The man had gotten Joe interested in some Scythian antiquities, some of which were gold. It was always a problem for Joe and for Lerner where they could be safely kept, so when the wall safe was discovered, it turned out to be the perfect place for the Scythian pieces to be hidden. They remained there until that office was abandoned for a larger one a block away when the antiquities were transferred to a safe deposit box at the Bank of New York.

"Joe was making money," Lerner remarked. "The way I could tell was that he would arrive every morning very gay and full of things he had bought. Then I knew he'd had a good day on Wall Street." The new works were usually delivered to Joe's office, Lerner's office or to the warehouse. Sometimes Joe's enthusiasm for an item was so great he would carry a new purchase out of the gallery himself if it was small, especially a small piece of sculpture. "Once I came down from the ACA Gallery, before I worked for him, and Wilbert needed something out of the trunk. When he opened the trunk of Joe's Cadillac there was a piece of sculpture, I think it was a small Rodin. He had forgotten it."

By 1962, the office on 67th Street had grown too small, so Lerner and his secretary moved to a larger one at 11 East 68th Street off Madison Avenue. Joe called the four rooms on the seventh floor, "My art office." From floor to ceiling, paintings covered the walls and were stacked along the corridor from the front room to the kitchen. Small Daumiers were placed along the mantel in Lerner's office among art objects spanning eleven civilizations. There were even pieces of sculpture in the tub in the bathroom.

Joe was buying at such a pace it was almost impossible to keep up. "Very often I went with him when he was [buying]," Lerner said, "and at those times I could take notes of the acquisitions. But when Joe returned home after a trip alone to Europe, 250 pieces might follow, some going to the warehouse, others to the art office or Callahan Corporation in Toronto, the villa at Cap d'Antibes, the apartment on Park Avenue or to his home in Greenwich. It was impossible to keep up."

According to Lerner, Joe was an *interested* collector. "He foraged. He was very curious. He would find out. If you talked to him about something, he wanted to know who, why, what. And he learned."

Joe studied art the way he studied mining. He picked the brains of everyone he encountered who was knowledgeable and

During his tenure as Curator of Joe's art collection Al Lerner contemplates multiple Daumier bronzes in the "Art Office," circa 1966. (Original photograph by Philippe Halsman/copyright Halsman Archive.)

experienced on the subject, whether they were artists, dealers or collectors. He read extensively and had a vast library of books on art and artists. He was born with what is known as a "good eye" and kept it sharp by learning. Over time, he stored an enormous body of knowledge about art in his own capacious brain.

Lerner was emphatic, "Joe was not a naïve collector. He loved the artists. One of them might do something terrible and I'd say to Joe, 'You know, so-and-so behaved badly,' and Joe would look at me and say, 'Well, you know, he's an artist.' He forgave them everything. Do you know how unusual that was? Because Joe was not the forgiving type. If you did him dirt, that was the end of it. He loved the product and he loved the maker. Joe often gave money to an artist he felt needed money. He would extract the wad of $100 dollar bills he always carried and peel off one or two. He even did this for artists whose work he didn't like or who rubbed him the wrong way." How many similar selfless gestures Hirshhorn made to all kinds of people will never be known, but we know he was generous to artists, many of whom he knew well and admired, seemingly above all other people. If an artist was in need, Joe would reach unhesitatingly into his pocket for a donation. And there were occasional artists Joe, for some unknown reason, just didn't take to.

Lerner remembered when the world-renowned British sculptor Jacob Epstein visited Joe's office with his brother. "You would never think he was talking to one of the great sculptors, Joe was very casual with him. He just wasn't serious. He didn't treat him like an artist. I think he thought they only came there because they wanted to sell him something.

"Even before I went to work for him he knew a lot of young artists like the Sawyer brothers (twins, Moses and Raphael) and Chiam Gross, too many to name. But they are, in a sense, provincial. It was later that he met world artists. In his later days he palled around with Picasso." He used to bring Picasso toys because Picasso loved them. But when Joe was with him, Picasso was in the driver's seat. "Joe was overwhelmed by his talent," Lerner said, "He was overwhelmed by just meeting him." Hirshhorn was able to be close to Picasso even though they had no language in common because, as Lerner has said, "No language was needed between those two guys." But, Joe's relationships with international artists included Picasso, Barbara Hepworth and Henry Moore. These relationships came later. A measure of the strength of those friendships might be assessed in how willingly Joe crossed the Atlantic to be with them or how far he would go out of his way once there, to see them.

One senses from the following letter dated May 20, 1968, to Barbara Hepworth, that while his regard for her work was substantial, his affection for her did not have the strength of what he felt for Picasso or Moore. The letter read:

Dear Barbara,
    I was thrilled to receive the photographs you sent and touched by your warm inscription.
    I am so sorry that Olga and I couldn't get over to the Tate

show but we have heard it was a great show. Charles Gimpel
keeps us informed as to how you are.

We plan to be in England sometime this summer. I understand that St. Ives is not a good place to visit then and so we will
miss you. However, we send our love.

Fondly,

Joseph H. Hirshhorn[*]

The friendship between Hirshhorn and Moore was quite another story. It was something special, something primary and in
response to its lure, Hirshhorn crossed the Atlantic many times.

"Joe was crazy about Henry Moore," Lerner stated with ab-
solute conviction. "I went to England with Joe to meet him the
first time and later accompanied Joe on other occasions when
they were together abroad. We went to dinners in Italy where
Joe damn near wept because Henry Moore was being honored.
He once said to me, 'If I had a brother, I'd like him to be Henry
Moore.' "**

An indication of Hirshhorn's affection and regard for Moore
is easily illustrated by the gesture he made in 1964, when the
Arts Council of Great Britain celebrated Moore's 70th birthday
with a party and exhibition at the Tate Gallery in London.
Hirshhorn made it his business to be present as his friend was
honored. At the celebratory dinner given by the trustees of the
Tate, Hirshhorn surprised the director, Norman Reid, by pre-
senting him with a check for $30,000 as a token of his friendship
with Moore. "They can do anything they like with it," he said,
"Henry is one of the greats of the twentieth century and a lovely,
simple human being." Joe added, "I wanted to do something in
his name."

The degree to which Hirshhorn loved and was devoted to
Henry Moore is even more apparent in a telegram Joe sent to the
artist in response to a letter from Moore dated 11th December,
1969 in which Moore identified three pieces of sculpture in Joe's

*Gimpel was Hepworth's gallery representative.
**Joe had three brothers, none of whom was still alive by 1960. Herman, who
  Joe was not close to, died in 1959; Abe in 1936 and Irving in 1939.

collection that Knoedler's and the Marlborough Galleries, who were jointly preparing to mount a show of Moore's work, wanted to include, on loan "for three or four weeks." Moore added a personal request for the loan of the Sundial, which had recently been sent to Joe, also for the pending show. Hirshhorn's telegram in reply reads as follows:

Hoglands, Perry Green Much Hadham, Hertfordshire (ENG)
YOUR LET RECEIVED STOP SUNDIAL ARRIVED STOP WILL
LEND YOU EVERYTHING INCLUDING MY SUNDIAL AND
MY SHIRT STOP YOU ALREADY HAVE MY HEART STOP.

The telegram closed with wishes to Moore, his wife, Irina and daughter, Mary, for a "Merry Christmas" and a "healthy, productive New Year" and was signed, "Love to all of you, Joe."

Wow. "You already have my heart!" Such a powerful declaration conveying such unmitigated, uncensored, unconditional love for Henry Moore and his family. *What I wouldn't have given for a sentence like that from my father.*

Henry Moore was born July 30, 1898 in Castleford, Yorkshire, England to Raymond Spencer Moore, a coal miner, and his wife, Mary Baker. After local schooling in Castleford, he attended Leeds School of Art from 1919 to 1920 and then the Royal College of Art from 1921 to 1924. From 1924 to 1932 he was a part-time instructor there, after which he became a full professor at the Chelsea School of Art in 1932.

Hirshhorn began buying Moore's sculptures in the mid-1950s after he had seen them in English museums. The strength of his figures appealed to Joe greatly and when he went out of his way to meet Moore in the early 1960s he fell for the man, his dignity, his lifestyle, his humor and vitality.

There were a number of threads in Hirshhorn's early life that had verifiable echoes in Moore's. These speak to the bonds between the two men. Both had suffered privations in childhood and had risen above them. While Moore had a hardworking, albeit Victorian, father and Hirshhorn had none, both had mothers who were the heart of their large families, women of exceptional character, energy, determination and dignity who held their families together with love, affection and neverending hard labor. It is understandable Joe felt a familial affection for Henry Moore. In some mystical sense, they had come from the same family.

The friendship between the two men was one of equals and was mutual. In the second, revised, updated and redesigned edition, done in 2003, of Berthoud's biography of Henry Moore, the author pays homage to Moore's loss, in 1981, of one of "his closest American friends, Jo Hirshhorn . . ." and underscores this by offering a brief biographical sketch of Hirshhorn.[*] This was an unusual gesture not repeated for a list of Moore's other good friends who died about the same time.

Joe's belief in Moore's work is substantiated by the fact that between 1966 and 1981, Hirshhorn gave a total of thirty-two Henry Moore works to the museum bearing his name. In his lifetime, Hirshhorn bought more than fifty of Moore's sculptures, nearly all of which were large and expensive pieces that, upon his death, found their way into the Hirshhorn Museum and Sculpture Garden.

Lerner concluded his comments regarding the friendship of these two men by saying, "Hirshhorn was never aggressive with Henry Moore. He could be short with artists on occasion. Even so," Lerner added, "he forgave them everything."

It wasn't just Henry Moore for whom Joe felt sincere affection. "Take Larry Rivers," Lerner said, "Joe loved Larry because Larry was Peck's bad boy and Larry was, to the end of his life, a very independent guy." Rivers had to support his new family and at the same time was building a studio for the family he divorced. He always needed a lot of money and he got it. He showed at the Marlborough Gallery in New York and he was never reviewed. "The critics ignored him," Lerner commented, "because he wasn't abstract enough for them. He didn't paint penises or something, I don't know. But Joe liked Larry because there was a kind of devilish quality to him and in his paintings that appealed to Joe. Larry was a musician, had been on drugs, was into everything straight-laced-Joe was supposed to abhor. He was a bum!

*Berthoud, p. 465, the author's spelling of the name "Jo."

And yet, Joe loved him." What he loved about Rivers' work in particular, he never told me. *My own fascination with Rivers was the architectural foundation that underlay his work.*

It is painful to accept the fact that my father could be so loving and forgiving of artists, yet so rejecting and suspicious of his flesh and blood.

In the early 1950s, Hirshhorn recognized Rivers as a talent and bought thirty-one oils, drawings, collages and sculptures, some of which have been identified as his finest work. In 1963 Rivers went to Greenwich, where he stayed several days, to paint Joe's portrait. In his autobiography written with Arnold Weinstein called *What Did I Do?*, Rivers says Joe "commissioned me to paint his portrait."[*] Rivers, a craftsman of outstanding ability, worked hard to produce two pencil sketches before embarking on the oil painting. He worked in the small library while Joe went through his usual behavior from pacing to relaxation, much of it on the phone. For hours, Rivers struggled to capture his subject until, in frustration, he threw down his brush, "Damn it," he bellowed, "I don't know what's the matter. I can't get your eyes right!"

"Oh," replied Hirshhorn, "is that the problem? Well, I'll tell you. It isn't your fault. I have two different eyes, one shrewd and one kind." Jennie's sister Ruth who knew Joe from the time he was ten years old, always said, "One of Joe's eyes says yesterday and the other says tomorrow." Not everyone had noticed, but some people did. Larry Rivers, an artist with an exceptional eye, refused to be stumped by the problem. He resolved it by painting Joe with one eye only. Hirshhorn entitled the portrait, "Cockeyed Joe." Eventually he filled in the other eye.[**]

In the same biography Rivers speaking of Hirshhorn wanting to buy his monumental painting called "The History of The Russian Revolution" to be hung in the Hirshhorn Museum in Washington and remarks, "If I'm [Rivers] to be recognized in this

[*]Aaron Asher Books, HarperCollins Publishers, 1992, p. 398.
[**]Rivers made two preliminary sketches for this portrait, one belongs to Olga Hirshhorn, the other to his daughter, Gene.

drama as some kind of Bohemian descendant of Michelangelo, Joe was Lorenzo de Medici in a business suit."

Once Lerner had his own office, everything stored in the warehouse remained there and, as additional pictures came in, more rooms were added to the six Joe had previously rented. It was then that Lerner began making trips to Toronto, six or seven altogether, because Joe had been and was still buying in Canada. His hotel suite in the Royal York was covered with his purchases, his closets were packed with pictures. Lerner arranged for the work to be packed and sent to the United States where they were numbered and cataloged. "Your father didn't even remember he had them. He'd already forgotten them," Lerner said.

Lerner was unable to control the buying in Canada. "Sometimes the purchases were sent down to New York, usually not. When he left Canada for good I can assure you there was an office full of works and whether it got to me or not I don't know because I didn't know what he was buying there." The collection was growing by leaps and bounds.

In 1963, for the 50th Anniversary of The Armory Show, the groundbreaking public display of modern art in 1913, Hirshhorn underwrote the updating and republication of Milton Wolf Brown's *Story of the Armory Show,* an unselfish tribute to the work he loved.

Joe also began buying in California. Both Naomi and I lived in Los Angeles but that wasn't the only reason Joe became involved in the Southern California art scene. Sometime in 1961 a woman named Joan Ankrum came to Lerner's office bringing with her some watercolors by her nephew, Morris Broderson, who happened to be deaf. She had recognized his talent when he was just a boy and encouraged him to pursue an artistic career, for which he had promise and where his handicap made no difference. Now she was trying to promote his finished work. Ankrum's background was theater and film, she had been an actress. She was pleasant, well-spoken and attractive, but not very familiar with the art world.

Lerner remembered the occasion in a letter to the author in 1988, after he'd learned Joan Ankrum was closing her gallery after thirty years.

. . . I remember her walking into my first curatorial office (it must have been in the late '50s) with some Broderson watercolors under her arm and no idea of what to do, driven by faith alone and a lot of guts. Her manner, even then, tended to be a little wacky but one also liked her for her enthusiasm and good nature and those qualities set the pattern for her gallery career. Sorry to have it come to an end.

Lerner looked at the drawings and, impressed with Broderson's ability, advised Ankrum to take the work to a curator at the Whitney Museum. "I gave her his name, she went to see him and he bought them." Ankrum knew Lerner was working for Joe. "I think she went from that sale to Joe and convinced him to buy something." He bought several things and, hearing her story, encouraged Ankrum to start an art gallery featuring her nephew's work as well as that of other artists. Joe, in addition to appreciating Broderson's talent, was taken with this soft-spoken, feminine, lively and naïve woman. He understood what she was trying to do for her nephew, whose handicap didn't prevent him from being a fine artist, and Joe was sympathetic. He contributed funds to help her start her gallery and over the years, he continued to buy Brodersons and other artists she represented, two in particular whose work he supported were William Dole and Irving Block. Other artists represented by Ankrum were: Hans Burkardt, Helen Lundeberg, Lorser Feitleson, Ben Shan, Marilyn Lowe, Phyllis Manley, Fritz Schwaderer, and Shirl Goedike and Joe's daughter, Naomi Caryl Hirshhorn. Hirshhorn bought many of these artists and never failed to spend time with Joan Ankrum in her gallery whenever he was in Los Angeles. The Ankrum Gallery on La Cienega Boulevard became a successful and a respected fixture of the Los Angeles art scene for three decades.

Besides buying from Joan Ankrum, Joe patronized the galleries of Rex Evans, a stout, red-faced Englishman who doubled as a character actor in many Hollywood movies; Felix Landau, who, like himself was a refugee from the Russian Empire who had made good; Frank Perls, Esther Robles and others in the area. He also bought from Esther Bear, a charming woman with taste and knowledge, located in Santa Barbara. Felix Landau who once described Joe as "one of the most important art collectors in America," suggested he could "see [Joe] as the hero of an enormously successful musical comedy, with his personage incarnated by Mel Brooks, who resembles him considerably . . ."[*] From Landau, who resented Joe's penchant for hard bargaining, he bought paintings by Bill Brice (the son of Fannie Brice), Paul Vonner, John Paul Jones and Jack Zajack. Landau, with some honesty, remarked, "I can well remember the feelings of satisfaction mixed with bitterness that followed each of Joe's forays into my gallery." Landau would have benefited from Al Lerner's low-key lecture on how dealers might have handled Hirshhorn's bargaining when he inquired, "Did he put a gun to your head?" In spite of Landau's anger, he continued to do business with Joe who also acquired a Max Weber from him that had come from Wright Ludington in Santa Barbara. For all the invective he directed Joe's way, Landau admitted he once or twice "had the good sense, courage and foresight to quote a price much higher than normal," thereby somewhat evening out the score.[**]

In Los Angeles, Joe's reputation as an important art collector brought him into the company of other noted collectors such as Edward G. Robinson, Vincent Price, Taft Schriber and Norton Simon. Joe enjoyed their company as men who were knowledgeable about art and not dilettantes who dabbled in collecting.

On some of those jaunts to Southern California, Naomi and I had occasion to suggest a restaurant where Joe could take us for dinner. It was almost always a place he'd never been to before and his first question was, "Is it dark?" This was a junction where Joe's requirement for cleanliness met his ever-present suspicion. "I don't want to eat in a dark restaurant," he would iterate, because if the restaurant had "atmosphere" or in his opinion, was "dark," he was suspicious the lights were kept low to mask uncleanliness!

Hirshhorn had other restaurant suspicions: Although generous Joe always picked up the tab in a restaurant, he was par-

*From an unpublished manuscript by Felix Landau, p. 96.
**Ibid., p. 100.

ticular about the charges. He would scrutinize the bill looking for a mistake, an attempt to cheat him. He totaled the bill carefully, verifying every item and if it was even a penny off, he would angrily summon the waiter. *This was behavior his children found embarrassing, albeit correct. His natural suspicion came out in other ways and restaurants seemed to provoke it.* Esta Carlen, Joe's niece, recalled a time when her uncle took Esta and her husband for dinner in New York at a very nice restaurant. "When the waiter took the drink order," she said, "Uncle Joe asked for Red Label," then added in a preemptive strike, "And don't try to give me Black Label because I know the difference."

For all his known generosity, having a poor childhood leaves all kinds of marks upon a man, even one as successful and confident as Hirshhorn. It made Joe a proponent of the "waste not want not" school of behavior. *He could be heard shouting, "Turn off the lights!" as we left a room. He ingrained the habit in me. I turn off the lights, still. Then there were his clothes. After his death, in his closets were found old suits of good material and manufacture that still had buttons on the fly. I seriously doubt he'd worn any of them for at least forty years but apparently was unable to give them away.*

In New York Hirshhorn had discovered David Smith, an American artist born in Decatur, Indiana in 1906. He bought his work from 1945 through 1963 when Smith made sculptures that framed the landscape with finishes that captured the light. Hirshhorn exchanged some limited correspondence with him. One exchange, in particular, regarding restoration of a work called "Autumn Queen" is revealing. In a letter to Hirshhorn dated January 7, 1963, Smith asked if Joe had taken out insurance on the sculpture, now restored,[*] inquired about the source of some drawings recently acquired, wished Joe good health and added a sentence which now seems quite poignant, "Stay good," the artist wrote, "stay with me long, so many of my friends drop out or mur-

---

[*]Hirshhorn had an insurance floater on all his art which, from the moment of purchase, covered each and every new art acquisition.

mur a heart or something." David Smith was killed in an automobile accident in 1965 while Joe lived another sixteen years.

Joe's marriage to Brenda Hawley had a short life. His endurance for wedding contracts could be charted on a decreasing scale: Joe's marriage to Jennie had lasted twenty-five years; his association and marriage to Lily, twelve. Now after only two-and-a-half years, Joe and Brenda were legally separated and in five were divorced. Years later, Joe confided to me that, while Brenda was "very clean," she "just didn't have the gray matter." Brenda bored him. She was predominantly a sweet, passive person whose limited interests left him without any stimulating interaction. Lerner's observation when told of Joe's explanation was, "Joe was also very good at finding reasons for why he had done something . . . like all people."[*]

Although Joe and Brenda didn't divorce until 1963, he didn't suffer a loveless existence for long. In Los Angeles he met and courted a woman named Anna White. He grew close to another woman who was between husbands and allowed her to assist him in decorating his newly purchased home in Greenwich, Connecticut. Whether or not they had an affair is not known but she may have been mentally measuring drapes for their bedroom by the time Joe had moved on to another lady. In New York he fell into unrequited love with a sculptress named Shea Reager whom he allowed to move into his Greenwich, Connecticut home with an elderly, sick woman companion she treated like a guru. There were surely more women whose names have fallen by the wayside. Lerner commented, "Joe was always on the alert and whenever he could sandwich it into his otherwise very busy days, he would have another affair." But as shrewd and accurate as Joe's judgment was in sizing up most people, this ability failed him when it came to wives and especially to his short-term affairs.[**]

---

[*]Brenda Hawley Heidi died June 20, 2001, in Woodland Hills, Los Angeles County, California at the age of eighty-seven. Her birth name was Mildred M. Hawley.

[**]After their divorce, Joe remained strongly attracted to Brenda. He bought and maintained an apartment for her in Manhattan at 225 East 63rd Street, off Park Avenue, where he frequently visited her even after his marriage to Olga.

"I knew three of Joe's four wives," Lerner commented, "and although I never met Jennie, it seems to me she was the real thing. She was the most cultivated, had the finest taste and she and Joe had a close connection. *The other things were sort of on the way.*"

XII
The Collection Draws Many Suitors

In 1959, Joe was already well known in Canada. Toronto, where he had his office on Bay Street, was not only the financial capital of the country, it was also the cultural center of English-speaking Canada. That year, the reputable Toronto Art Gallery arranged for an exhibition of some of Hirshhorn's art. Lerner, although already working for Joe, had little to do with the exhibition. It was the museum's curators who selected the objects to present from the 1,200 Joe already owned. The show was well received and word of it quickly got around the art world because, as Lerner observed, "The American art world is very conscious of what the Canadians do. The reverse is also true."

Because Joe was an American, interest began to stir at the Metropolitan Museum of Art in New York. Representatives approached Lerner about having a summer show of Hirshhorn's sculpture, to be exhibited in three or four sunlit galleries. From October 1960 through early 1962, Al met with James J. Rorimer, Director of the Metropolitan, a man Lerner described as "a well-dressed upper-class guy." Before discussing the anticipated sculpture show, Rorimer told Lerner an amusing story which permits a small peek behind the curtain of great wealth and art collecting.

For years, the previous director had tried to get John D. Rockefeller to visit the museum and when he finally came, the great industrialist was shown the various dedicated rooms in which paintings had been donated by specific contributors. After showing him the J. P. Morgan Room, the director commented, "Look at the outstanding paintings this man gave us."

"Very generous," remarked Rockefeller, "for a man who had no money."

The two men discussed in some detail what the Metropolitan had in mind for Hirshhorn's exhibit and it was clear the director and the curators were very excited about the prospect, but the show was never held. Lerner believed it was because the chairman of the board of directors, who had an office in the museum, opposed the plan.

"I gathered he didn't like the idea of a big summer show with somebody named Hirshhorn. I could smell it. He called a meeting that I attended at which he said, 'It's too large, too many things.' I said, 'Well, you're giving us a large space, you want things to be seen from it.' 'No,' he said, 'You're putting too many things into it. We could do a show with maybe fifty things.' I had figured maybe 300. I said, 'fifty? I could get a show like that at any gallery in New York.' His response was, 'Well, I don't think we can do anything then.' And that was the end of the discussion."

Fortunately, not long afterward, the Guggenheim Museum* stepped in and, in October 1962, presented 444 *Works of modern sculpture from the Joseph H. Hirshhorn Collection* among which were thirty-seven Daumiers, seventeen Degas, twenty-seven Henry Moores, fifteen Giacomettis, and many more by other artists. In the forward to the catalog, Lerner wrote: "The Hirshhorn Collection never aimed at an all-inclusive historical survey of sculpture. It was and is primarily guided by Mr. Hirshhorn's own inclinations and sensibility, as well as a passion for collecting which has long since passed the point of utilitarian need."

The show, wonderfully well received, opened the art world's eyes to the extraordinary breadth and quality of the works the collection held. An article in the arts section of *Time Magazine,* in an issue dated October 5, 1962, was generous in its praise. It said, ". . . if disasters there are in the Hirshhorn collection as a whole, they will not be found at the Guggenheim," and ". . . the exhibition provides a splendid survey of modern sculpture, all the more refreshing because Hirshhorn collected it with no pretensions and no esthetic doubletalk, but simply out of his own compulsive love."**

*The Solomon R. Guggenheim Museum in New York City.
***Time Magazine,* Volume LXXX No. 14, October 5, 1962 Issue, page 77.

From that time on, people began to ask for the collection or portions of it. At this point, the collection didn't travel but its reputation did. Several smaller shows were scheduled to give the public additional glimpses. The American Federation of Arts organized a show of paintings scheduled to open at the Knoedler Gallery in Manhattan in the fall of 1962 and then travel to fourteen different cities. And the Forum Gallery, in Manhattan, also had arranged a choice exhibition of sculptor's drawings from Hirshhorn's collection. The art world had awakened to the bounty and scope of Joe's art and several cities began to approach Lerner with offers to take the entire collection with a view to establishing a museum for its proper presentation.

Hirshhorn had never considered what might become of his collection until sometime in the early sixties when it finally occurred to him that the art he'd been acquiring with such drive and hunger didn't belong to one man. He now believed it should belong to the people, people who might be able to view it and enjoy it. As a result of this epiphany, he started "looking for a spot," for a permanent home for his art. He and Al Lerner went to London and to Zurich, Switzerland.

The first important request for the collection came from London. Suddenly, a phone call from the British Embassy in Washington, caught Joe in his office at 277 Park Avenue one morning, requesting an audience. "Can I come over to see you tomorrow? Will you be in your office?"

Hirshhorn replied, "Sure. What can I do for you?"

"Well," the diplomat* replied, "The Queen of England wants Lord Perth to talk to you." Joe was acquainted with Lord Perth, a Scotsman with whom he'd become very friendly as a result of the Rio Tinto uranium deal.

"I'll be glad to talk to Lord Perth," Hirshhorn replied. That was a Monday. Lord Perth was to call Hirshhorn that Friday. Instead, "He called on Wednesday. He was in New York. The Earl's name is David Drummond. I invited him out to Greenwich on a Thursday

---

*Joe was uncertain of the envoy's name. He thought it might be Martinson.

and he came. We sat down and talked. We had dinner. He said, 'You know, Mr. Hirshhorn, we'd like to have your collection.' "

That was how Joe learned that London desired to have the collection (on a permanent basis). He and Lerner and his wife were invited to come over to London as guests of the Royals to discuss the matter with them. The threesome traveled together to meet with the Englishmen who proceeded to treat them magnificently. Lerner remembered, "They made the most spectacular dinner I have ever been to. There was a servant, a footman, behind every chair, wearing white gloves. It was held in an incredible house [Carlton House]."

After dinner, the Americans were taken to Regent's Park in the center of London where the British were offering ten acres within the park and a plan to construct a building for twelve or fifteen million dollars to house Joe's collection. Lerner commented, "There were no public buildings in Regent's Park at all. They were going to give up such an important space for [the museum], it was as if we were going to put something up in Central Park." The offer included moving trees, building a lake and making Abram Lerner the Director.

"We were staying at the Savoy Hotel," Hirshhorn reminisced, "One morning they came over with a model of the museum they were going to build. We own the model now." David Drummond, whom Joe called "a darling human" took them on a tour of beautiful homes containing outstanding collections of art, one with a great Renaissance collection. It was a spectacular show, a masterful performance of salesmanship. "The morning before we left, they came over to see me again. I said, 'Listen, Gentlemen, I'm an American. Let me think about this.' "

Naturally, the Hirshhorns and Lerners were very excited. But when they returned to the United States and Joe told friends about what was being offered and of his inclination to accept, they were shocked. "How can you consider doing such a thing? How can you give it to England? You're an American. You made your money here, your life has been here, your children are here." So Joe decided against it. He knew his friends and critics were right. Hirshhorn had to tell his friend, Lord Perth, he couldn't leave the art to Great Britain. "We stayed good friends," Joe remarked, "The Earl of Perth, his name is David Drummond, a darling man, sweet, lovely. My wife and I when we go to Scotland we stay with them. Lovely people, and very nice."

Lerner's comment upon Joe's reaction to this incident, "Joe loved the game. He loved the game!"

The next serious offer to house the collection came from Italy. The same Italian curator who had mounted the great Henry Moore exhibition persuaded Joe to come to Italy to discuss the possibility. Lerner admitted it had been his idea to locate any Hirshhorn museum which might be in Italy, in Florence. The reason was not only ". . . because I love Florence, because that's no reason to put a collection there, but because there is no modern art at all in Florence. No American art, certainly, but no modern art at all."

Although Hirshhorn had rejected England on the basis that as an American the collection should remain in the United States, there were at least two reasons why he considered Italy as a possible home for his art. One was Al Lerner's enthusiasm for the site; the idea that there was no modern art whatsoever in Florence, a city known for its extraordinary wealth of great art. A second reason was certainly the marvelous building and location that was eventually suggested.

Joe and Lerner first went to Rome, where they'd been invited by Giacoli, who runs the Marlborough Gallery in Rome and accompanying him was a chap who was the Minister of Art. "They showed us the Borghese Palace, thinking that might be a place for the collection." But neither Al nor Joe felt it was right.

From there the two Americans went to Florence, where they met with Mayor Giorgio La Piera, who Hirshhorn was certain was very eager to have the art collection. He and his associates offered Hirshhorn a villa just outside the city but in a location that would certainly attract tourists. The villa was reputed to have been the home of Galileo. One cannot be certain that was the case, but when the Americans were taken to see it, they were awestruck. Not only was the interior gorgeous, according to Lerner, it had magnificent terraces that both Al and Joe immediately identified as the perfect setting for the collection's larger pieces of sculpture.

Joe was so certain this would be a great location for his art, he hurried to phone his New York attorney and trusted friend, Sam Harris, to ask him to find Italian lawyers in Florence who could represent him in the negotiations which were about to take place. All of this was in anticipation of meeting again with the mayor, who had the final say on the project. When they returned again to discuss the situation with the mayor in his office, they were served espresso and cookies. The mayor, an affable man, was exactly Joe's height and, although they couldn't communicate verbally, he and Joe seemed to understand each other despite the efforts of a hesitant, but determined, interpreter."* Joe's Italian lawyers were to be present when the formal meeting would take place the following day. Joe spoke not a word of Italian and Lerner, who had lived in Italy for more than a year, felt his Italian was not sufficient to act as a translator in a formalized meeting. Anticipating the scheduled negotiations, Lerner was greatly excited at the prospect of having the collection situated in Florence.

"I was jumping out of my skin," he said, "It was such a *great* idea. Everyone was traveling to Europe. Everyone would be going to the museum and the museum would be so spectacular!"

When the official meeting took place the next day, Joe's Italian lawyer was present, together with the lawyer's associates, the lawyers representing the city of Florence, an interpreter and the mayor. "It was quite a crowd," Lerner remembered. Joe claimed 200 Florentines were present, "beautiful people, very elegant, wonderful, very refined, really beautiful." Lerner was able to follow the proceedings with some understanding. "I sat there with Joe, who was not happy because it was all going on in Italian and he felt out of control, left out." However, Hirshhorn was following every nuance as the conversation was being translated into English. Always practical, at some point Joe spoke up.

"There's a road that leads up to that house which is almost impassible. I mean, it's not really a road. I would like assurance that it would be improved." Upon hearing the translation, Mayor

*From a letter to Gene LePere from Abram Lerner dated September 11, 1992.

La Piera's only comment according to Lerner was "Eh," which could have been taken to mean "Don't worry, we'll do it" or, more likely it meant, "Who can foresee the future? Or, who cares?" Both Joe and Lerner understood the mayor would not have upgraded the road and the Italians in the room also knew it. This didn't halt the discussions but it did sharpen Joe's natural suspicions. During the course of the negotiations, a funny and rather endearing exchange took place.

"In the meeting, Joe and I were sitting and the lawyers were discussing various points," Lerner said. "I knew a little Italian, because I lived there, and I heard them saying 'lui' this and 'lui' that and I guessed they were referring to the mayor and saying, 'he' this and 'he' that. Joe turned to me, somewhat impatiently, and said, 'Who the hell is Louie? There was no Louie in this.'"

The mayor's dismissal of Hirshhorn's request to improve the road to the villa, on a scale of importance, was a minor irritation. The next stumbling block was far more serious. The interpreter reported that the Italian lawyers wished to inform Hirshhorn that when he brought works of art to Italy, he had to pay a duty on them. Indignant, Joe immediately responded in a challenging voice,

"You mean, I'm going to give you my collection which I think is worth forty million dollars and you're going to charge me for giving the art to you?"

The nods all around made the situation clear. It was a condition that was a definite deal-breaker. In Hirshhorn's own words, "I said, Mr. Piera, you're a very nice man. I like you very much. Goodbye." The idea of Italy as a repository for Joe's collection was dead.

England, then Italy had both fallen through, giving Lerner the sense that all offers from outside the United States would ultimately fail.

Toronto, with somewhat more legitimacy, wanted the collection as well, and the officials were angry at his refusal to consider it because, they claimed, Hirshhorn had made all his money in Canada, which was untrue. But Joe was established there and perhaps the reason the museum had given him a show was in the hope that they might ultimately receive the collection.

Joe, remembering his spurned offer to gift a museum in Blind River with his art, never considered Canada seriously.

Baltimore showed some interest in the collection and Israel also made a bid. The incentive may have come from the well-known, personable Mayor of Jerusalem, Teddy Kollek, who knew Joe very well. The bid never seemed serious because, unlike England and Italy, countries that showed Hirshhorn exactly where they intended to put the museum, Israel never invited him to the country (although when he did travel there as a tourist, the possibility was discussed). In addition, they never gave any indication as to what they would do with Joe's collection if he gave it to them. Billy Rose, the theatrical producer, had intentions of donating his own art collection to the state of Israel and tried to interest Joe in some sort of participation, but the idea didn't appeal to him.

At the suggestion of Henry Seldis, art critic of the *Los Angeles Times,* Joe took a look at "Greystone," the Doheny family estate at the edge of Beverly Hills, that was for sale. Seldis had seen it as a possible location for a museum to house the collection. It wasn't the only private estate or large house Joe had considered buying, but the idea was discarded. Joe said the cost of purchasing any of the buildings, the renovation expense to make it suitable to house the collection, plus the ongoing maintenance costs, "would break me."

The only other genuine and appealing approach came from the Governor of New York, Nelson Rockefeller. It was Rockefeller's idea to locate a museum in Purchase on the site of one of the branches of New York State University he had developed during his tenure. It had drawbacks but one advantage, it was near Greenwich where Joe was living.

After his separation from Brenda, Joe had made a number of other changes in his life, some were more significant than others. He closed his Toronto office and gave up of his suite at the Royal York Hotel, thus closing the book on a twenty-eight-year-old lifestyle. He had arrived in Canada in 1933 when he was thirty-four years old. It was now 1961 and he was sixty-two. During those nearly three decades Hirshhorn had commuted endlessly between Toronto and New York.

Joe never, however, gave up his attention to his mining business. He had strong feelings about the difference between the work he did as a broker and the significance of what he accomplished in mining. "What is a broker or a banker?" he asked rhetorically. "What do they produce? They're parasitical people. But, when you're in the mining business, if you develop an oil field you're creating *wealth. You're creating work.* In my day at the top when I was in the uranium business, I had seventy-two engineers working for me and 12,000 people. We developed mines that will be there for the next 200 years with the reserves in the world that are up there."

After abandoning his Wall Street office years before, and now the Toronto office, Joe nevertheless still required a base of operations in Manhattan. He bought a two-bedroom apartment in a co-op on Park Avenue in the sixties which allowed room for a small office as well as comfortable quarters for him to sleep overnight whenever he chose. For his main residence, Joe fulfilled his cherished dream of owning property in prestigious Greenwich, Connecticut which still harbored the same prejudice against Jews it had when he and Lily looked for a home there years before. But money affords great leverage, even against bigotry, and Joe's wealth and status as an important art collector finally enabled him to engrave a new address on his velum stationary: "Round Hill," John Street, Greenwich, Connecticut. It also didn't hurt that Connecticut had no state income tax.

It was at this time, when Joe was between marriages, that he invited me to meet him in France to stay one week at his home in Juan Les Pins, the home he acquired when married to Brenda. He then proposed that we travel to Paris. I was living in Los Angeles working as a probation officer and jumped at the chance to have my father all to myself. I was able to arrange vacation time and Joe sent me a first-class ticket to travel on Pan-American Airways. That was a first for me. It was during this visit that I sat with him at the lunch table at the Hotel du Cap, the classiest hotel on the French Riviera where the Kennedys stayed when they were in town, and watched him suck the eyes out of the fish heads the chefs had saved for his lunch at his special request. He loved the hearty foods of his threadbare childhood, foods that butchers gave away in those days or for which they charged mere pennies. He never tired of eating chicken gizzards, chicken necks, chicken feet, boiled chicken in chicken soup with or without matzo balls, boiled beef and those fish heads. He was rarely able to obtain any of these foods, especially the bones that came with the cheap cuts of beef that were boiled or roasted to death. It was the same with chicken or turkey, he preferred the dark meat and bones. Occasionally I made some of the traditional Jewish foods for him but once I gave a fancy dinner party to which he came and at which I served boned chicken. His first question after cutting into his meat was, "Where are the bones?" During his marriage to Olga she learned to make him short ribs and even got a recipe for matzo balls from his sister Dora. She understood his love of those favorite foods of his childhood. But, on the Riviera, except for the fish heads, Joe ate food the French offered.

The visit was remarkable, I had never seen my father so relaxed. One day, sitting on the rooftop patio of the house at dusk, basking in the waning Mediterranean sunshine, after a shot or two of Scotch, he opened up as if we were confidants, sharing with me in an almost shy manner his aspirations to win the hand of an artist named Shea Reager. For me, the sharing was amazing and, like a good friend, I wished him well in his ambition.

After leaving the Riviera, we went to Paris as planned and what I remember most about that was getting up early one morning, having a quick breakfast, then walking down the Rue Fauberg St. Honore looking at the goodies in the shop windows, doing what I call "window wishing" as these beautiful, elegant, exclusive shops were just opening up. Standing in front of a jewelry store I noticed a ring in the window that caught my fancy. We walked three short steps up into the store where we were greeted by the shopkeeper. After asking the owner his name, if he was married, had children, etc., and introducing himself as J.J. O'Brien—the usual preliminaries—Joe asked to see the ring I had identified. To me it was absolutely lovely. Set in gold, it had a center diamond ringed with emeralds beyond which was a ring of rubies and an outermost ring of sapphires. Oh, how I coveted that ring, so when my father started bargaining for the purchase, something he did automatically and skillfully, my heart leapt. I *could see it on my finger. The dealer finally gave in, selling the ring to Joe for $700, about half the asking price. The jeweler's reason for acceding to Joe's persuasion? He said because we were his first customers of the day, it was good luck to complete the sale.*

Upon leaving the shop I was all smiles, excited and thrilled to have had my father buy this lovely piece of jewelry for me. His first words were, "You know, this ring isn't for you. I'm going to give it to Shea Reager, if she accepts me." I made him promise that if Shea refused his proposal, the ring would be mine. He promised.

Compounding the injury, upon arrival in the U.S. at the end of our trip and hoping to avoid paying duty, Joe had me wear the ring and told the customs official he'd bought it for his daughter, a probation officer in Los Angeles. "Show him your badge," Joe instructed me, as he knew I had one pinned inside my wallet. As soon as he got his way with customs, he took the ring back. No more "Mr. Nice Guy." The next time I saw the ring it was on Olga Cunningham's hand.

The new house in Greenwich had many advantages. It was a perfect baronial showplace for Joe's art, both inside and out. Its magnificent grounds offered numerous sites where his largest sculptures could be placed on pedestals, to be displayed for his own pleasure and the approbation of guests. Surrounded by well-groomed lawns, the sculptures could be seen from his windows, he could stroll among them over the twenty-two acres of landscaped lawns. The placement of those sculpture was determined by Joe and designed to have them seen with the most spectacular effect. The wonderful, oversized Giacometti dog was installed at the edge of a rise so that it was silhouetted against the sky with nothing to distract the eye from its wondrous form. *The Burghers of Calais*, of course, was set atop a pedestal within an oval of green grass just outside the front door to the baronial stone manor. To approach the house by car was to be forced to see the Burghers as one drove around the grass oval and stopped at the front door. As for the epic-size *Balzac* by Rodin, its hulking form leaned over you as you came around a curve of driveway on the way from John Street to the house. He took great care in showing the art to its best advantage. His eye and instinct were true. There was never anything, no matter where the sculptures were placed outside, to distract or confuse the eye from its main target: the art.

The interior of the three-story house contained twenty-three rooms, more than enough wall space to hang many paintings from his collection. There were multiple fireplaces, a great hall, gracious living and dining rooms, ideal for accommodating a large guest list. In addition, there were two large master suites as well as another seven bedrooms, most of which had their own baths. For Joe's loyal servants, Louis (chef/butler) and Gertrude (housekeeper/waitress), who, like Wilbert, seemed to be members of his family, there was a suite of rooms and a five-car garage where Hirshhorn parked his Rolls Royce and a station wagon to haul whatever was needed from town. An expansive stone terrace ran nearly the length of the house in back. Moreover, the property had come equipped with a swimming pool and tennis court. No one, not even a multi-millionaire with a 1,000 sculptures and 3,000 paintings could want more. And Joe had only himself to please, he was living alone!

*Soon after Joe moved into "Round Hill," at a time when he was working with a decorator I knew named Marion Gardiner, he phoned me at my home in Los Angeles.** "I'm going to buy you a sable stole," he announced, clearly in an ebullient mood. The offer came out of the blue. I was surprised and a bit troubled.*

"I want a mink stole," I said.

"I want to buy a sable stole," he shot back.

"No," I said, "mink, please."

"Okay," he replied, "If that's what you want." He sounded disappointed.

Within an hour I had reached Marion at her home in Los Angeles and told her about my conversation with my father. "Gene," she told me, "Sable is better than mink." I hadn't known that.

"I'll call him back," I said.

---

*Marion was allowed, only with his approval, to order the draperies, fabrics for upholstery, buy dishes, glassware, linens for the bedrooms and dining room. I suspected Marion of setting her cap for Joe.

When I called Joe and said I'd like the sable instead of the mink, he was quick to put me down. "Sure," he said in a voice dripping with scorn, "You found out sable is better than mink. Well, I'm buying you mink."

I was too humiliated to say, you're going to punish me because I didn't know sable was better than mink, but how could I know? Mother wasn't into fur coats, she didn't even own one, neither did Lily. If you hadn't been married to Brenda who had a closet full of full-length mink coats in several colors, ermine wraps, sable and mink jackets that you undoubtedly paid for, you wouldn't have known either.

It was during this time, when Joe was trying out new chauffeurs he had ordered up from a New York agency, that Nelson Rockefeller was making his pitch for the collection.

In response to Rockefeller's invitation, Joe and Lerner visited him at his home in Pocantico Hills, New York, where they found Rockefeller and his wife sitting on the steps to their property waiting for them. This informality indicated a lack of pretense in the scion of a notoriously wealthy family, a posture that suited unpretentious Joe to a tee. They were taken to the proposed site of the museum in Purchase, which Lerner, on a previous visit, had thought not only suitable but quite beautiful. The property originally was a dairy farm with a barn that, Lerner said, was "not like barn. It was like a palace." The barn had been tiled inside and the animal stalls and compartments for machinery were beautifully crafted of polished wood. This was Westchester County, New York, an area Lerner loved. But he had one reservation, he thought Purchase a little out of the way, which meant any museum situated there might not attract the optimal amount of tourist traffic.

After viewing the property, the men returned to Pocantico Hills to discuss the possibilities with Rockefeller, who tried mightily to persuade Joe to locate his collection in Purchase. Rockefeller's desire to have an art museum, particularly one as desirable as Hirshhorn's, was understandable. He was not only a patron of the arts, he was an important collector of pre-Columbian art himself. But when they left, Joe told Lerner, "Look Al, he's making all these promises and I think he means it.

But the minute he's out, the next guy's going to say, who needs this? It will not be supported." And Joe knew the museum would need support. The location Rockefeller offered at New York State University at Purchase which Hirshhorn turned down, is now the site of the Neuburger Museum, containing the works of American masters collected over half a century by Roy R. Neuberger.

Israel didn't make the cut for much the same reason. Not only was the country perpetually in turmoil in Joe's opinion, he doubted any proposed museum would receive the support it needed. Perhaps, had Joe been a Zionist, he might have been more inclined to leave his legacy to the Jewish state. In spite of his early religious background, Joe only minimally practiced Judaism. He and Jennie had helped raise funds that built Temple Beth-El in Great Neck, but that was in 1933. It had been many years since Joe had attended regular Friday night services although he did go to "shul" on the high holidays.

Zurich also made a bid for Joe's art but, while Switzerland was a frequent travel destination, many of his objections still applied. It was too small a country, not in the mainstream of tourist travel, and it was not the United States, where the collection seemed more properly to belong.

Joe's attempts to replace Wilbert, who had retired after twenty years with Joe, with a chauffeur hired through a New York employment agency were unsuccessful. He had tried two and found both unacceptable. Deciding his strategy had been mistaken, Joe concluded that to find a chauffeur for a Connecticut placement he should try a local agency. To this end he checked with the broker, William Pitt, who had sold him the property in Greenwich. Pitt suggested Joe try an agency called Services Unlimited. When Joe telephoned, it was the owner, Olga Cunningham, who answered the phone. Although she was not in the office to work—she had two employees to handle business that day—without thinking, she had picked up the telephone. Olga, who ultimately became the fourth and last Mrs. Joseph H. Hirshhorn, told the story of their meeting in an interview she gave in July 1975, at the request of The Greenwich Library.[*]

"I just picked up the phone very playfully and said, 'Services Unlimited,' and there was a voice on the other end that said, 'This is Mr. Hirshhorn. I've just bought the Sinclair Robinson house on John Street, and I'm looking for a chauffeur. I'm calling from New York, and this is my number. Call me back if you have anybody.' And down went the phone.

"I hung up and said to the girls, 'Imagine the nerve of this man! He's ordering a chauffeur like you order a loaf of bread. You've got to talk about it a little more.'"

She went on, "Well, I've since gotten to know Mr. Hirshhorn very well, and he's a very abrupt man. He doesn't waste any time with things that aren't important."

Having been challenged, Olga decided she would show him up by finding someone for him. But, after several unsuccessful tries, including one which had prompted an irate call from Joe who wanted to know why she had sent a drunk for an interview at 9:00 A.M., Olga continued to try to find a suitable chauffeur for him, without any luck. As Joe had someone who could drive him when necessary, he was able to wait. But by fall, he was looking for household help at which point Olga decided she wanted to see for herself just what the situation was at "Round Hill."

She called Joe. "I need to come out to see your place so I will know better exactly what you need." Joe invited her to do so. He was already intrigued by her voice and her efficiency. He'd already asked her how old she was: forty-two. She had immediately shot back: "And how old are you?" In 1961, Hirshhorn was sixty-two. He liked her spunk. There were many subsequent visits. During one of them Joe was sitting outside on his terrace while Laura Zeigler sculpted a bust of him. Sam Harris, his wife Madelyn and their two sons arrived. Olga was introduced to them and learned for the first time, from Zeigler, that Joe was a famous and important art collector. Olga found this not only in-

*Copyright 1976. *A First Generation in Greenwich,* The Greenwich Library, Greenwich, CT, p. 31.

triguing, she was captivated by all she saw and felt no need to hide her interest in Joe.[*]

Olga and Joe hit it off and they were well suited to each other. She was a petite, very pretty woman, inches shorter than Joe, with luxuriant brown hair and a full figure much like the women he grew up with, his mother and sisters. They shared common immigrant roots. Her parents, Nicholas and Barbara Chayka Zatorsky, had come separately from the Ukraine and married in the United States. They also shared childhoods of hard work and relative poverty although Olga, having been born and raised in suburban Fairfield County, enjoyed a far different childhood from Joe's. She was able to romp and play among children of a more refined class. Most important to their compatibility, Olga's energy was a match for Joe's. Like him, she was athletic—she'd been a junior champion tennis player—and graceful; she loved to dance and was ready in an instant to join him in any endeavor. Olga was as ambitious as Joe. Her ambition had enabled her to attain a measure of financial independence. Given it was still the days before the Women's Liberation Movement, Olga had shown initiative and done well. And, significantly, like Hirshhorn, she was a pragmatic narcissist.

Imaginative, resourceful, quick and shrewd, all characteristics she and Joe shared, Olga was not a woman who was ever likely to bore him. There was only one hitch in this pretty picture. At the time when Joe and Olga met, she was married and living with her husband John Cunningham in a house in Greenwich with their three teen-aged sons. Likewise, Joe, although separated from Brenda, was not yet divorced. None of this deterred either of them from enjoying each other's company more each passing week.

Joe found his new "interest" to be capable, quick, bright, energetic and eager to please. Olga embarked on a program of making herself indispensable to Joe and he, accustomed to using the

---

*For a more detailed description of the courtship of the couple, according to Olga, consult the transcript of her interview with Penny Bott in the above-cited *A First Generation in Greenwich.*

willing, gladly took advantage of whatever services she was anxious to provide. Olga began acting as Joe's secretary, giving him three days a week for a salary that compensated her for the time she was taking away from her own business. In that capacity she was also eager to run any errand that would please him. He liked her organizational ability, work ethic, willingness and, on a more personal level, he was attracted to her as a woman. She did, indeed, make herself indispensable.

Due to a health issue, I had taken a long leave of absence from my job in Los Angeles and was living with Joe in Greenwich at the time Olga entered his life. Her version of the events of their courtship differ somewhat from mine. My father, in those first weeks Olga was around, complained that the first time she came to look over the house for the reason she gave "to be able to determine what his requirements were," he couldn't get rid of her and that day and the next several times she came, when he offered her a drink, she became shikker (tipsy) and wouldn't stop talking. But she kept coming and he kept offering wine or sherry and they seemed to be getting along. Over time, especially when she started working as his part-time secretary and demonstrated her eagerness to run any errand, he complained less.

Eventually, after they became intimate and he started taking her out in public, Olga began to take liberties. I think she was feeling competitive with me as I was ensconced in the second master bedroom and my father asked me to play hostess when he entertained. One morning she came into my bedroom quite early in order to get me out of bed. She invited me to have breakfast with her and my father in his bedroom where the cook and butler would serve us on trays.

Olga was dressed in one of Joe's dressing gowns so it was clear she'd stayed overnight without her own nightgown or pajamas. When I entered my father's bedroom, I saw Olga had jumped back into the bed with Joe where they both sat up awaiting the breakfast trays which were being brought up from the kitchen. *

*It was the servants' choice to serve breakfast on trays in the bedroom rather than clutter up the formal dining room.

My reaction to her performance was not one she would have liked. I felt her need to establish her new relationship with my father in my eyes, and method for doing so, was crude, tactless and offensive. When she had left the house that day, I spoke to my father about it. "Daddy," I said, "I am aware you are an adult and have a perfect right to your relationships, but Olga's behavior was unseemly. It is not necessary for her to shove it in my face. It's none of my business." Joe took my words seriously and must have spoken to her. It never happened again.

In time, when Olga pressed for marriage, Joe consulted me. "Do you think the townspeople will accept her as my wife?" he asked. He was thinking about her humble beginnings right there in Greenwich where she was born and raised by her gardener father and a mother who took in wash. "I could send her to finishing school, I suppose," he added. I told him he had to do whatever he wanted to do. If he wanted to marry Olga, he should. In truth, it wasn't my life and I felt if I got involved, whatever I advised, would be the wrong thing. Moreover, I wasn't in competition with Olga. It was never my intention to continue living in my father's home, acting as his hostess. I had been independent since I was nineteen years old and enjoyed being master of my own fate. Let him make his own choices, right or wrong. I would make mine.

Not long afterward, in March, 1963, I married James E. LePere, an antique dealer, and moved out of Joe's home into my own in Cos Cob, Connecticut.

XIII

The Smithsonian Wakes Up

When all other offers to accept Joe's collection had been considered and refused, the Smithsonian Institution suddenly reached out. Even before any discussions were held, before appointments were made, before terms were considered, the notion that his collection might go to the United States and be housed in Washington felt right to both Lerner and Joe, given that the details could be worked out to Joe's and Sam Harris's satisfaction. The importance of Harris as Hirshhorn's attorney and close friend cannot be overlooked.

Harris, a founding partner in the prestigious law firm of Fried, Frank, Harris, Shriver & Jacobson, was unusual, perhaps unique. Handsome, personable and principled, Harris was born in 1910 in New York City. When he attended Yale University he was a brilliant scholar and after graduation became a senior attorney at the Securities and Exchange Commission in Washington during its formative years at a time when he encountered Joe Kennedy, who had been charged with developing the S.E.C. There Harris earned the reputation as one of its most gifted lawyers. From 1940 to 1942, Harris was counsel to the trustee in the complicated and protracted reorganization of Associated Gas and Electric Company. During World War II, still a very young man, he served in the Judge Advocate General's office after which he was associated with Justice Robert Jackson at the Nuremberg trials, carrying the major responsibility for the presentation of the case against chief of the German Luftwaffe, Herman Goering. Committed to Democratic politics in New York, Harris took an active role in the campaigns of Adlai Stevenson in 1956 and John Kennedy in 1960. In 1962, Kennedy appointed Harris as one of the first directors of the Communications Satellite Corporation where he subsequently became acting chairman of that board. Harris's reputation in the legal profession and in the investment banking community was so greatly esteemed, his services were widely sought and he was elected a director on the boards of many distinguished multinational corporations.

His unique gifts were his integrity and his outstanding ability to objectively assess any problem as both a lawyer and a businessman.

Joe met Harris during negotiations with the Rio Tinto company over his Rio Algom uranium holdings at a time when Harris was representing the principals of Rio Tinto. Recognizing Harris' unique abilities, respecting his qualifications, liking the man himself and having lost his longtime friend and attorney "Chic" Corson, Joe began to retain Harris as his attorney in the United States. Now, in the negotiations that were about to take place with the Smithsonian Institution regarding Joe's art collection, he was well-represented with Harris at his side. The opening gesture began with a telephone call from S. Dillon Ripley, Secretary of the Smithsonian, who asked for an appointment with Joe.

Sidney Dillon Ripley was scholarly man. Tall, bald and slender, he had the bearing of an aristocrat and the tact of a diplomat. Born into a family of wealth, his mother was interested in and supported art, particularly the Museum of Modern Art in New York. This left him with a legacy of connoisseurship and a continuing interest in art. Ripley had spent eighteen years at Yale as a professor of biology and ecology and as director of its Peabody Museum of Natural History. Before that, he had served on the staffs of Philadelphia's Academy of Natural Science and the American Museum of Natural History in New York, had written four books and had served a hitch in World War II with the Office of Strategic Services, all of which well qualified him to assume the post of Secretary of the Smithsonian Institution in February 1964.

New in the post, desiring to prepare himself for its responsibilities, while researching the legislation governing the Smithsonian, Ripley came upon the Congressional Act of May 17, 1938.

This act provided that the President assign a site on the Mall for a museum of contemporary art as a counterpart to the National Gallery, which had been constructed with funds provided by Andrew Mellon to house his collection of Old Masters. A contest for the design of a modern museum had actually been held in 1946, and it was won by Eero Saarinen for a prize of $7,000. But the plan was rejected after a speech by William Delano, the Capital Planning Commission's most influential member, who cited and repeated the dictum of Frederick Law Olmstead.

"Let no touch of modernity sully the Mall."

Ripley had read *The Proud Possessors,* with its lively portraits of art collectors, written by Saarinen's widow, Aline, and was inspired to fulfill the 1938 mandate, he said, "in one giant step, by finding someone who had already done it." Joseph Hirshhorn, delightfully limned in her book, immediately came to mind.

While Mellon, Frick and Freer had collected Old Masters, Joe was the first to gamble on living artists, and predominantly American ones. What could have been a better fit for a museum of contemporary art on the Mall in the capitol of the United States?

Ripley got in touch with Roger Stevens, counsel on the arts to President Johnson. Stevens had been staying in London at the Savoy Hotel when Joe was there at the invitation of Queen Elizabeth to hear the British proposal for a museum to house his collection in Regent's Park. Ripley urged Stevens, "Convince him our need is greater." Stevens then contacted Lerner and went to see him in his office where he noted with approval the quality of the scattering of fine small sculptures that covered the tables and desk. Lerner, of course, referred the envoy to Joe.

After receiving Stevens' report, Ripley sent off a letter to Hirshhorn meant to persuade him via a combination of national pride and good sense that the best possible future for his collection resided with a location in the United States. Dated June 15, 1964, it said in part, "The Smithsonian Institution has a lively interest in establishing an American equivalent to the Tate Gallery in London emphasizing American contemporary art. The National Gallery of Art with its emphasis on the arts of Europe and the past leaves the capitol and the nation with no proper equivalent to the Tate. The need for such a museum here has been widely recognized. We would be most happy to explore the concept with you."

The letter reached Joe two months after he and Olga Cunningham were married in a small ceremony held at "Round Hill." Conducted by a local judge and friend, Archie Tunick, the wedding took place on April 27, 1964, on the grounds of Joe's Greenwich estate under the *Glenkiln Cross* statue by Henry Moore. Both Joe and Olga had managed a timely discarding of spouses to make this union possible and none of their accumulated nine children had been invited. The butler/cook and upstairs maid, Louis and Gertrude, stood up for them. Afterward, Olga's family arrived to share wedding cake and champagne. None of Joe's children attended this wedding as with the others that followed their parents' divorce. They were never asked.

Olga reported in her several transcribed interviews after Joe's death that although Joe had children, the reason they didn't attend the couple's after-wedding cake and champagne celebration (to which Olga's three sons were invited and came) was because "they were scattered." She said: "Then, he had three daughters living in Provincetown, Massachusetts; two daughters living in California; and a son living in Stamford [Connecticut]."

Olga was mistaken. Only one of Joe's children, Naomi, in Los Angeles, was living too far away to have attended the wedding or its after-party. Jo Ann and Amy were living in Provincetown; Robin, lived in a suburb of Boston, not that terribly far away; Gene and her husband were living in New York City and Gordon, in Stamford, a twenty-minute drive from Round Hill.

To be fair to Olga, it is not easy to be the fourth wife of any man, especially one with six children. The four of Joe's older children who once owned him all to themselves and their mother and, since then, had been forced to relinquish him to three other women and their collective six children, found it hard to embrace one more wife. A fourth one, at that. Hirshhorn's personality of exclusion only exacerbated the coolness. While I felt no affection for "numero quatro," I honestly felt she was the wife most suited to Joe's personality and, in that respect, would make him a good wife. For all the benefits she derived from her marriage, she inherited an insoluble mess of family baggage.

Not long after their wedding, Joe and Olga came to visit me in the Stamford Hospital where I had just undergone surgery for an ectopic pregnancy. In what was, in retrospect, Joe's awkwardness with illness and his inability to show tenderness even when he may have felt it, he entered the room where I lay in bed still groggy from an anesthetic and barked, "What are you trying to do?" That was the best he could do to show concern.

Before her wedding took place, Olga, committed as she was to her future position as Mrs. Joseph H. Hirshhorn, had not considered abandoning the Greek Orthodox religion into which she was born. Although she attended the traditionally important religious occasions with her husband at the reform temple in Greenwich, it wasn't until 1973 that Olga converted to Judaism. The impetus for her conversion, she readily admitted in a taped interview she gave for the Smithsonian Archives after Joe's death, was so that when she died she could be buried beside her husband in the Greenwich Hebrew Institute Temple Shalom Cemetery.

No one was more excited by the letter from Ripley than Olga. Having already traveled with Joe and been exposed to people, places and events exciting and unknown to her in the years before meeting him, she clearly saw a future filled with more such opportunities and loved the idea of being in the center of national celebrity and fascinating activity. A whole new world was opening up for her. She had made a difficult pact in order to secure her place at Joe's side where the spotlight of his notoriety would shine on her as well.

Before Joe would agree to marry her, he set one non-negotiable term: Olga's youngest son, who had yet to graduate from high school, was not to live in their home as a member of his family. He reminded Olga he had little contact with his own children, had no desire that any of them live under his roof, and didn't want to have more contact with her children than he had with his. He was beyond the time of life when he wanted to deal with children of any age, in particular, a teenager. Olga, on the threshold of the most important phase of her life, was faced with a difficult and, undoubtedly heart-wrenching, choice. Her future in the sun or the son in her future.

The couple reached a compromise: Olga's son would live on the third floor of the "Round Hill" mansion, he would use the back stairs reserved for servants, and he would take his meals with the servants, not with Joe and Olga. That Joe would require this as a condition of marriage underscores his self-concern; that Olga would accede to this demand in order to become Mrs. Hirshhorn, reflects hers. It may have caused her a good deal of guilt. One wonders what such a marginalization did to her son or to their relationship.

The couple set off on an extended honeymoon trip to Europe, spending time in London, Paris and Switzerland, then traveling to Israel where Teddy Kollek and Billy Rose made an effort to interest Joe in gifting his collection to Jerusalem. But Joe, having already decided Israel was not the right place for his museum, remained polite but uninterested.

In September, an appointment was arranged between Ripley and Joe through Mrs. Verner [Permilia] Reed "with whom Ripley took tea in Greenwich and then together drove to Round Hill for more tea." It was merely a friendly meeting in which Ripley chose only to commend the Smithsonian to Joe. Back in Washington, Ripley, seeking to muster more weight with which to convince Joe, tried to enlist President Johnson's aid by describing the collection and telling the president that it was, at that time, valued at $40 million. That number caught Johnson's ear.

Meanwhile, his interest piqued, Joe asked Harris to get in touch with Ripley in response to his June 15th letter. Harris, accompanied by Max Kampelman, a partner in the Washington law office of Fried, Frank, arrived at Ripley's office in the Smithsonian "castle" where he let Ripley know of the offers which had come from England, Italy, Israel, New York State and Toronto.

"Would Mr. Hirshhorn consider giving his collection to the Smithsonian?" Ripley asked.

Harris hesitated a moment before answering, "He would want his name on the museum."

"That," Ripley replied with no hesitation, "is simply the identification of a building, not an impediment to other gifts."

Harris questioned further, "On the Mall?"

"I don't see why not."

"You mean," Harris said, barely containing his astonishment, "a Hirshhorn Museum on the Mall?"

"This is 1965," Ripley replied, having discerned that the underlying meaning of Harris' question concerned anti-Semitism, answered in measured tone, "and I think America has grown up."[*]

Eager to obtain the collection, Ripley continued working behind the scenes. He knew Abe Fortas, the Supreme Court Justice, was a friend of both the President and Joe. Ripley suggested to Fortas that a timely word from the President to Joe might have a favorable impact. Fortas, who trusted Ripley's appraisal of the collection, told the President and Mrs. Johnson that in view of Hirshhorn being wooed by such important rivals, perhaps a luncheon with Mrs. Johnson might shift his interest to favor Washington. More than that, Ripley also knew Lady Bird had a strong interest in art and, in fact, had been hoping to acquire a Thomas Eakins painting for the White House collection during her husband's presidency. He sent word to Elizabeth Carpenter, her staff director and press secretary, that Joe owned the largest group of Eakins paintings in private hands. That, he thought, should whet her appetite for a luncheon meeting with Joe.

Ripley was working both sides of the street or, as they say in marketing circles, he was using both *push* and *pull*. In a second letter to Joe, he emphasized three crucial points. "under the aegis of the Smithsonian, the collection would retain its independent identity; annual attendance of twelve million on the Mall would assure the collection the greatest possible prominence and more accessibility than any other place in the world; and it guaranteed the collection against change and interference."[**] Ripley made other comments he felt would appeal to Joe

*Hyams, Barry. *Hirshhorn: Medici from Brooklyn,* p. 143.
**Ibid, Loc Cit.

and concluded the letter by saying, "Mrs. Johnson is herself aware of the importance of your collection to the nation. She would be happy to discuss this with you and Mr. Lerner at a luncheon, and I hope you will be able to arrange to visit both the Smithsonian (especially the Freer) and the White House."[*]

This letter encouraged Joe and also provided Harris with a rebuttal to Lerner's objection to removing the collection from New York. Harris pointed out that while New York gets a million tourists a year, Washington gets twelve million. In early May, Mrs. Johnson wrote a warm note to Joe suggesting their meeting on May 21st should start at 12:30 P.M. as she wanted to spend some private time with Joe and Olga to show them the paintings in the White House before the other guests joined them a half hour later. This personal attention was appealing, but Joe was cautious. He was more than willing to follow the advice of an attorney whom he respected and whose counsel he trusted.

In reply to the invitation, Joe wrote out some conditions of his own to the President and First Lady, conditions which had been outlined by Harris. They set forth the understanding that resulted from conversations with Ripley: that 1) the collection would be housed in a modern museum to be erected on the Mall; that 2) it would be maintained, preserved and developed by the Smithsonian and operated by a board of trustees in accordance with plans and proceedings to be agreed upon by the Institution and himself. In addition, Joe would contribute $1 million in cash for further acquisitions.[**]

Hirshhorn went on to say, "I would, of course, want binding assurance that the museum would bear my name in perpetuity; that it would be adequately maintained and operated in such a manner as to assure the fulfillment of my objective of a better understanding and appreciation of modern art."[***]

This letter of May 17, 1965, contained the basic terms which

[*]Ibid., pp. 143 & 144.
[**]Loc Cit. p. 144.
[***]Loc Cit.

emerged, after debate and refinement, as the statute which Congress enacted two years later.

There were two aspects of the negotiations incorporated into the final contract and statute which, over time, were criticized. One was the Smithsonian's insistence on their right to de-accession works that were given in the original and any additional donations. The second was that there would be a board of directors.

Lerner thought the Smithsonian's reason regarding the right to de-accession was sound. "They had had great problems with the Freer Gallery because it was left with the understanding that *no work of art could ever be sent out of the museum,*" Lerner said. "No art could be sent out even on loan. None could be sold. They were not permitted to add to the collection except by gift." This had caused a serious problem, one which the Smithsonian didn't want to repeat. As an example of how it caused severe difficulties for which there was no remedy, Lerner gave the following example: "Freer was a great patron of James McNeil Whistler. He had bought a great many of Whistler's paintings, including one which is considered the most famous Whistler in the world. If another museum wants to present a Whistler exhibition, they cannot get the greatest Whistler for the show, nor any other Whistler in the Freer Collection. Conversely, the Freer can only mount a Whistler show using pictures that already belonged to the gallery. I understood this condition, it was valid.

"On the other hand," Lerner admitted, "it was I who thought we should have a board of trustees, unlike most museums that have advisory boards. I made a big mistake. We should have had an advisory board which is not the same as a board of trustees. An advisory board doesn't have any power and I know that because I used to sit in as a guest on the advisory board of the Museum of American Art and I saw exactly what they did, which was altogether different. The reason I thought a board of trustees was a good idea is because I knew it would be bringing a lot of modern paintings and sculpture to Washington. Washington is, or was at that time, very provincial. I mean, they had the great National Gallery, but that was Old Masters and everybody likes Old Masters. I was afraid all the time of some redneck in Congress getting up and saying, 'Why the hell are we spending public money on this stuff? What's that? A de Kooning? It's crazy.' I thought that if we had somebody like Pat Moynihan on the board, and he did come on the board almost immediately, he could stand up and tell them very reasonably why they should have it. So, I thought we could be defended in Congress and in the Senate, because we had one or two senators—they're dead now—who were very favorable and who knew Joe."

On May 21, 1965, S. Dillon Ripley, Sam Harris, Abe Fortas, Roger Stevens, and their wives assembled for lunch in the upper dining room of the White House. Thirty minutes before they arrived, the Hirshhorns had entered the Southwest Gate to be greeted in the Diplomatic Reception Room by Mrs. Johnson.

"We had a delightful time," Lady Bird recorded in her diary. "He [Hirshhorn] enjoyed seeing the White House collection and I love showing it to people who enjoy it."[*]

As they toured the White House rooms looking at the many paintings, some good, some bad, some indifferent, Mrs. Johnson held back from saying anything about the Eakins she hoped to have Joe donate to the White House. She had asked Ripley, Stevens and Fortas to approach him instead, saying she was a poor saleswoman. There was no discussion at the luncheon about the museum, or the terms and conditions of Joe's gift. The purpose of the gathering was only to assure Joe that Washington wanted the collection. The rest would be up to the President, who was, as most everyone knew, a great salesman. Fortas was certain that given agreeable terms, Joe would donate his collection.

"While dessert and coffee were being served, Harris unobtrusively passed a paper to Ripley. The secretary retained his composure as he read the contents of a letter in which Governor Rockefeller proposed that a New York State bond issue provide $10 million for a Hirshhorn museum at the university campus in Purchase."[**] But at that moment the President, who had been

*Johnson, Claudia T., *A White House Diary*, Holt, Rinehart And Winston, 1970, p. 275.
**Hyams, ibid., p. 145.

delayed by a meeting with his cabinet in a nearby room, entered. He was introduced to the guests, took a seat next to Joe whom he addressed familiarly and upon whom he proceeded to let out all the warmth of his personality with gracious subtlety. He was seductive and charming. Joe Hirshhorn had met his match.

The President was a salesman *par excellence* and when he put his arm—the legendary Johnson ploy—around Joe over whom he towered like a huge bear, Hirshhorn went down for the count. Boldly, Johnson said what Lady Bird was unable to say, "It is wonderful the people of the United States are going to be able to enjoy your artworks, but it would be downright selfish if the White House itself didn't get an example." In her diary, the First Lady had written, "Mr. Hirshhorn could appreciate Lyndon, I think. They are both aggressive and strong." Mrs. Johnson was right.

Nevertheless, Hirshhorn, knowing he'd been seduced by a seducer as artful as himself, turned to his attorney and asked, "What do you think, Sam?" and Harris, borrowing a page from Joe's own playbook, answered, "We ought to think about it."

"You leave it to me," the President told Joe earnestly before he left to return to his tightly scheduled day, "to see that the conditions are fulfilled."

Ripley, feeling assured that Joe's collection would be coming to Washington after the President's magisterial performance, was overjoyed. He believed it would be the greatest art gift to be made to the nation since Andrew Mellon had given the collection that formed the nucleus of the National Gallery in the late 1930s. Abe Fortas was reassuring. He told Joe that there was nothing to worry about, he should just "do as the President says." But Harris wasn't going to leave anything to chance. He believed that regardless of the power and position Johnson exerted as President, an accident, a heart attack, a loss of his power could invalidate any promise made. "Over my dead body," Harris stated firmly, "are you going to get this collection without the conditions written into the contract and a statute passed."

When Lerner said that Harris was a crucial factor in dealing with the Smithsonian regarding the transfer of Joe's collection to the United States, he did not overstate the situation. Lerner had more to say about Harris.

"I liked him and I thought he was awfully smart and he handled the thing with the Smithsonian so well. He was a very impressive man. I also thought he was very loyal to Joe. I once said to him, 'What do you think of Joe?' He said, 'He's a genius.' I said, 'What do you mean?' And he said, 'You know, Al, I can call him up and ask him what he paid for a certain stock in 1922 and he'll tell me. He has a fantastic memory and a genius for what he does.' "

With Rockefeller still making attractive advances, Ripley worked even harder to increase the visible interest and active intercession of the President and Mrs. Johnson. He was determined to win the competition for Hirshhorn's collection. He went so far as to begin assessing design possibilities for the museum even before the contract had been signed or the statute had been passed.

To add to Ripley's anxiety, in early June, a clipping from the (London) *Daily Observer* revealed that Joe was in England as a house guest of the Earl of Perth. The *Washington Post* then published a full account of the protracted Smithsonian negotiations and the "fierce competition for the multi-million-dollar treasure trove." Regardless of the *Post*'s suggestion that Joe was "considering accepting an offer by the British Government in which a special museum would be built in Regent's Park," Hirshhorn told the British, "But I love the United States and I belong there. Let me think about it." The disclosure of the negotiations in the *Post* angered Joe and he temporarily suspended further discussions.

In August, Mrs. Johnson paid a successful visit to "Round Hill" with her daughter, Lynda Bird and her secretary, Bess Abell. Joe found Mrs. Johnson vitally interested in and appreciative of his paintings and sculpture displayed inside and out on the lawns. Lerner, who was present at the time, said he honestly didn't know if their visit had any influence on finalizing the agreement but said that he was "quite taken" with her.

"She was a very nice woman and very smart. We showed her around the garden where all the big pieces were and I showed the first piece and said, 'This is by an English sculptor named Henry

Moore,' and by the time we got to the second Henry Moore, she said, 'That's a Henry Moore.' Now, that's a good eye."

Joe liked her for a different reason. Upon her arrival at the house, she said, "I really know nothing about art. I'm prepared to learn."

"That was honest," Joe recalled, "I respected her."

Mrs. Johnson reported in her diary her fascination with all the works of Joe's collection she saw on the visit and added, "But nothing that I saw was more interesting than our host, himself. Mr. Hirshhorn told me he had been collecting for forty years and delighted in finding art which had not struck the eye of the world, acquiring it at a moderate price, watching it appreciate in value and bear out his judgment."[*]

Between 1965 and 1969, Joe and Olga Hirshhorn were invited not only to lunch at the White House several times but even more prestigious, also were invited to dinner. On one memorable occasion, the couple was invited to an overnight stay at the LBJ Ranch. In this way, they cemented their relationship with the Johnsons.

Things began to move quickly after Lady Bird's visit to Round Hill. Lerner prepared lists and descriptions of paintings and sculpture and obtained fair market values from auction firms, dealers and insurance companies. At a meeting with Ripley that Lerner attended, Joe told Ripley, "You understand, Al Lerner is to be the first director of the museum," and Ripley agreed it would be so. Lerner then proceeded to orchestrate the myriad preparations, tedious as they were, with increased pleasure. An enormous amount of work had to be done wherever Joe had not cataloged or even organized the purchase slips for much of the art. In Greenwich, Olga, who was an excellent organizer and tireless in her dedication, took it upon herself to list all the artworks in the Greenwich house and to look everywhere for misplaced sales slips.

At the same time as the huge array of art in the warehouse, the "art office," Joe's office and Greenwich was being organized

*Johnson, Ibid, p. 308.

Group photo of Joe's family, taken at Round Hill, Greenwich, circa 1966. All children and grandchildren are present except Michael and Daniel Cohen, Robin's sons, who were away at University and Naomi Caryl who was in Los Angeles. Front row (l. to r.): Rebecca and Rachel Hirshhorn; Deborah Cohen; Jennifer Hirshhorn. Second row (l. to r.): Gordon Hirshhorn with his wife, Helen; Robin Cohen; the fourth Mrs. Joe Hirshhorn, Olga; Joe Hirshhorn; Robert Cohen, Robin's husband. Back row (l. to r.): James LePere, Gene's husband; Amy Hirshhorn; Jo Ann Hirshhorn; and the author, Gene LePere.

and cataloged, there were hitches in the proposed designs for the museum building itself. Ripley had approached Nathan Owings of the architectural firm of Skidmore, Owings & Merrill to produce a model. The result was one that both Lerner and Harris disliked intensely. Due to the location of the site, Owings had found what he thought was an ingenious solution, devising an original museum entrance off Constitution Avenue, raising the street level and lowering the level of the gardens. Al Lerner called it a "bomb shelter" and when Joe saw it he reacted with his usual outspoken frankness, "You're not going to bury me underground," he told Owings.

Thereafter, Owings' partner, Gordon Bunshaft, a member of the Commission on Fine Arts and, as it happened, also a close friend of Henry Moore, took over. He included Joe in the planning as much as possible, accepted his input into the building's development and made him a part of the ultimate creation of what became the Hirshhorn Museum & Sculpture Garden. Bunshaft believe the site for the museum could be improved upon and suggested an alternative to the original site chosen at Constitution Avenue at 9th Street. He was able to obtain agreement from the government to use his suggested site due south across the Mall at Independence Avenue and 7th Street where there was an old, half-used building scheduled to be razed, a building that had once been the Armed Forces Medical Museum before it was relocated in 1955 to the grounds of the Walter Reed Army Medical Center.

After that, things began to fall into place, but the stress surrounding the project took a toll on Joe who, early in 1966, suffered a heart attack. Hospitalized for four weeks in La Quinta, California (at a home he had bought after his marriage to Olga), he spent another month convalescing there. Afterward, he was confined two more weeks in Greenwich.[*]

While recuperating, Joe received a sympathy letter from President Johnson to which Joe replied, "Your letter came as a

*While Joe was recuperating from his heart attack in California, Jennie died of cancer. Due to his own poor health, he did not attend the funeral.

pleasant surprise. I was touched . . ." The next month, when
Johnson was hospitalized in Bethesda Naval Hospital after the
removal of his gall bladder, Joe wrote to him from Greenwich.
"At Temple, on Yom Kippur, our congregation joined our Rabbi
in prayer for your well-being and speedy recovery. My wife and I
are delighted to see you up so soon. Keep it up. We all need you
and love you." Although Hyams stated in his book, "From that
moment, negotiations governing the art gift went forward in
tranquility,"[*] the tranquility did not extend much past the signing of the agreement. There were many troubled days, weeks,
months and even years ahead before the museum became a reality.

On May 12, 1966, Hirshhorn confirmed his commitment to
enter into a signed agreement to donate his collection to the
United States under the auspices of the Smithsonian Institution.
In a personal communication to the President, he said, "I am delighted that you and Mrs. Johnson have encouraged me to arrange for the establishment in Washington of a museum and
sculpture garden to help achieve our common objectives and contribute to the improvement of our cultural environment. It has
now been agreed that the Hirshhorn Foundation and I will donate our collections to the Smithsonian Institution."

President Johnson replied with a gracious letter which said,
"Yours is an act of patriotic generosity which will be treasured by
this and future generations of your fellow men. Mrs. Johnson
joins me in expressing our profound appreciation of your contribution to the nation."

Shortly afterward, in an atmosphere of relief and pleasure,
the bill to Congress, the purpose of which was to pass the statute
necessary to the agreement, was drafted. In preparation for its
presentation the following week, Senator Jennings Randolph,
Chairman of the Committee on Public Works; Senator Stephen
M. Young, Chairman of the Subcommittee on Buildings and
Grounds; and Representatives George H. Fallon and Kenneth J.
Gray, Chairmen of the House's parallel legislative bodies were

*Ibid, p. 152.

all notified it was on its way. "Everyone we saw," McPherson reported to the President, "was enthusiastic and offered full support. Ripley told each one that 'Mrs. Johnson was the decisive factor. Hirshhorn is crazy about her and the President.' If we were to strike a medal for the occasion, Mrs. Johnson and Dillon Ripley should get it. Because of them—and because of Hirshhorn's affection and respect for you—we have beat out Rockefeller, the Queen of England, the Governments of Israel, Canada and the State of California." He left out Italy and Switzerland but it was a generous compliment to be sure.

At noon on May 17, 1966, the agreement was signed between Joe and the Smithsonian. Hirshhorn and his wife followed the President and Mrs. Johnson from the White House out to the Rose Garden where Vice-President and Mrs. Humphrey, Dillon Ripley, Sam Harris, Abram Lerner and their wives; Supreme Court Justice Fortas, Roger Stevens, Harry McPherson, Secretary Stuart Udall, and Robert McNamara were already gathered. In front of this assembly, the President signed his message to Congress urging the adoption of the measure to affect the acceptance of the gift.

"This is a magnificent day for the nation's capital," Johnson proclaimed, "and for the millions of Americans who will visit Washington in the years to come. I know that Joseph Hirshhorn will go on seeking the best in modern paintings and sculpture for years to come. But, he will never have a finer hour than this; for today he offers the fruit of a lifetime in the service of art to the citizens of a grateful nation. Now we must build a museum worthy of the collection and worthy of our highest aspirations for this beautiful city. Washington is a city of powerful institutions, the seat of government for the strongest nation on earth, the place where democratic ideals are translated into reality. It must also be a place of beauty and learning. . . ."

In reply, Joe spoke briefly and simply. He said, "I am deeply touched. You know, I am an American, and I'm giving this to the capital of the greatest nation in the world, I'm glad to be able to do it."

Afterward, Ripley asked Joe, "Will you miss your collection?" Fortified by a couple of sherries, Joe replied, "I don't feel any sense of loss at all. In fact, I'm going to go on collecting like I always have. My only regret is that I can't go back to the beginning and start all over again. It's been an adventure. Nobody in the world had a back garden like that." He added with a touch of sadness, "I feel like I've given away 6,000 children. But we're going to live near here—to be close to the children like a mama and papa should." *It was not the first nor the last time my father referred to his art as "my children."*

Asked for a comment on the addition to the Washington art scene of the Hirshhorn collection, James Harithas, curator of the prestigious Corcoran Gallery in Washington, said, "The collection is staggering. It will have an enormous effect on the museum scene. It will embrace many of the things the Corcoran and Phillips and the Gallery of Modern Art have been trying to put together. We are all very pleased but it will be difficult to compete."

In the delirium of self-congratulations among the movers and shakers of the as yet unrealized Hirshhorn Museum, Ripley experienced a quiver of misgivings. Paragraph nine of the agreement stipulated:

> In the event that legislation containing provisions substantially as set forth in *Paragraph Second* hereof is not duly enacted by the Congress of the United States and duly approved by the President no later than ten (10) days after the close of the 90th Congress, or in the event that said Museum and Sculpture Garden shall not have been constructed and completed as provided in *Paragraph Third* within five years after such legislation shall have been enacted an approved [by 1971], this Agreement shall be null and void and the proposed gifts by the Donor and the Hirshhorn Foundation shall not be consummated.

There were rough seas ahead.

The Hirshhorn Museum bill reached Congress and began its journey through the legislative process. It was the first museum proposed for the Mall in almost thirty years. What should have been greeted with great fanfare was met with an overwhelming attack of criticism, private prejudice, animus, conflict of personality and ego, bifurcated loyalty and self-interest. Every aspect of the museum and its construction came under fire. The site was contested, its name opposed, its donor disparaged, the two encounters Hirshhorn had had with Canadian authorities back in 1935 were dredged up, its sponsor was investigated and its appropriations were delayed. Senator Richard Clark of Iowa, in contradiction of the President's pledge and the signed agreement, demanded that the name of Franklin D. Roosevelt be substituted for Joseph H. Hirshhorn. Not every charge and counter-charge is worth repeating. Suffice it to say, the museum was brought to the brink of extirpation. The storm that broke over Hirshhorn's museum even threatened to spill over onto Lyndon Johnson, himself.

The battles raged on in the capitol. The Congressional Record of 1966 details the extent to which each Congressman and Senator spoke up for or against the museum and outlined their arguments and counter-arguments. Experts representing museums, dealers and respected collectors were asked their opinion of Joe's collection. The comments from the art world varied depending upon personal taste, self-interest or generosity of spirit. All of this infighting was deeply disturbing to Joe and Olga. For these ignorant and/or self-serving men to attempt to deny permission to such a gift, especially when the President of the United States had clearly been its champion, was beyond Joe's comprehension. More than that, he was deeply hurt and angered by all the ill will. Dillon Ripley, vigorously fighting for the passage of the statute, urged the committee members to visit Greenwich, to satisfy themselves as to the breadth and quality of Hirshhorn's collection. By the summer of 1966, some members had done so. But not many.

Meanwhile, as the budget for the escalating war in Vietnam increased, inflation was having its impact on the planned financing for the museum. Now, instead of a cost of $10 million, the new estimate totaled $13 million. When Sam Harris apprehensively sounded out Richard Goodwin (who had figured prominently in investigating the *Twenty-One* quiz show scandal during the late 1950s) on the matter, the White House aide suggested an appropriation of $15 million to which Harris responded that, given this was an "austerity" Congress, $15 million was "a hell of a lot of dough." Goodwin's response was intended to be reassuring. He said, "In my opinion, they will be enamored of the idea of a modern museum." What he had based his optimistic opinion on is not known, but as it turned out, his belief was providential.

Late in August, the Senate Public Works Committee authorized construction of the Hirshhorn Museum and Sculpture Garden at a cost of $15 million, plus an annual $1,388,000 for maintenance and operation and, together with the Rules and Administration Committee, reported Bill S-3389 favorable out of committee. The Senate passed the bill on September 1, 1966.

It was mid-October before the House prepared a companion bill which authorized $7.5 million for construction of the AFIP (Armed Forces Institute of Pathology) addition to the main building of the Walter Reed Hospital as an alternative to any new building on the Mall for the museum. Congress was anxious to adjourn and the elections of 1966 were fast approaching. Ripley was pensive as the House Public Works Committee held the museum bill in suspension and the AFIP was stalled in the Senate's Armed Services Committee. Passage of both bills by this 89th Congress was essential. The Smithsonian timetable needed both sessions of the 90th Congress to process appropriations for planning and construction to meet the completion deadline of the museum by 1971.

On October 18, after a nudge from the White House, the Armed Services Committee cleared AFIP at its final meeting. In the wake of that passage, HR-15121, the bill for approval of the museum was approved and went to the House for signature. Now, only the President's signature was required. Johnson, at his ranch in Johnson City, Texas, received the bill authorizing construction of the Hirshhorn Museum with all its concomitant specifications and signed it into Public Law 89–788 on November 7, 1966. The *New York Times,* reporting on the passage of the Act, said it represented "Johnson's boldest stroke as a patron of the arts, a personal triumph, a national victory over foreign bidders, and an inestimable enrichment of Washington's cultural resources."

XIV
Washington Backlash

Almost immediately, an unexpected fallout descended from the art community which previously had praised the collection to the skies. Aline Saarinen, who had written so approvingly about Joe in *The Proud Possessors,* took him to task and utterly by surprise. "Joe," she wrote in outrage over the passage of the Act, "took the government as it's never been taken before." She believed Ripley had oversold the President and Mrs. Johnson; that instead of bargaining shrewdly and persuading Hirshhorn to selectively give the best of the collection to form a base for an *anonymous* "National Collection of Modern Art," they had allowed the collector to have his name on the museum and to exert indirect control over the museum by allowing Joe to handpick its director.

Sam Harris coolly responded to the idea that Hirshhorn had "put anything over" on the U.S. government. "They were all grown boys," he said. "They knew what they were doing. They wanted the collection. They were only one of a great number of people and institutions who wanted it." Anyone who read Saarinen's profile of Joe would be as shocked as he was when he read her diatribe against him and the collection she had once described with such admiration. Joe wondered if she had been unaware of the offers made by Toronto, England, Italy and Nelson Rockefeller. In his joy at securing the future of the museum, Joe put Saarinen out of his mind but, as Lerner observed, Hirshhorn was not a forgiving person. He would hold a grudge against her from that time forward.

Not all the negative observations were stilled and, while plans for the building and its construction moved forward, Joe and the government had to suffer additional complaints. Be-

216

cause Gordon Bunshaft, when he was a member of the Commission on Fine Arts, was awarded the design contract, an
accusation of conflict of interest arose. This matter was appropriately resolved and nothing more was heard about it. The appointment of Abram Lerner as director of the museum agitated
the museum community, chiefly because he hadn't risen through
the ranks. The fact that he had twenty years of firsthand knowledge of the collection (ten years as its curator), was frequently
called upon to lecture on art and was teaching at Brooklyn College, didn't cut any ice with Lerner's critics. They chose to ignore
the fact that Lerner was in good company with two distinguished
museum directors and scholars, John Pope-Hennessey of the
British Museum, and Kenneth Clark, formerly with the National
Gallery in London. Both these men were also self-educated in art
history.

Charles Blitzer, a Smithsonian official, summed up the fun-
damental cause of the controversy. "Who [won] in this case? It
was a name on the Mall against the acquisition of a unique collection. The same and better were offered by England and New
York State."

There were supporters. One fair-minded appraisal was
made by art critic Vivian Raynor shortly after Johnson enacted
the law. She said:

Half the pictures and sculpture I have seen are excellent. The rest
are mediocre, including a sprinkling of choices I would call unfor-
tunate. But a just estimate can only be made relative to other collections, and those in museums have been carefully weeded—as
the junk-filled basements would testify. The point is, Hirshhorn
has bought as a private individual, unprotected by the
tastemakers "union." It's a fantastic gesture this man has made;
it could turn out to be as eccentric as a Watts Tower—and as
beautiful. . . . Modern artists [have expressed] consciously or un-
consciously that something is desperately wrong with civiliza-
tion. Hirshhorn is a man of the 20th Century; the swath he has cut
through its art may well be true history, not the edited kind.

Unfortunately, in the six years that passed before the museum's opening date, Raynor, possibly affected by the swirling

controversy regarding the quality of the art in the collection, had changed her mind and now seemed to be on the side of its detractors. There were many moments when Joe felt like withdrawing. Only weeks before this, the art world had paid homage to him and to his collection. He couldn't understand what had caused the reversal of such widespread initial approval. The negative voices left him bewildered and hurt.

Once the bill had been passed, the collection immediately transferred responsibility for its costs, including staff, warehousing, maintenance, restoration and insurance to the U.S. government vis-à-vis the Smithsonian Institution. Joe's relationship to what formerly was *his* art collection changed. Although he still had many pieces that had never resided in the Hirshhorn Foundation and remained in his private ownership, he continued collecting as if he were starting over. Olga joined him in this second phase of collecting. They traveled to France, met new and important artists and enjoyed the company of those who were already their friends. But most of all in the years immediately following the passing of the Act, Joe continued collecting and was intensely involved in the development of the plans for the building and grounds that would ultimately house the Joseph H. Hirshhorn Museum and Sculpture Garden.

Lerner, no longer working for Joe but rather as an employee of the Smithsonian, found "a lot of things were available [to me] that I didn't have before." Lerner's offices were moved to a three-story brownstone at 135 East 65ᵗʰ Street in New York City where he had the use of two floors. "Before this I had one secretary and a warehouse man to help me move things in the warehouse," Lerner said. "Now I started to hire people to help organize the collection."

In 1967, Fran Weitzenhoffer was hired as a researcher and Cynthia McCabe came aboard as a curator. An art library was started which grew to several thousand volumes. More staff was hired, so the entire operation was moved to six rooms in the brownstone on East 65ᵗʰ Street where Anna Brooke joined them in 1971 as librarian. The kitchen of the brownstone was her office. Brooke, the last original hire for the new museum is, as of this writing, still Head Librarian at The Hirshhorn Museum in

Washington. The staff enlarged as fast as Lerner could find good people. Curators Inez Garson and Frank Gettings, photographer Walter Rosenblum and secretary Rita Jaros nearly completed the core staff. Soon security dictated moving most of the pieces from the office to the warehouse where one man, Myron O'Higgins, entitled registrar, was located to record the avalanche of incoming artworks. By the time the gift went to the museum, the collection occupied most of four lofts at Morgan Manhattan Storage on West 21st Street.

Although Joe no longer directed Lerner's activities, a restriction he understood and respected, he telephoned Lerner throughout the day exchanging details of purchases and deliveries. Joe had not stopped buying. Nor had he lost interest in an intimate association with the art or the employees who would be staffing the museum bearing his name. During a brief pause in the activities of his day or on his way home, he might stop by the office "to enjoy art." At those times, phone calls from stockbrokers and other insistent business associates would be routed to the art office, disturbing the very serenity he'd come to enjoy. Even if the visit lasted only a half an hour, the office vibrated in his wake long after he'd left. To a certain extent, Joe and Lerner maintained the same intense relationship as before. They not only discussed art, but Lerner was still marking catalogs of auctions for Joe's attention and, when possible, went along to enjoy the excitement Joe generated when his enthusiasm to own a work on the block sent bids spiraling in thousand-dollar units. Lerner estimated that in the decade ending in 1967, Hirshhorn spent $5 million for the works of twenty-one sculptors, from "Archipenko to Zogbaum, including Grooms, Manzu, Moore, Nadelman, Picasso, Rickey, Rodin and David Smith.

"When I first came (to work for Joe)," Lerner said, "I knew every painting personally. I could look at each one and recognize it." He added ruefully, "But now, I don't know them anymore." Still, Hirshhorn kept buying and more art was delivered.

At his downtown office, George Courtney was irritated and claimed each new delivery was a "pain in the ass. One day," he related, "they walked in with an eight-foot statue by some Italian . . . or maybe it was an Epstein. It arrived at the building from Italy. Couldn't get it in the elevator. About 200 people gathered to watch. I was supposed to be handling securities and there I was wrestling an eight-foot statue. I had to get it out or there'd have been a riot on Cortlandt Street. I gave the cop five dollars to disperse the crowd. Finally, the moving people gave up and took it to the warehouse."

The artwork proved to be Jacques Lipshitz's monumental *Figure*—87½ inches tall. It was meant to have been sent to Greenwich where eventually, it was placed like a sentinel on the lawn of Round Hill.

Joe and his wife would remain at the house in Greenwich until 1977, nearly three years after the museum opened and almost five since the art was removed from the property. But as long as the epic-sized sculptures remained on the grounds and the interiors of the house were lined with the finest paintings, Joe and Olga opened the house—to more than 500 private tours—a courtesy for which the viewers were overwhelmingly grateful. Lerner and his wife occasionally found their way to Greenwich. On one of those visits he had a brief but unforgettable vision of Joe as he sat with Hirshhorn who was being interviewed by a reporter for an article in the *New York Times:*

> Right after the collection was given to the Smithsonian and the building hadn't yet begun, the *Times* sent over an art critic to interview Joe for the (paper). And it was a big article as I remember. (The interviewer was) a very smart British girl who'd been to an American school. Joe had a sunburn, a very, very bad one where he couldn't stand anything on his body. So, Joe sat there stripped down to the waist giving the interview. I tell you, I don't remember what he was wearing but it looked like a toga—it wasn't, but it formed itself like a toga and he looked like a Roman emperor. With that nose and a strong kind of face, he looked like someone off a Roman coin.

In the New York brownstone, the staff was being transformed from a private organization to one under federal jurisdiction. The General Services Administration (GSA) was assigning civil service ratings to all the personnel and every expenditure had to be accounted for, from the cost of a restoration and setting up a reference library to money spent on paper clips. Petty cash vouchers had to be forwarded in triplicate for each and every purchase. Humor can be found even in this mundane, tedious task. When the staff worked nights, the government provided sandwiches and coffee. On one such occasion, Fran Weitzenhofer ordered a bagel for which, as required, she submitted a voucher for eleven cents. Some days later, when her phone rang, she was alarmed to have the caller announce it was the treasurer's office at the Smithsonian on the phone. "Can I help you?" Fran asked.

Without hesitation, a Southern voice inquired, "What is a bagel?"

On January 10, 1967, Joe fulfilled Lady Bird Johnson's wish by donating a Thomas Eakins to the White House. The painting was a portrait of Ruth Harding, painted in 1903, showing a little girl in a white dress and pink ribbon. The child was a niece of sculptor Samuel Murray who was a close friend and early student of Eakins. On the back of the canvas the inscription read, "To Laura K. Harding from Thomas Eakins." Joe had bought the painting two days before its presentation to the White House from the Knoedler Gallery for $40,000. Within a few years its value had increased tenfold.

The attacks on Joe continued throughout the years before the museum opened. Many, if not most, were spurious. Joe was able to deflect all those that came to his attention and were based on incorrect suppositions instead of facts. The *Washington Post* reported that he was getting a big tax write-off for the gift. Joe replied, "I'm taking no tax deduction on my personal gift." He added, "You want to talk about taxes? In 1955, I sold my Rio Tinto interests and paid the U.S. government $9 million on my long-term capital gain."

The original target date for the museum's opening was 1969 but, with the war in Vietnam accelerating, the Smithsonian's budget was in serious danger of being struck down. To request the additional $14.1 million of the appropriation for the construction of the Hirshhorn Museum in one sum would have swollen the Institution's annual allowance by sixty-five percent, which was an unseemly increase. Yet, without it, Ripley had no authority to contract for construction even though plans had been approved. That meant the museum could not be completed in the agreed upon time. Harry McPherson referred the problem to the White House Budget Bureau noting that LBJ was "determined that nothing be left undone that will help secure the bequest. We must not lose the Hirshhorn gift." It was the bureau's recommendation that Ripley request $2 million to start construction along with authority to enter into future contractual arrangements for the remaining $12.1 million. Against Gordon Bunshaft's warnings that this procedure invited trouble, Ripley submitted the revised request and Congress approved.

In January 1968, a letter from President Johnson to Joe suggested the museum appeared to be on its way to construction even though "with the budgetary pressures we are facing, it's not easy to convince some members of Congress they should spend for art." And when, at the end of March, the President halted bombing in Vietnam and made his historic announcement that he would not seek a second term, Sam Harris' insistence at having both a signed agreement and a statute to protect Joe's gift seemed providential. Given the previous delays and changes ahead, Joe authorized Ripley to amend the agreement that deferred major funding for the museum to the 91st Congress and rescheduled completion of construction by the end of 1972.

As if in a reaction to what was happening to "his" museum, Joe began an art-buying spree that continued throughout 1968 and culminated in his acquisition of 960 additional works, among them Dubuffet's *Glass of Water II* and Agram's *Transparent Rhythm II*, both destined for Washington. Some of his buying took place when he and Olga were traveling, which they did every summer, spending time on the Riviera at the house on the Boulevard du Littoral. In 1969, Joe continued buying but at a reduced pace. At the end of the year, he had acquired only half the number of artworks he had purchased the previous year and the pace slackened with each succeeding year. Joe was getting older.

XV
Breaking Ground:
The Battle's Not Over

It was January 8, 1969, a morning when the winter sun barely warmed the forty-degree air before, at last, ground was broken for the construction of the Joseph H. Hirshhorn Museum and Sculpture Garden. In a ceremony at 7th and Independence Avenue, on the Mall, under a tent erected for the occasion, members of the Supreme Court, Congress and Smithsonian officials gathered along with Joe, Olga and all five of Hirshhorn's daughters. Gordon was not present. He was in England packing up his family to return to the United States after his North Sea oil venture failed or, as he put it, "after Joe destroyed my English deal." The President accompanied by Mrs. Johnson and their daughter, Lynda Bird Robb, arrived at 11:30 A.M. to perform one of his final, official acts in office.

To ward off the morning chill, Johnson was wearing an overcoat "so long," said one observer, "that it could have been a hand-me-down from General Pershing," while Joe, sporting his usual bowtie, was enveloped in a thigh-length dark mink coat, a gift from Taft Schriber, the Hollywood mogul. Despite the heating elements under the tent, it was uncomfortably cold. The army band played as the President and Chief Justice Earl Warren took their places. Towering over the lectern, Dillon Ripley opened the formalities, addressing the shivering crowd of about 400 with words from a letter written by John Adams to his wife regarding the importance of art and architecture. He closed his remarks by saying, "In this setting . . . no building presently planned could add more to the spirit of the place than this one, a fortunate and humane partnership of Joseph Hirshhorn and our enlightened government."

Ripley then introduced Joe, who had to stand on a box to reach the microphone. Positioned between Ripley and Johnson—both well over six feet tall—with typical good humor, Joe commented wryly, "They should have given me a high-chair." He then began to read with sincerity and heartfelt emotion this address:

Mr. President, Mrs. Johnson, Dr. Ripley, Chief Justice Warren, Congressmen, honored guests, friends, loved ones, ladies and gentlemen:

There are special occasions that celebrate a lifetime of effort and commitment. Even when they are formalized to fit the pattern of ceremony, these are the golden moments that have the greatest significance. They are very, very rare. Today is such an occasion for me.

I have spent the greater part of my life with art, with artists, and as a collector of art. When I began to collect, it was considered absurd to believe that American art could ever achieve international significance, that it could ever become a vital world art. I am proud that I began by collecting American artists. I am proud that I believed in them and championed them and stayed with them. I am proud that I felt from the beginning that American art had an explosive energy that would one day affect and influence art all over the world. The past twenty years have proved it.

This is a proud day for me. I feel fortunate that I should be here sharing this podium with such distinguished Americans, to initiate the construction of a great museum. Mrs. Hirshhorn and I are grateful to all of you who have taken the time on a chilly day to help us celebrate this occasion. It was an honor for me to give my art collection to the people of the United States. I think it is a small repayment for what this great nation has done for me and others like me who arrived here as immigrants. I repeat, it is an honor for me to give my art collection to the people of the United States. I think it is small repayment for what this great nation has done for me and or others like me who arrived here as immigrants.

Ladies and gentlemen, I want you to know we Americans are a great, wonderful, generous, kind people and I am proud to belong to the family of Americans. I was six years old, sixty-three years ago, when my mother brought me here from Latvia. I am grateful to that momma of mine and I hope she is here in spirit. What I have accomplished here in the United States, I could not accomplish anywhere else in the world.

I want to express my deepest thanks to President Johnson, whose interest and encouragement have made this day possible. He championed not only the creation of this museum, but also the cause of all the arts in America. In my memory, he is the first President of the United States to have been so deeply concerned with our national culture, and his administration was the first to recognize the importance of art in American life and to legislate in its favor. This is a matter of record. All of us who are concerned with the cultural heritage and future of our nation recognize the magnificent contribution President Johnson has made.

The President is fortunate in having at his side a great, darling and charming lady. Mrs. Johnson's concern for beautifying our nation and our capital made her an indispensable ally to our cause. Her unique personality, vision and lofty purpose have brought a new significance to the title of "First Lady."

Dr. Dillon Ripley was instrumental in bringing my collection to Washington. I want to pay my respects to this amiable diplomat who conducted the entire proceeding with exceptional grace and courtesy. It is not easy to work out the details of a gift of such proportions, but Dr. Ripley was persistent, cooperative and a charming seducer throughout.

There are several others who deserve my deepest thanks: Mr. Roger Stevens was one of the first to speak to me regarding a museum in Washington. As head of the nation's art programs, he has earned the respect and gratitude of all our citizens for his unstinting efforts in behalf of the arts and the wise manner in which his programs were accomplished. He has destroyed the myth that government in art means censorship and bureaucracy.

My friend, Justice Abe Fortas, that wise, good and gentle man, did much to shape my decision. His lively interest in the arts and his sympathy for what we are trying to accomplish make him a particularly valued and understanding friend.

Mr. James Bradley, assistant secretary of the Smithsonian Institution, who helped work out the details of our agreement, was an angel throughout: my attorney and good friend, Sam Harris, was a key person in my decision to bring my collection to Washington. He worked hard to bring this about: Mr. Abram Lerner, my former curator, the first Director of the Joseph H. Hirshhorn Museum. His dedication and help over the many years have made him a cherished friend and a valuable associate: Mr. Gordon Bunshaft of the architectural firm of Skidmore, Owings and Merrill, has designed a beautiful museum building, an exciting structure that will contain an equally exciting assemblage of art. It is my great hope that this museum will dedicate itself to public service, that it will be the nation's showcase for the widest range of contemporary artistic expression, that it will become involved with the community as well as the nation, and that it will be a productive center for recreation, education, and study for all our people.

Thank you.[*]

"When he began to talk," wrote Paul Richard, the art critic of the *Washington Post,* "standing on a box so he could see over the podium, the [red and white] tie and the mink coat both made sense. There was poverty mixed with money in his voice."

President Johnson, who was the last to speak, connected the start of the museum to the next day's scheduled welcome for the three astronauts returned from orbiting the moon. "Today and tomorrow are memorable days for our Capitol," he said, "and for this country. These two events," he added, "tell us something about this country and its people." He continued by saying he and Mrs. Johnson "have great respect for Joseph and Mrs. Hirshhorn," and that "I will take great pride in turning the first spade of earth and dedicating this new museum to 'the increase and diffusion of knowledge among men.' "

At this point, the President left the platform and, with a silver-handled shovel, turned the first spade of earth. Chief Justice Warren and Dillon Ripley followed, each shoveling a spadeful of dirt. When Joe's turn came, he dug in with such vigor, his bowtie unclasped and fell to the ground. He retrieved it and Ripley bent to refasten it on Hirshhorn's collar.

Joe's sisters were not present at the groundbreaking, but years later when they saw his photograph with Johnson in Hyams' book, their appraisal of the photograph had nothing to do with their brother's accomplishment. They wondered aloud that "the President is such a clean-looking man."

---

*Hirshhorn wrote none of his speeches. Al Lerner wrote them. Joe would explain in detail to Lerner what he wanted to say and Lerner, skillful with words, would fashion them into a speech. Before giving his speeches, Hirshhorn practiced them diligently so as to deliver the words effectively.

Joe with President Lyndon Baines Johnson at the groundbreaking ceremony for the Hirshhorn Museum. In the background can be seen, at far left, Lady Byrd Johnson; also, behind and between Joe and the President are Lynda Bird and Lucy Baines Johnson.

After the ceremony, the exterior design of the building was first revealed to the public. The model disclosed a cylindrical structure resting on four legs and floating fifteen feet above a plaza. Reporters variously described it as "a gargantuan bagel," "the Pentagon with the corners knocked off," "the biggest tomb since the pyramids," and "a magnificent pillbox from the Maginot Line." Ada Louise Huxtable, architecture critic of the *New York Times,* denounced it as "the biggest marble doughnut in the world." Everyone, including Gordon Bunshaft, took the criticism in stride. They had confidence in the beauty and functionality the building would have after it was completed and the art was installed.

The museum had been designed to have a marble face of

pale travertine or, alternately, white marble from Rome. But when it went out for bids, congressmen from marble-producing states were up in arms. Either the marble had to be native or, at least, the fabrication had to be done in this country. No one in the U.S. could compete with the prices from Europe and the project, due to rising costs in 1968, was already $1.5 million over budget. Adjustments had to be made. Bunshaft flew to Cap d'Antibes, where the Hirshhorns were summering in August, to show Joe the changes in design he'd had to make and get Joe's approval for them. The public restaurant and kitchen had been eliminated, the ground floor area had been reduced by 40,000 square feet, the sculpture garden had shrunk and gravel had been substituted for the dark flagstone pavement originally specified. The marble facing was definitely out. It would be replaced by a granite-chip concrete, approved by the Commission on Fine Arts. Faced with the inevitable, Joe, ever the pragmatist, acceded. Before the new drawings were ready, it was December and costs had escalated once more.

Throughout the '60s, before and during the struggle to bring the museum into existence, Joe and Olga traveled extensively in Europe, using the villa on the Riviera, which Olga did not like, as their base. They went to Paris, London, Rome, Milan and Switzerland. They visited Picasso, Manzu, Marino Marini (who executed a portrait of Joe) and with Henry Moore as well as the European gallery owners Joe befriended over the years. They entertained many visitors at the villa including Marc Chagall and Pierre Matisse. On one occasion, they traveled to Ireland with Henry Moore and on another, met with Peggy Guggenheim in Venice. It was a life filled with excitement and stimulating friends. But back home, things had not improved.

When the new bids, regardless of the concessions already made, proved to be over budget again, Bunshaft traveled to New York, where, over lunch, he broke the bad news—again—to Joe. It meant further reductions in the structure: no fountain in the plaza, no stairway and underpass connecting the sculpture garden to the plaza. "It made Hirshhorn ill," said Bunshaft. "He went out and bought something for $30,000." The "something" was the Picasso bronze, *Kneeling Woman Combing Hair.*

An additional appropriation was out of the question. Dillon Ripley suggested to Joe he apply his million-dollar endowment for further acquisitions to defraying some of the increased costs of construction. Joe agreed and then supplemented his original gift with an additional million dollars worth of art.

Actual construction began in March and whatever could go wrong, did. The process seemed typical of the births of all previous museums in Washington, D.C. As a result of the many delays, Ripley had to request further extensions, which he accomplished with his usual aplomb. But the criticisms and suggestions that the Hirshhorn Museum be abandoned continued. In a note smacking of hysteria, printed in the *Washington Star,* Gilmore D. Clark, a former member of the Commission on Fine Arts (1932–1950) decried, "The whole project should be stopped. The Hirshhorn Gallery has no place on the Mall." When further letters to the newspaper questioned Joe's respectability, setting forth his unworthiness to have a place on the Mall, the same paper retorted with an editorial that seemed to frame the matter more realistically. In addition to examples of other men whose names are linked with the Mall and whose reputations may have been questionable, it said, "On the Mall itself, Charles Freer, whose name is memorialized in the lovely gallery of Oriental art, had a well-deserved reputation as a rake and died of a disease acquired in gaining that reputation." Gilmore went on, "The nation is not, as our correspondents imply, erecting a monument to Hirshhorn. It is accepting and suitably housing his gift of a magnificent collection of modern art. In doing so, the nation is enlarging the art enclave along the Mall. All of this is perfectly proper and completely within the tradition." This balanced editorial, however, did little to still the clamor. But it did apply a somewhat soothing balm to Joe's wounds. Shaking his head, he wondered, "What is wrong with these people?" Perhaps it evoked memories of Blind River's rejection of Hirshhorn City.

John Canaday, art critic of the *New York Times,* wondered if "anyone [in the American museum field] really likes the idea of this project going through?" Ripley's assistant replied in response, "The museum and sculpture garden have been under construction since March. Full contract authority and the necessary appropriations have been legislated by Congress. Completion is assured, scheduled in the fall of 1973."

Dillon Ripley felt for Joe, who had gained his unfaltering respect and admiration. He thanked Joe for his additional gifts of art and bolstered his spirits with his own optimism. "I am sure," he wrote, "all this reads like a strange tale to you but I have found there is a way to get things done in Washington despite the system. . . ." And he reminded Hirshhorn of something Joe had already learned and practiced; that it required "the grace of patience." Little did they know that virtue was soon to be put to the test by events looming on the horizon like a storm cloud.

A man named Robert Hilton Simmons, disgruntled and feeling personally wronged by the Smithsonian, the FBI and the government in general had a contract with the Institution cancelled because of a claim of malfeasance concerning two paintings in the Institution's collection. Because of this, Simmons set out to have the perceived wrong righted. Believing he was defending the public interest, Simmons took his complaint to his Congressman, Hastings Keith. Keith moved the complaint upward until the Comptroller General was induced to cite "various questionable policies and practices in Smithsonian financial management."

Although the Board of Regents of the Institution stood squarely behind the administration, Simmons pursued his claim. Three bills for expanding the Smithsonian were pending in 1970, one of which concerned the Hirshhorn Museum and Sculpture Garden. Simmons chose to concentrate his attack on the Hirshhorn. Foraging in Canada, Simmons returned with new ammunition with which Clark Mollenhoff, the *Des Moines Register* Washington Bureau Chief and ombudsman to President Nixon, fired the first shot. "The truth is this isn't a gift, it's plain theft," he said, recommending that the least that could be done was to get Hirshhorn's name off "that building."

Within months of Mollenhoff's first barrage, Jack Anderson, the right-wing columnist known for his anti-Semitic, anti-progressive views, a man given to distorting facts in order to paint as lurid a picture as possible, jumped aboard the get-rid-of-Hirshhorn bandwagon. He found a sixty-seven-year-old woman in Florida who claimed she was unable to attend the opening of the Hirshhorn Museum because she could not afford the bus fare having "lost her savings," wrote Anderson, "through a stock hustle by Joseph Hirshhorn whose name will now be honored alongside those of George Washington and Abraham Lincoln."

The accusations against the Smithsonian financial management underwent a full-fledged investigation by the General Accounting Office (GAO) involving Congress, the Smithsonian Board of Regents, the Chief Justice of the Supreme Court, the vice president and several senators. Although little was found amiss, the Hirshhorn Museum remained a focal point of negative allegations. While Congressman John Brademas of Indiana commented, "When I think of what goes on over in the Department of Defense, my blood does not boil very much about the Smithsonian's shortcomings. . . ." Sherman E. Lee, Director of the Cleveland Museum of Art, reiterated to the committee the misgivings he still harbored about the Hirshhorn Museum ever achieving first-class stature. Al Lerner testified that Lee had never seen the Hirshhorn collection and, being a specialist in Oriental art, he would have no standing for evaluating Joe's collection. Lee, unable to give up or shut up, continued his diatribe by demeaning the museum building and the sculpture garden, which he said was an "encroachment" and therefore damaging to the Mall. "This," he said, "is the nose of the camel under the tent which may provide an excuse for future encroachment." The arguments and counter-arguments continued.

In rebuttal to Lee's disparagement of Joe's collection, Ripley requested an opinion from H. Harvard Arnason, art historian and former director of the Walker Art Center in Minneapolis, MN, a museum of impeccable reputation. His letter to Chairman Frank Thompson, Jr. was placed in the record. It said in part, "Hirshhorn has built up the most comprehensive collection of American painting of the 20th century in existence." It outlined the highlights of the artists included in the collection and went on to describe the sculpture in these words. "In my opinion and that of most other specialists in the field, [it] is the most important collection of modern sculpture in existence. I do not believe any museum of modern art, including the Museum of Modern Art in New York, possesses as comprehensive and important a collection."

Still, Simmons continued his diatribe by placing columns by Jack Anderson in the record and repeating the news accounts of Joe's fortunes and misadventures in Canada. He claimed that the Depression of the '30s was caused by the "fiscal irresponsibility" practiced by men like Joe and characterized him as unpatriotic for engaging in "illegal activities while Americans [lay] dying on battlefields in Europe." His accusations extended even to Ripley. If the matter hadn't imperiled the museum, much of what was going on would have garnered laughs.

Joe's attorney offered his opinion of Simmons' activities. "He made all sorts of wild charges," Harris stated. "In my view, some of the statements were scandalous, but I have a general philosophy," he continued with typical candor, "you don't get into a pissing contest with a skunk."

The controversy continued in hearings that were reported in news articles replete with accusations and frequent demands that the whole notion of the Hirshhorn Museum be cancelled. Along with counter-arguments, the war of words continued through the 1960s into the '70s as the building rose on the Mall.

Then the unexpected happened. Lyndon Johnson, out of office, died of a massive heart attack. The newly elected man in the White House, Richard M. Nixon, hadn't inherited Johnson's passion for the arts along with the mantle of President. Resistance to Gordon Bunshaft's cross-Mall design mounted as several important institutions added their voices to the melee. The National Sculpture Society declared it was "unalterably opposed to the use of any part of the Mall by the Smithsonian Institution for a sculpture garden as an adjunct to the Hirshhorn Museum." The Capital Planning Commission, wielding authority over all federal installations in Washington, stated its refusal "to violate the sacred sweep of the Mall" and vetoed Bunshaft's transverse design. All of this led to a meeting between Sam Harris and Leonard Garment, Nixon's advisor. Garment passed along Nixon's position on the matter, "The President would not go for the garden across the Mall."

Harris wanted to remind Garment of the previous administration's commitment to the museum but Garment's response killed further discussion. Harris was forced to confront an exasperated Bunshaft who was, understandably, opposed to any further changes. "Gordon," said the attorney, "if you had a choice between a sculpture garden across the Mall or no garden at all, which would you take?" No further discussion was needed. Bunshaft got it. He went back once more to his drawing board, reduced the two football fields to one-tenth the original size, and pivoted the garden ninety degrees to parallel the Mall between Jefferson and Adams Drives. The Fine Arts Commission gave its approval to the new design in May and the National Capital Planning Commission agreed to it July 1, 1971.

Two days later, a full year after the names of nominees had been submitted to him, Nixon announced the trustees of the museum. Joe had submitted fifteen candidates of whom Nixon chose only four: H. Harvard Arneson, Taft Schreiber, Hal B. Wallis and Elizabeth Houghton. The fourth of Joe's submissions that Nixon named, Houghton, died before the opening and was replaced by Anne d'Harnoncourt. The other appointees were Leigh Block, Theo C. Cummings, George H. Hamilton and Daniel Patrick Moynihan, at the time, Ambassador to India. Two ex-officio members were Chief Justice Earl Warren and Dillon Ripley.

In spite of the resolutions—each a contentious roadblock—and although the appointment of trustees seemed to underscore progress, the controversy would not abate. Now James P. Allen, the freshman Senator from Alabama, introduced a resolution to rescind Congressional approval of the agreement between the Smithsonian and Hirshhorn. Threatening to place before a subcommittee hearing, "questionable legalities" regarding the Hirshhorn Museum, he cited "Congress in making the Chief Justice an ex-officio member of the Hirshhorn Board of Trustees," saying, "it violated the Constitutional separation of powers." Congressman Allen hadn't done his homework. The illustration he cited would have been embarrassing had he the capacity for embarrassment. The Chief Justice of the Supreme Court had, for 125 years, been appointed by statute to a post on the Smithsonian Board of Regents. Errors in judgment on the part of Hirshhorn's opposition approached the level of farce when, in a summer session, a subcommittee heard testimony from a former gangland dealer in stolen securities using the pseudonym George White, who accused Hirshhorn of fleecing the investment public.

Meanwhile, at 7th and Independence Avenue, the four acres were completely excavated and concrete was being poured into foundation forms. The museum construction was on its way, well behind schedule.

In anticipation of the museum's opening, Joe sold his home in La Quinta, California and replaced it with one in Naples, Florida. It was less tiring to fly between Naples and Washington or Greenwich than to make the long, cross-country flights to and from California. A three-hour difference in time between the West and East Coasts was also eliminated. The warm climate in Naples inured Joe from winter chill and was on par with the warm winters in La Quinta. By 1972, Joe was a reasonably healthy seventy-three years old. He'd had gall bladder surgery in the early '60s and a heart attack in the mid-'60s that dictated he be monitored on a regular basis by his surgeon, Dr. Kaare Kristian Nygaard. Nygaard, a Norwegian by birth, had a large surgical practice in White Plains, New York, and an abiding interest in the visual arts, especially sculpture. Nygaard had suggested open-heart surgery as a possibility, but Joe opted against it.* Weighing the odds, with his age as a factor and the fact that open-heart surgery was still in its infancy, Joe deemed the procedure not a good bet.

Clark Mollenhoff was still on Hirshhorn's case. In January 1974, he went to press with a full column on tax dodges. Referring to deductions taken by President Nixon and former Vice President Hubert Humphrey on their executive papers, Mollenhoff called for an examination of Hirshhorn's tax returns. "It would be advisable," he said, "to examine the still-pending

*Nygaard, four years Joe's junior, outlived him by nearly eight years. He died in Scarsdale, New York in 1989 and was buried in the town of his birth, Lillehammer, Norway.

multi-million dollar art write-off on a collection Joseph H. Hirshhorn is giving to the Smithsonian." Mollenhoff, a Pulitzer Prize-winning journalist, claimed that "the tax write-off of Hirshhorn's agreement with Dillon Ripley is reported to be at least $50 million—one hundred times the tax advantage President Nixon received on his papers. . . ." Mollenhoff went on to demean the value of the art Hirshhorn was donating which he suggested would give Joe a write-off of $80 million.

"That's complete rubbish," Sam Harris replied, "It's flagrantly false and, in my opinion, it's libelous. Joe did not receive a write-off on anything like $80 million. The gift was so enormous in terms of value that it would be impossible for him to realize tax benefits during his lifetime in deductions that would be available. His deductions, not as Mollenhoff figured, are to be taken within a five-year period, not a lifetime. Joe hadn't the slightest concern about taxes when he made the gift. We never even discussed it, or the tax consequences of his gift. Taxes had nothing to do with his decision at all. Mollenhoff was assuming that making that magnificent gift, Hirshhorn automatically obtained a tax benefit. He was out to smear Joe. What he wrote was irresponsible and absurd, and a flagrant abuse of freedom of the press."[*]

Contradicting reports that the value of the collection was exaggerated, in 1970 just four items of Joe's gift—Rodin's *Burghers of Calais*, Brancusi's *Sleeping Muse*, Moore's *King and Queen*, and Eakins' *Portrait of His Wife*—were evaluated at $1.3 million.

---

[*]Sam Harris' death in November 1980 at the age of seventy, came as a shock to everyone who knew him. Joe was devastated. Not only did he rely on Harris' counsel, indeed, Sam and his wife Madelyn were among Joe's closest friends. Sam's death remains a mystery. All Madelyn Harris could offer was that they were both at home in their New York apartment: she was in one room and Sam in another. Madelyn heard a noise, went into the room where Sam had been and then heard a ruckus outside. She looked down to see her husband on the pavement below. Al Lerner shared these facts with me and added, "Part of what made his death so traumatic," Al Lerner said, "and why it was such a tragedy was that no one had an explanation for why he might kill himself. But, the only sound thing I've ever heard," Al summed up, "is that he was slowing up terribly. He was possibly in the early stages of Alzheimer's disease. He had been so in command. He was a very impressive man."

Perhaps to counter the outcry from both the art world and the politicians, Joe kept expanding his gift. He added two more works by Eakins, bronze reliefs produced in 1893 for the Trenton Memorial Monument. They were the *Battle of Trenton* and *American Army Crossing Delaware* which had gone on loan to an exhibit at the Corcoran Gallery, after which the state of New Jersey wanted them placed permanently in the Trenton Museum on the provision that two castings were made, one pair to replace the original on the monument and the other to go to whoever paid the costs. Joe stepped forward and the bronzes became part of the collection.

Other items were bought to expand the gift. A dozen paintings and sculptures by Leger, Matisse, Mondrian, and Picasso were added to other works by Calder, Pollock, Miro, Rauschenberg, Giacometti, Magritte, Houdon and Bacon, among a total of 321 items valued at $7 million.

Finally, in March 1974, after suffering interminable delays and the many insults during Congressional hearings, about which one congressman said, "the fear among politicians of the anti-Semitic label was Mr. Hirshhorn's most important protection," the GSA certified the structure of the museum "substantially completed." At last, on April 17, 1974, the pact was consummated and title to the collection passed to the Smithsonian Institution. Somewhere along the way, the "Joseph H." was dropped and the name officially became the Hirshhorn Museum and Sculpture Garden. All principals concerned breathed a huge sigh of relief. But much hard work had yet to be done. Rounding up the art from all the various places where it was stored, wrapping it, packing it and arranging for it to be transported to Washington D.C., took more months and the efforts of an army of planners and workers.

"Nobody," commented Al Lerner, "has ever opened a new museum with a collection that could fill it four times."

Many of the events in Joe's life were less about the man and more about his art. Things that went on behind the scenes in order to bring the museum (the crowning achievement of his lifetime) into being never came to the attention of the public. What happened *after* the preliminary work was done, was very much on public display. While there was overlap between the two processes, the hidden efforts came first.

Thanks to Olga's dogged assistance, a workable inventory now existed of the art stored or displayed in Joe's offices on Park Avenue and East 65th Street, in Greenwich and Naples, and in warehouses in New York and Connecticut. Since 1972, Lerner had been considering the pieces to be shown in the opening exhibit, visiting the warehouse several times each week, systematically examining the works of each artist to select one or two to be included. Identifying 1,015 works he wanted to display, Lerner arranged for a catalog to be printed and bound in Japan, published by Harry Abrams and Company. For each of these items, researchers and curators in New York compiled lists of artists, authenticated signatures and dates, noted the position of data on canvases, frames, labels or on the body or plinth of sculptures. Because such exacting data was included in all professional art catalogs, this information was required before the catalog could be printed.

Concurrently, as the works to be displayed were being chosen, Douglas McAgy, curator of exhibits, who was in charge of arranging their placement for the opening, found the available space wouldn't permit room for Lerner's 1,015 pieces and cut the number down to 900—375 paintings and 525 sculptures. Soon after, models of the museum's interiors were constructed and the art scaled down to three-eights of an inch. Using mirrors and an architect's periscope to view the effects, McAgy designed the layouts which, but for a few adjustments, were ultimately used.

In December 1973, even before the lower levels of the museum were completed, the staff was installed in the offices on the fourth floor where they began preparations for the delivery of the art the following May. Joe, prior to the delivery, had added another 209 works, among them another Eakins, two Jackson Pollocks, a Toby, a Man Ray, Joseph Stella, Franz Klein and three Max Webers. It took four men six months to wrap and crate the total of 6,211 pieces of art at the warehouse and at Greenwich. Each piece had to be examined to verify its condition for insurance purposes. The move from the warehouse began in May. In June, trucks started leaving from Greenwich with paintings and the "light stuff."

The day of the removal of the sculptures, Joe and Olga, his fourth wife, sitting atop Henry Moore's monumental *King and Queen*. (Photo by Wide World Photos)

But, it was the transportation of the large pieces of sculpture from the lawns and gardens of Round Hill that garnered much public attention. Because trucks moving over the lawns and gardens would have badly damaged them, the heaviest sculptures were lifted by helicopter and "cherry-picker" cranes from the positions some had occupied for twelve years. Practice flights were staged that experimented with various methods of lifting these tremendously heavy pieces, using slings, cradles, nylon and padded cables and depositing them at a staging area. Having decided on which specific methods to utilize, a three-week-long airlift began on August 5th. Hyams gives an excellent description of the circus-like atmosphere which accompanied the airlift.

> . . . over a hundred spectators stood spellbound as they watched pilot John Roatch hover over Round Hill in his Sikorsky S-58. He dropped a 75-foot cable from its belly and swung Manzu's *Monumental Standing Cardinal* 50 feet into the air. The crowd gasped as the 1,200-pound bronze gyrated above the trees like a ceiling fan. To stop the spin, which threatened to snap the cable, the pilot lowered the Manzu gently onto the grass. Slowly he raised the bronze again and, with the aid of six men handling guy ropes, set it down on a flatbed truck. Two camera crews in additional helicopters filmed the airlift. The downdraft from all the blades blasted acorns from the surrounding oaks and fired them like buckshot at the onlookers. Nobody stirred.[*]

These maneuvers were repeated with Moore's *Glenkiln Cross*, which weighed 1,700 lbs., his *King and Queen*, that weighed 1,250 lbs. and Marini's *Horse and Rider*, at 1,110 lbs. In quick succession, more than $3 million worth of art left their pedestals to soar through the air from the rear lawns "over the house and its gables, turrets, towers and cupolas" to settle onto trucks in the driveway.

The *Burghers of Calais*, Rodin's monumental sculpture, defeated all pilot Roatch's efforts to hoist it up by helicopter. "It's listed at 4,000 lbs. and my helicopter has a capacity of 4,000 lbs,

Hirshhorn: Medici from Brooklyn, p. 182.

Joe standing in front of Rodin's *Burghers of Calais*, on the day all of the sculptures were removed. (Photo by Wide World Photos)

but I gave it everything she's got and she couldn't budge it." A huge crane was brought in and the *Burghers* was removed. The airlift, which completed the delivery of the art to the museum in Washington, was covered by local Greenwich and New York papers. In Washington, the arrival and placement of the *Burghers* was also captured on film.

When asked how he felt as he stared at the empty bases and pedestals that dotted his lawns that day, Joe replied in a voice husky with emotion, "We'll chop up the stone and plant new grass." Then moving toward the house, he sought the refuge of the familiar. "You'll have to excuse me," he said, "I have to make a phone call to see if the real world is still out there."

Later, when a reporter asked, "How much did [the move] cost?" He replied, "What's the difference? I'm paying for it." In fact, the move, the most economical way to transport the art, cost $215,000.

The only way to describe Joe's reaction to the transfer of his "children" from Round Hill was conflicted. He had done what he wanted to do and was proud and happy, but at the same time he was bereaved. And, to assure himself he would once again be able to see "his" art on an "as needed" basis, he and Olga began to scout around for a suitable home in Washington. They had been talking about finding a house in Washington since 1966. However, once the art had been removed from Greenwich, especially the sculpture on the grounds, the search became more focused. The new Washington residence would have to be large enough to house the art Joe had retained for his own pleasure and for the additional art he expected to buy. Moreover, it would have to be comfortably close to the museum.

Every weekend in September, Joe flew down from the White Plains airport to visit the museum and watch his collection being installed in preparation for the important date. "I went one Saturday," he said, "and things were all over, on the floor, everywhere. I looked at them and wondered, *Did I buy that? When? My God, it's great! If I had it to do all over, I'd buy it again.*" Joe and Olga didn't expect to leave Greenwich until sometime after the museum had its official opening on October 1, 1974. In fact, Joe didn't move to Washington until 1977.

Joe embracing Henry Moore's *Reclining Nude*, just before it, too, was removed. (Photo by World Wide Photos)

XVI
The Dream Is Realized, but Real Life Goes On

At this time, when Joe continued living in Greenwich, he maintained his apartment/office on Park Avenue at 76th Street in Manhattan. *At the same time I was living in Mt. Kisco and working in Manhattan. I had become increasingly troubled by Joe's lack of interest in and feeling for me. I decided we should have a heart-to-heart talk during which I could explain that I loved him, wanted to be closer to him and ask for some explanation of why he seemed so unloving and so loathe to include any of his children in his life. At first he was wary and reluctant to see me. When he finally consented, I asked if we could meet in his apartment in the afternoon. I would take off from work early. He adamantly refused. Our meeting had to be in a public place. "But," I argued, "I'm sure I'm going to cry and I'll be embarrassed at crying in a public place." But that was as far as he would go: Meet in a public place or not at all.*

We met in a Longchamps restaurant on Madison Avenue within walking distance of Joe's apartment. While I talked and wept about how hurtful his rejection felt, Joe listened. What he felt, how much he accepted, I couldn't tell, but the fact that he was listening at all was some kind of small victory. It was my father who decided the session had gone on long enough. Apparently satisfied he'd heard the essence of my position, the man of little patience for drama or emotional intimacy said we were going back to his apartment. His immediate actions once we were there were to place phone calls. Our conversation was over, his interest in me was over. He had moved on to the next item on his daily agenda without comment or closure.

243

That night I received an unusual phone call from him. "Gene," he said, "I'm really glad we had that talk today." I felt a fleeting moment of closeness, of being understood and accepted. But, in the end, our relationship didn't change. Joe was simply and clearly an absentee father.

When I reflected on our meeting in Longchamps, I thought I understood why he initially refused to allow me to have the "talk" in his apartment. Remembering some gossip Jennie had told me (no matter that she often repeated rumors that turned out to be untrue) I considered the possibility that her story about a manicurist trying to kill Joe may, in fact, have been true. What Jennie had said was brief in the extreme, I had no details and I'm sure it came out of her hurt as a betrayed wife. But it involved an affair Joe had been having with a woman whose name was May. As a result of Joe's attempt to break off the affair—or in her anguish or dissatisfaction with his attention—May allegedly brought a gun to what turned out to be their terminal meeting and threatened him with it. After remembering this tale, I believed my father was afraid I would be carrying a gun and might shoot him as May was alleged to have done. There was no other possible reason why he would have been afraid to see me in private and it underscored how paranoid Joe could be. It was the only scenario which could have accounted for Joe's fears. I would love to know how, in the end, Joe made this unsavory situation with his paramour manicurist go away.

Meanwhile, preparations for the opening of the museum continued. Invitations had been extended to friends, relatives, the press; the art world in the form of artists, gallery owners, and museum directors; to politicians, to everyone suitable and politic. Three dates were set for the three successive openings.

Several days before Joe was to leave for Washington, his daughter Naomi who had come east for the events, saw him in one of his softer, humbler moods. She wrote:

In 1974, just before the opening of the museum, I was visiting with [my father] in his New York apartment on Park Avenue. He was walking around the living room in this soft, silk paisley robe, his hands in his pockets and a slight boyish smile on his face. I don't remember his exact words but what he said in essence was,

"Just think of me, little Joe Hirshhorn, my name is going to be on a building on the Mall in Washington, D.C.—in perpetuity. Do you know what that means? It means forever! Me, little Joey Hirshhorn, my name on the Mall of the capital of the United States, forever!" In his voice was a sense of wonderment that this could have happened to him.

The Hirshhorns arrived in Washington two days before the opening and ensconced themselves in the Hay-Adams Hotel where Joe had reserved rooms for his five daughters, one son, two grandsons and four granddaughters, and his one sister, Dora, who was able to attend. In addition many nieces, nephews and others close to Joe were invited to the first opening, as well as his second wife and mother of his two younger daughters, Lily Harmon, whom Joe considered "family."

The day before the opening, the Hirshhorns viewed the exhibit at the museum because they knew they wouldn't see much the night of the opening. Joe was thrilled and excited. It was the realization of a dream. He said about the coming event, "I tried to be calm. You know I had trouble with my heart. I wondered how people would respond. I made up my mind not to let it bother me. And it didn't."

Olga said: "He had this sense of humor and he'd kid a lot during the night of the opening; he kidded a great deal. He talked about his mother, Amelia Friedlander, wishing she were there to have seen this. And he went to bed very happy. All along I kept hoping that he would live long enough for the opening of the museum."

On October 1st, the celebration began at 10:00 A.M. with a preview for 350 news reporters who were greeted in the museum's basement theater by Charles Blitzer, who introduced Secretary of the Smithsonian, Dillon Ripley. With him onstage were Ambassador Moynihan, Gordon Bunshaft and Abram Lerner. Each made a contribution to the presentation. Ripley announced that Joe, in honor of the occasion, had donated four new sculptures: two gigantic Ruben Nakians, one Kenneth Snelson and an additional Henry Moore, the *Two-Piece Reclining Figure; Points*, which had been featured at the sculptor's retrospective exhibit in Florence two years earlier. Lerner's statement to the press was, "The museum enters its most important phase, the arrival of the public." Bunshaft's contribution was, "It's been eight years since I was selected to design the museum. If the building doesn't speak for itself, words won't do it." Moynihan invited the press to tell him what they thought after they were given six hours to wander about the premises, served drinks, sandwiches, shrimp, fruit and pastries.

The premises consisted of the lobby on the ground floor which provided elevator access to the main galleries on the second and third levels where the exhibition rooms (with 168,000 square feet of floor space) encircled a fifty-foot-wide walkway. Paintings were hung in the galleries with sculptures positioned along the walkway. Other, larger sculptures, were situated in the garden. The top floor, reached via elevator in one of the piers, housed the library, administration offices and the storage/study facility. The storage and study arrangement was the "envy" of "all museum professionals," claimed Bunshaft, proudly. "Even the Museum of Modern Art's study room didn't have adequate space and light you find in an attic or basement." It was the museum's storage space that created the biggest stir. There, 141 double-faced panels suspended on rails could be rolled out at will, each fifteen feet high and thirty feet wide, providing 84,000 square feet of surface on which to hang far more than the roughly 4,400 paintings in the collection.

The basement of the museum contained, in addition to the small theater, a gallery for temporary exhibits, a sales shop, storage for sculpture and over 1,000 drawings and prints, a photo library and restrooms.

What the press corps reported back to Moynihan after they had leisurely toured the museum is not known. What they reported to their newspapers and magazines is well recorded. Overall, the reviews were mixed, more positive than negative, nationally and internationally. Hilton Kramer, arguably the most influential and respected art critic in the United States and who reported for the *New York Times,* was positive. He represented the immediate reaction of most of the mainstream press.

The real festivities began at 7:00 P.M. when 200 dignitaries and Joe's family dined in the Smithsonian's "castle" with the evening's principals. I was fortunate to be seated at a table graced by Lady Bird Johnson. The room was noisy with the clatter of silverware against dishes, the clinking of glasses, footsteps of wait-staff and the chatter of two hundred dining guests striving to make themselves heard above the din.

Then, at 8:00 P.M., almost 2,000 additional guests arrived at the museum itself, to join the 200 who walked to the museum from the "castle" fifty yards away. Tables in the court were laden with pastries, three-foot sculptures of fruit and glasses for the champagne being iced in buckets. There was music provided by the National Symphony Orchestra and more by the Marine Band whose twenty-four musicians, in full dress, marched in and played a medley overture as Lady Bird Johnson; the Smithsonian Regents; the museum trustees, designer, and director; Mayor Walter E. Washington and the Hirshhorns took their seats on the dais. Dillon Ripley, as Secretary of the Smithsonian, made the opening remarks.

"This building and its attendant garden of sculptures have been appropriately controversial. If it were not controversial in almost every way, it would hardly qualify as a place to house contemporary art. . . ." He continued:

The Hirshhorn challenges you to make what you will of it on the exterior but works beautifully within as no one can deny. Without Mr. Hirshhorn there would have been no single way the Smithsonian could have lived up to its Congressional mandate. This is a fact easily forgotten or glossed over by those without a broad understanding of the recent history of art and art collection. . . .

We are lazy, most of us, and our eyes are veiled, accustomed to patterns, the familiar landscape, the gray blob of the "tube." . . . The purpose of the Hirshhorn is to remind us all that life is more than usual, that the human mind in its relentless diversity is capable of seeing life subjectively and being stirred by objects into new and positive ways of thought. That is what the Hirshhorn is for and why we are so grateful to the donor.

Sen. Moynihan read a letter from President Gerald Ford, in office a mere two months after the resignation of Richard Nixon. Mrs. Ford was ill and neither was able to attend. Al Lerner paid tribute to the officials and to all of his staff whose devotion had brought the museum into being. Then Ripley introduced Joe to the audience, calling him, affectionately, "Uncle Joe," which the press picked up and subsequently dubbed 7th and Independence Avenue "Uncle Joe's Corner." Then it was Joe's turn. Behind the lectern someone had placed a wooden case for champagne on end upon which he stood to reach the microphone. It brought his head level with Ripley's.

"This is a day to remember," he began, "the proudest day of my life. Tonight's ceremony marks the beginning of the museum's dedication to public service. No one individual can do more than plant a seed and hope that a living museum will grow from it. This is what I have done."

The audience rose to its feet and gave Joe an ovation. When Ripley concluded the formal exercises, inviting the assemblage to "wander about as they pleased," some surged to the podium where Joe stood, smiling, accepting congratulations and blowing kisses. He later said, "I was in a fog."

Champagne flowed and Howard Devron's Orchestra played as dancers took over the plaza, Joe among them. "Play a foxtrot," he called to the bandleader, and as the orchestra swung into his requested tempo, Joe took Olga in his arms and, as a circle of distinguished guests looked on, danced in the light of a clear, harvest moon. There was a spontaneous burst of applause. Later, sitting beside the fountain while he autographed about 250 programs, Robert McNamara, president of the World Bank, bent down and whispered into Joe's ear, "You are going to be remembered for 1,000 years." It was midnight before the last guest departed.

The night of October 2, the Smithsonian played host to the international art community with a dinner in the "castle." The guests included artists, museum directors, scholars, art patrons, gallery owners and dealers—450 in all—who dined on lamb chops, acorn squash, Southern-style peas and, for dessert, cherries jubilee. Ripley toasted the assembled guests with champagne and called them the "important" guests as opposed to the previous night's "influential people." Joe knew virtually everyone there and had a personal relationship with most of them. He toasted their health and remarked with characteristic enthusiasm, "I love everybody. We have people here from Japan, Italy, Pakistan, Mexico, France—did I miss anyone?—England, Israel—and a lot of people from the Bronx. I thank you for coming. It's an honor to have you here."

After dinner, the guests were invited to "get over to the museum" where they joined nearly 4,000 people: artists, dealers, museum directors and curators. The next evening, October 3, two two-hour previews each accommodated 4,000 "Friends of the Smithsonian Institution." Those three nights concluded the special openings and festivities which cost, in total, about $60,000—money which came from private, not federal, funds.

On Friday, October 4, the Hirshhorn Museum and Sculpture Garden opened its doors to the public. Promptly at 10:00 A.M., with 200 people waiting patiently outside, the doors opened and inside the public was greeted by Secretary Dillon and Director Lerner. Soon afterward, Joe arrived. He was stopped near the entrance with requests for autographs. Olga set a chair for him in the lobby where he sat signing catalogs and brochures. Not long afterward, a kindergarten class arrived with their teacher. When Joe looked up and saw them, he exclaimed, "That's what's great!" and led them across the plaza to the sculpture garden where the photographers got a shot of the proud founder with the five-year-olds who Joe named "the class of '74," in front of the *Burghers of Calais*. Then he toured the museum as one of the crowd. "It's the first chance I've had to see the exhibit," he said, stopping to admire fourteen caricature figures by Daumier in a display case.

Just before lunch, Mayor Washington presented Joe with a key to the city, praising his contribution to the culture of the city as the band played "Hail Columbia," which ended the ceremony. Immediately afterward, Joe took the elevator to the fourth floor and, from Lerner's office, called New York to get the latest quotations on stocks of interest to him. When the museum closed for the day and the public had departed, the staff gathered in the lobby to celebrate with a small cocktail party; the completion of the successful first day in the life of the museum. While everyone was marking the occasion by taking photos, "Uncle Joe" sat autographing copies of the catalog, inscribing each to the staff. From time to time, Joe threw back his head and broke into song, "Oh Rosemarie I love you. . . ."

Joe, "in seventh heaven," as his wife described him and over-stimulated by the celebrations of the past four days, hated to leave Washington to go back home to the relatively quiet life they lived in Greenwich. In part, his reluctance was because he didn't imagine he would be back in Washington soon or how often they would visit. He was eager to learn how the collection, as exemplified by the opening exhibit, would be received and read all the reviews in all the newspapers. They were uneven in spite of the praise Hilton Kramer heaped on the museum and its contents in his review in the *New York Times* of Wednesday, October 2.

With the opening of the Joseph H. Hirshhorn Museum and Sculpture Garden, all of this uninformed carping—the apocryphal anecdotes, the condescending criticisms and general gossip-mongering—can now be consigned to the oblivion it so richly deserves. The private collection has become a public collection. It belongs to a new national museum—a museum devoted to the achievements of modern art—and for its inaugural exhibition, Mr. Lerner, now installed as director, has filled the galleries and garden with approximately 850 works selected from a total of some 6,000.

It is a marvelous exhibition, containing some superb paintings and especially notable for the scope and quality of its sculpture. On the basis of this exhibition alone, in which less than one-sixth of the collection is represented, the Hirshhorn museum joins that body of institutions essential to the study of modern art.

The sculpture collection is surely one of the greatest in its field. From Daumier and Degas in the 19th century to Alexander Calder and David Smith in the 20th, the major sculptors of Europe and America are represented in remarkable depth. There are whole anthologies of the works of Rodin and Matisse and Henry Moore, of Medarlo Rosso and Elie Nadelman and Raymond Duchamp-Villon. Along with this massive representation of the major figures, there are excellent examples of virtually every notable sculptor of the period, whether avant-garde or academic.

Offhand, the only significant omission seems to be the work of Claes Oldenberg.

Kramer commented on the volume of works by Eakins contained in the collection. He said, "The constellation of paintings by Thomas Eakins, the greatest of American realists in the 19th century, is fairly staggering, and it is augmented by six sculptures by the same artist." He also commented on the volume of works by a second important artist. "Willem de Kooning is another of the major American painters represented by an entire constellation of pictures—nine in all. . . ."

Kramer completed his long, detailed review by saying, "Mr Hirshhorn's magnificent gift to the nation is unlikely to be equaled in our lifetime. He has given us a great collection, and Washington has responded to the challenge—and the opportunity—with a rare combination of intelligence and vision. Bravo."

Although Kramer had praised the collection and predicted that "all the uniformed carping could be consigned to the oblivion it so richly deserves," the carping by professionals, however, was not over. They found fault with "gaps in the collection," its "unevenness and embarrassments," and one critic used the word "junk" in connection with what he saw as the lesser works on display. Another critic cited the fact that Claes Oldenburg was not represented and several complained that the Abstract Expressionist canvases were "by no means first rate." Emily Genauer, in her syndicated column, took Hirshhorn to task for the poor representation of Red Grooms and Jackson Pollock. Douglas Cooper in the *New York Review of Books* found fault with the building, the catalog and the collection. There was a mixture of other reviews, some praiseful, others punitive. Ada Louise Huxtable reiterated her disapproval of the exterior of the building but found positive things to say about the interior.

All in all, Joe, as well as the staff and administrators of the museum, took the reviews in stride. They were confident that time would establish the true worth of the museum and its collection by virtue of the traffic that passed through its doors and the pleasure derived by the visitors.

The conclusion of the various initial celebrations marked a

subtle but significant change in the life of Joe Hirshhorn and his wife.

Olga had had the great good fortune of marrying Joe when his achievement in art collecting was becoming internationally recognized. It was a time when she was able to participate in most, if not all, of the events that culminated in the establishment and opening of the museum. It was a once-in-a-lifetime opportunity for anyone, especially someone whose life had previously been proscribed by a small town, albeit a town like Greenwich where the rich and famous resided. Olga's marriage gave her an opportunity, rare in the life of most people, to meet the great and the near great in America and Europe. More than that, having attained the heights, Joseph Hirshhorn, at seventy-five, was, in a sense, treading water. No longer dedicated to making his name and fortune and his young man's energy slowly leaching away, Olga was able to be at Joe's side as, for the first time in his life, he began to relax a bit. Now, having reached and passed the crest, Joe was able to gradually ease back to a pace more agreeable to companionship.

A few months following the museum opening, Joe, in a voice that betrayed his own amazement, admitted to Barry Hyams, "I did something today I never did in my life before. I left my desk at noon. I went for a walk, dropped in on a couple of galleries to chat. I didn't buy anything. I had lunch with a little wine. It made me feel good. I didn't get back until 1:30 P.M. I didn't do anything but relax." This signaled a sea change in Joe's life and one in his wife's as well. Their lives together took on a new kind of routine.

Although Joe and Olga no longer required as large a house as Round Hill, they hesitated to give it up and move to Washington, although they had already purchased a four-story, red-brick townhouse on Bancroft Place in 1969. The house, located in the Embassy District of Washington, was in need of considerable renovation and Joe vacillated as to whether or not he was going to make the necessary alterations. The couple was committed to attending the openings of each successive exhibit that the museum executed. Olga arranged to make one bedroom in the Bancroft Place house livable so they could fly down for the day, go to an opening or attend a special dinner and, if they liked, stay overnight in the yet-to-be renovated house, returning to Greenwich the next day.

It was a makeshift arrangement not without its difficulties but Joe loved the visits to the museum. Occasionally, memorable events took place on those visits. This was especially true when notables were expected and Al Lerner always made sure the Hirshhorns were aware of the pending visits so Joe could be there.

"Nelson Rockefeller came [to the museum], we were told he was coming," Lerner said.

He was the Vice President at that time (and) came officially. Your dad knew he was coming so he was there to meet him. And, although I was there, it was your dad who was walking around with him and explaining everything. Now, there was no reason to explain anything to Nelson because he was one of the big collectors. But, I can understand it was of great pride in what Joe was doing and what he had done.

We finally got to the end of the tour and I think Nelson was very impressed. He said, "Joe, I think you've done a terrific job, you've done a great job." And Joe said, "Nelson, if I had your money, I would have done better."

Nelson said, "You know, Joe, my wealth is very much exaggerated." At which point Joe put his hand in his pocket and pulled out the roll of $100 bills he always had on him and said, "If you need a couple of dollars. . . ."

There was a photographer preceding us. I thought he would drop his camera he laughed so hard. He came over to me later and said, "That was the funniest thing I ever heard. I can't imagine anyone would offer a Rockefeller money." Nelson took it good-naturedly. It was so funny.

Joe really enjoyed coming to Washington and pulling up to the museum. He was very proud, and rightfully so. Olga remembered that the first time they came to Washington after the museum had opened, she said to her husband, "Let's see what happens when we say to the cab driver, 'The Hirshhorn Museum.' When we got into the cab and we said, 'The Hirshhorn Museum,' and the cab driver knew where to take us. That, to

[Joe] was the culmination of everything. The cab driver knew where to go."

Joe and Olga found it exciting driving up to the museum and seeing family groups being photographed in front of the Henry Moore. On several occasions Olga suggested she introduce Joe to the group and when she did, asked the person holding the camera, "Would you like to include Mr. Hirshhorn? He's right here," she said. "They always acquiesced and Joe would get into the picture, putting his arms around the children." Olga's comment, "So quite a few people have Joe Hirshhorn in their photographs from those early days."

Going to the museum was, especially in the early years, one of Joe's greatest pleasures, but he was careful not to get too involved with its operation and, even after they moved to Washington, made certain not to be there all the time. Out of his regard for Lerner and a sensitivity to their relative positions, he never tried to impose his opinions on what was taking place. When Joe and Olga attended the new exhibit openings, he loved to mingle with the crowds. Even when he was there on an average day just to walk through the museum, Joe would introduce himself to strangers. He also made it a point to shake the hands of all the guards when he went in so all of them would know him. The museum was Joe's playground, a place where he felt at home, where he could play host and exercise his penchant for getting to know people. This continued long after the couple moved to Washington.

After the museum's successful opening, Joe was approached with offers by universities and associations wanting to bestow awards and honorary degrees. In 1976 Joe was recognized, together with a number of other well-known men including Rod McKuen and Art Linkletter, by the Horatio Alger Society. Hirshhorn was certainly a prime example of the Alger work ethic and initially felt honored to have been tapped. Later, when he learned he was expected to donate $10,000 to the organization as part of his acceptance, he agreed to their terms but shrugged off the "honor."

Between 1965 and 1981 Joe had been the recipient of a number of awards and honorary degrees beside the already mentioned Horatio Alger Award which was presented by Norman Vincent Peale for philanthropy. Among the other philanthropic awards were: the Annual Art Award by the Arts Materials Trade Association, 1967; the James Smithson Award by the Smithsonian Institution, 1973 and 1977; a Citation by the National Association of Schools of Art, 1975; Award of Merit by the Lotus Club, New York, 1965; the Gertrude Vanderbilt Whitney Award by the Skohegan School of Painting and Sculpture, 1979; the Award of Excellence by Friends of Moore College of Art, 1980; and the Swan Award by the Tennessee Botanical Gardens and Fine Arts Center, 1981. There were a scattering of honors from various institutions: Union College, George Washington University, Moore College of Art, Wake Forest and Baltimore Museum of Art.

It was the honorary degrees that impressed Hirshhorn even more, especially when he considered his lack of formal schooling. He was very proud of them. Among them was one that had special meaning for him: Doctor of Humane Letters awarded him by Boston University in 1975. Part of the reason it was so meaningful was because he had become personally acquainted with its President, John Silber, who had come to view Joe's collection when the art was still in Greenwich. A second reason was that Boston University was the school with which his son-in-law, Robert Sonné Cohen, was associated. In fact, Bob Cohen helped dress Joe in his red gown in preparation for the ceremony and has reported that Joe was quite taken with the red robe and opined that he thought the color was very becoming to him.

In 1975 Maryland Institute, College of Art granted Hirshhorn a Doctor of Fine Arts degree as did Wake Forest University in 1976. In 1979, when he was eighty years old, Skidmore College bestowed upon Joe their Doctor of Humane Letters and in 1980, at the age of eighty-one, Hirshhorn received a Doctor of Humanities from Pratt Institute.

Eventually the trips from Greenwich to the capital became more tiring and Joe made the decision to renovate Bancroft Place with a view to relocating permanently to Washington. Olga, full of ideas, was put in charge of creating a residence that would work for them. She supervised the alterations inside and out and made sure to install a small elevator so that Joe wouldn't have to navigate four flights of stairs. As she was still acting as secretary and organizer, she arranged an office for each of them, upgraded the kitchen, added a garage where there had formerly been a pool and created an outdoor porch above it where they could entertain. On the fourth floor she designed an apartment for servants. Olga thought of everything and the house became livable, comfortable, utilitarian.

The Greenwich house went on the market and, in time, sold—not for the $2.5 million at which it was first offered in a soft market—but for $1 million less. The move was made in 1977, and the Bancroft Place house was filled with paintings and sculpture. Joe couldn't really live without the art. Now their lives took on a more comfortable pattern. Naples, Florida with its income tax benefits was a good substitute for Greenwich where there also was no state income tax so, although Joe and Olga spent more time in Washington than they did in Florida where they avoided the coldest months of the year, Naples became their legal residence. The trip between Washington and Naples was also far less taxing on both of them. They were now entirely on the East Coast, in the same time zone. No more getting up at 5:00 A.M. so Joe could talk to his brokers in New York or catch a plane from Palm Springs to Manhattan or White Plains. In Florida, life was as easy as it had been in the Southern California desert. Joe loved the sun and Olga was a fine swimmer. In 1977, the year of the move to Washington, he gave an additional gift to the museum—a gift from him personally rather then from the foundation. It included forty-nine paintings, five sculptures and 204 prints or drawings, 258 items in all, some of which were works Lerner had wanted for the collection. In addition to that gift, Joe decided that since they were moving, it was also a good time for everything the foundation owned to go to the museum. The 1977 foundation gift was also a very large one. It included 242 paintings by 104 artists and 182 pieces of sculpture, many of which were Benin pieces from Africa.

By 1978, when Joe was seventy-nine years old, it occurred to me he might have something special he could leave to his children. With that in mind, I asked him if he still owned anything that Jennie, my mother, had given him. He replied that he had a

*set of evening studs and cuff links, made from platinum and dia-
monds, that she had given him. He also had a platinum pinkie
ring he wore all the time set with a star sapphire. I asked what he
planned to do with them and suggested they should go to his children. I was hoping he would give them to me and I would dispose
of them as I saw fit to his grandchildren. He decided he would
specify in his will that the ring go to my brother Gordon, the diamond and platinum evening set to his eldest grandson, Michael
Cohen (Robin's son) and he would give her second son, Daniel Cohen, another evening set he owned (not from Jennie) of gold set
with sapphires. He left nothing personal to his daughters or
granddaughters. However, during his lifetime Joe gave his
daughters pieces of jewelry from time to time. We never knew
where they came from as they were never wrapped as a gift or in a
box. They arrived loose as if he'd bought them at a garage sale.
But they were usually beautiful and usually "estate sale" quality.
I received one I always called the "purple boil." It was **not** one of
the most beautiful.*

XVII
Retirement Doesn't Mean Retiring

Previously, summers were pretty much committed to spending time on the Riviera. But once Joe had rid himself of the house in Cap d'Antibes by trading it for seven paintings by Clyfford Stills, he and Olga were free to extend what had become their annual cruise to include longer trips, even a trip around the world. For the eight years following the opening of the museum, the Hirshhorns planned and went on a cruise or a long trip each year. This kind of relaxation was new in Joe's experience but, when at home, his life followed a definite pattern.

Five days a week, in whichever home they were living, Joe had a routine that rarely, if ever, deviated. He arose every morning, washed, shaved (surely wiped out the sink!) dressed with a shirt and tie and began work at his desk. In Florida, to get to his office, he walked the length of the large house to his study which was at the end farthest from the master bedroom. In Washington, he went down the stairs to his study on the first floor. His occupation throughout the morning was trading—buying or selling stock, or both—and getting quotes from a variety of brokers at regular intervals. It was his lifelong habit to buy with one broker and to transfer the stocks to a different broker to be sold when he was ready. He didn't want the right hand to know what the left hand was doing. Over the many years of trading, Joe regularly set up brokerage accounts, usually in Toronto, in the names of his children, his sisters, his friends and associates. All this was done for the purpose of manipulating the prices of the stocks he was promoting. At what time he may have discontinued this practice I do not know. It often cost me money on my income tax returns which I resented and for which I tried to get him to compensate me. I was not always successful. This was all part of his preoccupation, part of his "work."

He might chart stocks, *schmooz* with his broker friends, men he'd done business with for more years than he cared to remember. There was his lawyer, Sam Harris, to talk to and his accountant, David Tarlow, still with him after more than fifty years. He might have time to call his younger sister, the only sister still alive. He might speak with his children. He undoubtedly spoke with Leo Gold, a nephew of whom he was very fond and with whom he regularly traded. Leo went to work with Joe after he graduated from high school during the Depression and, having gone off on his own, he'd done very well in a brokerage business called Gold-Freedman. Leo worked on the floor of the American Stock Exchange. His partner, Mac Freedman, was the inside man. Joe was in frequent touch with his office, greatly reduced in size, in Toronto and also with the Callahan office that contained his mining interests which had recently moved from 100 Park Avenue to Darien, Connecticut.

Each day Joe broke to have lunch with Olga who made sure she was in the house whenever Joe might want her. Afterward, he returned to his office where he worked until the market closed. Until the end of his life, Joe "played" the market. He liked instant communication and required immediate and frequent quotes on his stocks. The way he structured his business in order to operate in a largely secretive manner was complicated. If Joe had lived another ten years he would have been able to trade on the Internet, a far simpler, more immediate method. It would have *thrilled* and amazed him and he would have taken to it like the proverbial duck to water. Talk about your "day-traders!"

After the market closed at 4:00 P.M. in New York, Joe took a nap. Then, for the remainder of the afternoon, he and Olga would do something together. They might go to museums or galleries, although Joe preferred galleries to museums "because the art in museums isn't for sale." Saturday mornings and part of the afternoons, the couple sometimes visited galleries and, although Joe never became attached to the dealers in Washington the way he was still close to those in New York, it did give both Joe and Olga a chance to become acquainted with the Washington art scene. It had been their plan to do the galleries one Saturday a month and to have lunch with a different dealer each month. It was a good plan but, since it was only initiated in late 1980, the couple was never able to complete the list. This was pretty much the Hirshhorns' routine even in Florida where there were also museums and galleries to explore. Only if he and Olga had gone on one of their yearly trips, did the activities of their days vary; although, even at sea or in Europe, with modern communications, Joe was able to maintain contact with the New York stock markets.

The first lengthy trip (around the world) they took together was in 1977. It came about at Olga's urging because Joe would never have proposed a trip that took him away from market activity for so long a period. The first leg took them by air to Rio de Janeiro where they spent several days. From there they flew to Johannesburg, South Africa, where they stayed several days more. Then on to Cape Town, again by air, for two days before boarding a ship which sailed up the east coast of Africa, stopping at the Seychelles. Next, the ship put in at Madagascar and went on to Bombay, from which they flew to Agra to see the Taj Mahal, returning to Bombay where they again boarded their ship. Next came several islands in the Pacific, until they debarked in Sri Lanka where they were met by a helicopter arranged by the Sri Lankan Ambassador to the United Nations with whom Olga had played tennis. The helicopter flew them to Kandy (Sri Lanka) where they were treated to lunch at a tea plantation and then flown back to again board their ship which set sail for Malaysia and Singapore.

The next part of their journey found the couple in Hong Kong, from which they took a train into China proper. They spent four days in Canton, returned to the ship and went back to Hong Kong, where they remained for a week before returning to the ship once more. During that week in Hong Kong both of them indulged in a grand shopping spree. While Joe had shoes, coats and suits custom made, Olga bought dresses and jewelry.

During this stay in Hong Kong, Joe was suddenly taken very ill. It happened that there was no doctor in the hotel and, as it was Sunday, no doctor appeared to be available anywhere. Olga

was frightened and desperate. She rushed all over town following leads to possible medical help, worrying frantically about
having left Joe alone. Finally, she located a doctor at the opposite
end of town who refused to make the trip until she begged and
pleaded. After nearly prostrating herself before him, he agreed
to accompany her back across town by taxi to the hotel. When
they rushed into the hotel to the couple's suite, there was Joe
standing in the middle of the room being measured for a suit by a
Hong Kong tailor!

Leaving Hong Kong, Joe and Olga flew to Japan, visited a
friend and then flew back to the States via Los Angeles where
they spent a few days with Joe's daughter Naomi. *By then I was
living on the East Coast and not in Los Angeles where I had been
from 1947 through 1962.* After having been away from Connecticut, Florida and Washington for several months, Joe and Olga finally returned to Greenwich which at that time was still their
home. There was to be more travel in their future.

Two years later, the couple returned to China, which they
had enjoyed greatly on their first visit. This time they traveled
with two other couples, the David Lloyd Kreegers and Dr. and
Mrs. Krongal, good friends of the couple's, on a pre-arranged trip
which began in Beijing. With six people making up the group, the
three couples hired a van and driver, guide and interpreter to es-
cort them throughout the two-and-a-half-week tour. Besides the
van, the six Americans also traveled by air and train to various
cities. Olga proclaimed it a marvelous, albeit tiring, trip.

It was a novelty for Joe to travel solely for leisure, pleasure
and enlightenment. But now, as he had grown older and was suffering from hip pain which caused him to limp, most of the yearly
trips the couple made were cruises planned to accommodate his
diminishing health and energy. Cruising was far easier to tolerate than traveling by plane, train and/or bus from city to city.

During the first twelve years of their marriage, Joe had been
the one who dictated his and Olga's activities. He was clearly in
charge during those years and could be harsh with Olga, at times
demeaning her even in front of guests if he felt she was dominating the conversation. Joe had always been put off if his wives or
daughters gained excessive weight, and obesity was one of Olga's

problems. That was another issue Joe could be bluntly accusative about. Occasionally he would embarrass her publicly with demands she regain the figure she'd had when they met and married.

Joe was slowing down. After a day of working and visiting galleries, after the market closed and before dinner, he would sit in the living room of his New York apartment and have a couple of Scotches, neat. It relaxed him. *It also made him less guarded, more apt to speak about his feelings. I caught him in one of those moods one afternoon and we spoke about his life and loves. There had been so much strife between my parents, such anger from the time of the divorce and he'd been married three times since then. I felt moved to ask him:*

"Daddy, did you love Jennie?"

"Yes," he said without hesitation, "your mother was a good woman, a little bit crazy, but I did love her." I could see by his body language and hear in his voice that he did.

"And Olga," I asked, "do you love Olga?

"Love her," he said with fire, "sometimes I hate her. If I was younger I'd divorce her. But I'm too old to go through that now."*

His admission may have been just the mood of the moment but it was clear that as Joe aged and lost some of his vitality, Olga emerged as the one in control. He was less likely to stand up to her demands, perhaps out of a sense of conserving his flagging energy. He was a man easily irritated, especially in his youth, and while advancing age was not changing how he felt, it seemed to make him more tolerant. Anger expends too much energy and Joe had less to spare. He accepted the fact that it was too late for him to make drastic changes in his life.

For the most part, Olga paid close attention to Joe's needs. She could see he was able to walk down the stairs every day and through the museums and galleries without pain. She kept a supply of oxygen by his bed which she administered to him twice

---

*This statement served to remind me of something Daddy Joe would frequently say when the subject of divorce arose, "Divorce may not be nice, but it's much better than murder."

a day. However, there were times when there was something she wanted very much to do, that she overrode his wishes. How eager Joe was for the last, long trip they took is uncertain. It occurred not long before he died so it is hard to imagine Joe really was eager to go and, although Olga was a very attentive, caring wife, clearly she wanted the trip believing it would be stimulating for Joe.

The couple flew to Los Angeles and boarded a ship that took them to Tahiti, Australia, New Zealand, Tasmania, Indonesia, Thailand and various locales across the South Pacific. Each of them, overtaken with a case of the "I've-got-to-have-its," Joe and Olga bought so many items that they returned with twice the amount of luggage. Olga claimed she had caught the "buying bug" from Joe. Both were astonished and dismayed when they returned home to realize how much they'd acquired.

When Joe and Olga were at home in Washington, they were greatly in demand socially, receiving many invitations, more than they could possibly accept. In turn, Joe and Olga did considerable entertaining. It was not difficult, as they maintained a full staff in the Bancroft Place house. They both enjoyed the theater, saw movies, visited museums and galleries, and spent time at the Hirshhorn Museum. Olga kept busy with her own activities, especially tennis, which contributed to her excellent health while Joe maintained his daily participation in the stock market.

On one of my visits to Washington to spend a weekend with my father near the end of his life—he was about eighty-one at the time—he spoke about projects he would never undertake—opportunities to make money, challenges that appealed to him. He added, with a penetrating look in my eyes, "I'm ready. I'm not in a hurry, but I'm ready." Then he added with a shake of his head, "I can't believe it went so fast."

Joe celebrated his 82nd birthday on August 11, 1981. He had outlived every other male member of his nuclear family: His own father died at forty-five, his brother Herman at seventy-five, Abe at forty-two, and Irving at forty-two.

On August 31, 1981, Olga spent the day with a friend in Baltimore Harbor where they had gone to see the National Aquarium. Joe remained at home with a friend, Bob Kogod, who offered to take him to see Crystal City where they had lunch and spent the day. Joe returned home in time for a nap and change of clothes, Olga joined him for dinner at 6:00 P.M. They ate early because they had theater tickets to see the musical "Annie" which was playing in town. After dinner Olga drove herself and Joe to the theater in the Rolls Royce.

"Annie" was the kind of musical Joe liked. It was fun. He was familiar with the songs and was singing or humming "Tomorrow" as they left the theater and in the car on the way home. In an established routine, upon reaching home shortly after 11:00 P.M., Olga pulled into the driveway and waited as Joe exited the car and went to open the garage door so she could put the car away. He always opened the garage door for her.

Joe never reached his destination. As he walked toward the garage, Joe suffered a massive heart attack and dropped to the pavement. Olga, seeing what had happened, raced from the car to his side and applied CPR, a technique she had studied just in case something like this should happen. But her efforts were futile. Joe had died instantly.

Devastated, Olga called the police and then telephoned Robin Cohen, the eldest of Joe's children, to tell her of his death, asking her to call her younger siblings to inform them. Olga alerted Lily Harmon to advise Amy and Jo Ann and reached out to her own family and friends for support.

According to Biblical tradition, Jews are to be buried as quickly as possible after death but, September 1st was already upon the household before Joe's internment could be arranged, including the transportation of his body to Greenwich where Joe was to be buried. Therefore, the funeral was held September 2, 1981, at the Reform Jewish Temple in Greenwich. The burial following the service took place at the Greenwich Hebrew Institute Temple Shalom Cemetery off Riversville Road in Glenville, Connecticut.

Before the funeral, the family had an opportunity to gather at the funeral home on Putnam Avenue in Greenwich where Olga held sway. All of Joe's four elder children were there. Jennie had died in April 1966, and now, foolish as it may have seemed, we felt for the first time what it was like to be orphans. When a child has even one parent, there is comfort in knowing there is an "older" generation standing between their generation and death. But now, Robin was nearly fifty-eight; Gene, almost fifty-five; Gordon would be fifty-two in less than three weeks and Naomi had just turned fifty. Joe's daughter Jo Ann was present but Amy was unable to come. Their mother, Lily, was still alive and well.

But the main reason we felt his loss with such agonizing pain was because his death forced us to give up the hope of ever being close to him, of ever feeling his love. Olga was too self-involved to offer support or understanding. She let Joe's children know, in an unfeeling dismissal of their pain, that losing a husband was far worse than losing a father. By devaluing the children's feelings and loss, she did not endear herself to me.

Two weeks later, after a memorial service for Joe in Washington, the divided family gathered again at the house on Bancroft Place where Olga's children, under their mother's protection and emboldened by her sense of entitlement, took over the house, drinking Joe's liquor and ensconcing themselves in the rooms from which they had been barred while he was alive. These events went further to alienate Joe's children from his widow.

Joe was memorialized in every newspaper, his death was noted in the various news magazines. One of the more fascinating notices comes from the *Toronto Globe & Mail*, dated September 2, 1981 and entitled "Joseph Hirshhorn: Canada Recalls 'Uranium King.'" It is reprinted here in its entirety.

The death in Washington of Joseph Hirshhorn, once known as the uranium king of Canada, stirs memories in both mining and art circles in this country.

There are still those who remember when Mr. Hirshhorn, who died on Monday at 82, moved to Toronto from New York in 1933 and opened a modest office on Bay Street.

Banks in the United States were closing their doors, victims of the Depression, but just before the crash Mr. Hirshhorn had sold his stocks, saying later that "when doctors, lawyers, dentists left their professions to play the market full time, I knew it was time to quit."

He once said he made money naturally—"just like breathing." Of his move to Canada, he said: "I brought lots of money with me. I was no carpetbagger."

He ran a full-page ad in the *Northern Miner,* which said: "Canada, your day has come. The world is at your feet, begging you to release your riches cramped in Mother Earth. . . . You have the courage! You have the energy, enthusiasm and the will to carry on! Carry on until the pick strikes the hard, firm, yellow metal, until the cry of Gold resounds through the virgin forests. . . . And as for us, we believe to the extent that we have investments in gold mining and other industries in the Dominion and shall continue to do so."

In his first business year in Toronto, his methods of lightning deals and brutally simple methods sent outraged mining barons howling for an investigation of "conspiracy to manipulate." But Ontario securities authorities gave him a clean bill of health.

He stunned the Canadian mining industry when he pulled off one of the most sensational coups in mining history—a secret six-week staking bee that wrapped up most of the Algoma Basin before Bay Street heard a word of it. Than he quickly organized more than a dozen companies to exploit the claims.

One man who remembers him well is Duncan Derry, a consulting geologist who was involved in the deal that made millions for Mr. Hirshhorn in the 1950s: the sale of part of his uranium holdings in the Blind River area to Rio Tinto for about $58 million.

"He was a very interesting man," Mr. Derry recalled yesterday. "He was an exuberant character, so completely different from the Rio Tinto people from England."

He remembered him as a jolly sort of person who was easy to talk to, "but he was very, very shrewd. . . . I'm sorry to hear the old man is gone."

He also remembers his love for art; when he visited Mr. Hirshhorn's New York office he was shown paintings side by side on every wall. "I really don't think he knew anything about art when he first got into it, but he certainly got to."

Mr. Hirshhorn caused considerable concern in the Canadian art world when he withdrew artwork he owned from such places as the Toronto Art Gallery and the Royal Ontario Museum to take it to the Hirshhorn Museum in Washington. Many felt that the artwork bought with money made in Canada should have been left here.

"I buy art like someone else buys neckties or horses, or yachts," he said in 1962 in a *Newsweek* interview. Reputed to be worth $130 million at that time, he called himself "a little Jewish boy brought up in the gutters of Brooklyn."

One of his Canadian dreams never came about: founding a town called "Hirshhorn" near Blind River, a grandiose scheme he saw as helping Canada, art and the little man in one stroke.

"This is going to be an esthetic town—laid out for growth," he announced. "It'll have a big square—like Italy—with sculpture. I'll have a museum there, too. Maybe the miners won't be different because of the beauty, but their kids will."

The scheme fell through when Blind River protested that the new town would compete with it for prosperity from the uranium boom. "I had wanted to help Canada," Mr. Hirshhorn said, "but I didn't want to impose a town on them."

The final tribute to Joseph Hirshhorn that bears repeating here is comments by Dillon Ripley, in the November, 1981 issue of the *Smithsonian Magazine.*

Joseph H. Hirshhorn died on August 31, less than three weeks after his 82nd birthday. To me the event was incomprehensible, and I am sure to his friends also. It was unthinkable that my old friend Joe would not help to preside at my own funeral. Joe could dance better than I could. He was young and merry at heart. He was curious and passionate and humane. He exemplified Jonathan Swift's observation that "Every man desires to live long, but no man would be old." I could not imagine him old.

I first met Mr. Hirshhorn in 1964, not long after I came to the Smithsonian. One of my own passions was to make up, somehow, for generations of neglect which seemed to proscribe forever the possibility of the Institution's catching up with the present in the field of art. In 1938, Congress had instructed the Regents and the administration to encourage contemporary artists, give scholarships, and create a modern art museum on the Mall. Perhaps this unusual language had been inspired by the example of New York, which was pioneering with two museums—the Museum of Modern Art and the Whitney Museum of American Art. But Washington in 1939–40 was a different place; and although the Smithsonian did hold a competition for a new building for modern art, won eventually by Eliel and Eero Saarinen, the design was quietly shelved by those whose dictum seemed to be "Let no touch of modernity ever sully the Mall!"

But the 1960s were full of vigor, if not daring. And it was then that contemporary art galleries were springing up all over the country, even in Washington. The poor Smithsonian, if it ever was to catch up, must find a collection already made. Joe Hirshhorn had been collecting with unimaginable personal zeal and competence for 35 years in the field of contemporary sculpture and painting. He was a mega-collector who already possessed more than 5,000 objects. He was happy with his collection, in the prime of life, and seemed an unlikely candidate for a donation to the Smithsonian.

If I ever thought so, I was soon disabused. To me Mr. Hirshhorn seemed utterly realistic, as well as curious. Why had I come to see him when he was so happy with his "children," as he called them, surrounding him in every nook and cranny? Of course, underneath, he was concerned about his "children's" fate. He had already been approached by three other nations and some cities. He knew little of Washington and, a common failing, even less about the Smithsonian.

But Joseph Hirshhorn was a patriot. His remarkable "Horatio Alger" career had instilled that in him, along with his essential honesty and decency. Of course he would think about it. Joe and his lovely wife, Olga, and ourselves became fast friends. Together we helped President and Mrs. Johnson and the Congress to understand this extraordinary man could do something for the Institution, for Washington and for the nation. Thus the Hirshhorn Museum and Sculpture Garden was born.

Now, in death as in life, he has continued to add to his unparalleled gift with additional works of art, with a generous endowment for acquisitions, and with an unforgettable memory of his joy in life.

Signed, S. Dillon Ripley

For the remaining doubters who, in spite of all documentation, still believe Joe "pulled a fast one" on President Johnson, the Smithsonian Institution and the people of the United States, a summary of his gifts to the nation in the form of art and cash, during his lifetime and after his death are included below.

The original gift of art which established the Hirshhorn Museum was evaluated at the time at $60 million. He also had initially contracted to give $1 million for a fund for acquisitions which went instead to defray construction expense when the building cost escalated beyond the existing budgeted funds. Following this, Joe further donated an additional $1 million in art.

Upon his death, the terms of Joe's will included the following:

I give and bequeath to the SMITHSONIAN INSTITUTION, Washington, District of Columbia, for the exclusive use and benefit of the HIRSHHORN MUSEUM AND SCULPTURE GARDEN:

1. My paintings in all media, all sculpture in all media, all pottery and ceramics, all graphic art in all media, all watercolors, all photographs, all engravings, and all other works of art which I may own at the time of my death (all of the foregoing being hereinafter collectively referred to as "my works of art"); and
2. The sum of five million dollars ($5,000,000) and
3. I give, devise and bequest all right, title and interest owned by me at the time of my death in and to the Overriding Royalty Interest in petroleum produced and saved from certain lands located in Canada as reserved to me under a certain agreement dated the 2nd day of August, 1960, between myself and John B. Aird, and under all other agreements amending or supplementing the same, as in effect at the time of my death, to the SMITHSONIAN INSTITUTION, Washington, District of Columbia, for the exclusive use and benefit of the HIRSHHORN MUSEUM AND SCULPTURE GARDEN. The works of art so purchased shall be subject to the provisions of the agreement between me, the JOSEPH H. HIRSHHORN FOUNDATION, INC. and the SMITHSONIAN INSTITUTION, DATED May 17, 1966, as supplemented and amended. All receipts of overriding royalties from the property bequeathed under this paragraph I shall constitute income.

Lastly, out of an art trust held in Zurich, Switzerland which amounted to between $10 and $15 million, the lion's share—an amount approximating $13.5 million—also went directly to the

Smithsonian Institution for the exclusive use of the Hirshhorn Museum and Sculpture Garden. By comparison, to each of his eldest four children, Joe left $1.5 million in trust.

Altogether, Hirshhorn's gift and bequest to the nation was proof of his sincere wish to create a lasting, cultural center of art. His bequest to the family of emotional loss was lasting as well. But the great achievement of the individual and his keen eye remain.

BIBLIOGRAPHY

Books

Berthoud, Roger. *The Life of Henry Moore,* Giles de la Mare, Publishers, Ltd. London, 2003 (second, revised, updated and redesigned edition), p. 542.

Dixon, Catherine. *The Power & The Promise: The Elliot Lake Story,* Cillidix Publishing, Inc. Lake Elliot, Ontario, 1996, p. 396.

Harmon, Lily. *Freehand,* Simon and Schuster, New York, 1981, p. 350.

Hyams, Barry. *HIRSHHORN, Medici from Brooklyn,* E.P. Dutton, New York, 1979, p. 206.

Johnson, Claudia T. [Lady Bird]. *A White House Diary,* Holt, Rinehart and Winston, New York, 1970, p. 806.

Saarinen, Aline B. *The Proud Possessors,* Random House, Inc., New York, 1958, p. 421.

Stevens, Mark and Swan, Annalyn. *De Kooning: An American Master,* Alfred A. Knopf, New York, 2005, p. 732.

Von Drehle, David. *Triangle: The Fire That Changed America,* Atlantic Monthly Press, New York, 2003, p. 340.

Oral Interviews

Hirshhorn, Joseph H. Interviews for the Smithsonian Archives of Art, 1976 (transcript) New York City, New York.

Hirshhorn, Olga. *A First Generation In Greenwich,* The Greenwich Library, Greenwich, Connecticut (transcript).

Hirshhorn, Olga. Interviews for the Smithsonian Archives, 1988 (transcript).

Lerner, Abram. Personal Interviews conducted by Gene LePere, 2001.

Moss, Tobey C. Personal Interview conducted by Gene LePere, 2004.